The Story of

Scripture Press

"THE WHOLE WORD
for the
WHOLE WORLD"

The Story of Scripture Press

"THE WHOLE WORD *for the* WHOLE WORLD"

A history of a remarkable publishing company that God brought into being to make solidly based Bible curriculum available to Sunday Schools at a time liberal teaching was corrupting curriculum of many denominations.

JAMES R. ADAIR

SP Ministries
Glen Ellyn, Illinos

Cover photographs: Bernice and Victor Cory
Cover design by Paul Higdon
Interior design and composition by Design Corps: Batavia, IL

Published by SP Ministries

250 Pennsylvania Avenue, Glen Ellyn, IL 60137-4327

Dedication

To Eunice Fischer, whose letter to Dr. Gray triggered the start of Scripture Press, and Lloyd Cory, my longtime boss and friend who not only stood up for me over the years at work but also when I got married.

Acknowledgements

SPECIAL THANKS to the many who aided in the making of this book, especially Gil Beers, for his enthusiasm toward preserving the history of Scripture Press and his encouragement along the way; Lloyd Cory, for editing the manuscript in the early stages; Lorraine Ackley, who supplied valuable information that contributed to the accuracy of many details; and Myrna Hasse for helping select photographs as she sorted those in the SPM Archives.

Contents

Note: Though the text in this book refers to an Appendix for further information, the collection of sources can be examined only in the SP Ministries Archives. These historical items were too voluminous to be included in this book.

Foreword

This is a story that must be told, for it is too significant to fade away with the passing of time and principal players. Like most great stories, the heroes were reluctant participants in a plot too fantastic for them to imagine. In their wildest dreams, Victor and Bernice Cory could never have imagined the global influence of their early dream. But the Lord God who made the earth also engineered the process of developing Scripture Press, and the Corys were His instruments. It is a reminder to us all that to accomplish God's purposes we must submit ourselves to the God who manages those purposes.

Two years ago, the Board of Trustees of Scripture Press Ministries commissioned Jim Adair to develop this work so that we could preserve a glorious chapter in the history of the church and Sunday School. Jim was the obvious choice, having written other books and serving now for 53 years under the Scripture Press "flag." Jim leaned on people who contributed significantly to SP's history, especially on Lloyd Cory, son of the founders (still a Trustee of Scripture Press Ministries); former Presidents Wilfred Frykman and David Hall; Bob Walker (55 years of service on Scripture Press boards); and many with 30 or more years of service to SP.

Scripture Press was born in a "fullness of time," at a moment in history when it met an enormous need. It was neither too early nor too late. God ushered in the advent of SP when SP was uniquely needed.

Prior to 1872, Sunday School curriculum was a mixture of almost everything, creating the term "the babel period." Then in 1872, the International Uniform Series was created and is still amazingly strong today, more than 126 years later. This was a great idea—the whole family studying the same Scripture on the same Sunday. But it forgot to factor in age-level differences. Preschool children don't learn the way older children, teens and adults do. When denominational publishers did something about it, they created age-appropriate materials, but at a time in history when major denominations were liberal in theology. So curriculum became educationally sound but biblically and theologically liberal. An obvious need arose—couldn't there be a curriculum that was both educationally sound and theologically and biblically sound? The Corys responded to that obvious need and Scripture Press was born.

Victor and Bernice Cory proved another important point. They were not alone in their vision. There were thousands of people in the churches who agreed with them, so their passion and the passion of these thousands met at the next intersection, and Scripture Press became a reality. More than that, it became a global influence. What better system has ever been developed than Sunday School, a weekly Bible study for the entire family meeting at one place to learn Bible at their own age or interest level? And what better perspective than a strong evangelical world view with a passion for evangelism and missions?

But there are cycles of life in companies as there are with people. As people are born, grow, mature, and change, so also do companies. To assume that most companies will be born, mature and continue forever at a fixed level denies reality. The maturing of Scripture Press coincided with the maturing of the parachurch movement, born in the fullness of time about the same time SP was born in the fullness of its time. The two matured together and reached the world for Christ in magnificent ways together. In a very real sense, Scripture Press was a significant contributor to the literature of the parachurch movement.

The ever-accelerating pace of change in society and the church caused the more traditional pace of maturity of both SP and the parachurch movement to become a premature aging of both to keep pace, and thus in a very real sense to age faster than society and the church. Looking back, there may have been another "fullness of time" for the parachurch movement and Scripture Press to change, anticipating the emerging change in society and the church. But looking back is far easier, but less helpful, than looking ahead. If we're not careful, we engage in the old 20-20 hindsight syndrome while we lose our vision for the future.

During the past 20 years society and the church not only changed, but the acceleration of change became unprecedented. Only the naïve would say that society and the church have not undergone radical change during the past two decades. Simultaneously, the "bar was raised" in the expectations of users, conditioned by the entertainment syndrome and the cost of meeting those expectations.

When I became president of both Scripture Press Publications and Scripture Press Ministries in June 1990, we faced the challenge of meeting these demanding expectations on a "Sunday School publisher's budget" rather than a "Hollywood budget." The Executive team, the Boards, and I went through an extensive six-year strategic thinking/planning process which led to the conclusion that merging or selling the Publications company may likely be the best way to secure its future, especially in curriculum. This led to SP Ministries (official corporate name since 1994) selling Scripture Press Publications to Cook Communications Ministries (David C. Cook Publishing Company) in February 1996.

Some mourn the loss of SP as it once had been and that is understandable, for it has had a glorious history. But it may be more appropriate to mourn the change in society, church, and Sunday School from what they once had been, forcing all traditional Sunday School publishers, not merely SP, into difficult choices. But let our mourning not continue too long, for we must set it aside to look to the future of what society, church, Sunday School, and Scripture Press may become.

Within the Cook context, SP Curriculum and Victor Books (now ChariotVictor Publishers) are alive and well, more alive and well than they may have been alone. There is yet great hope for the future of Christian publications, even the future of curriculum. All of us who love the Lord should pray for wisdom for those who plan for that future.

Part of our ability to cope with the past and maximize the future is to understand the nature of change and the inevitability of change. When we understand that, we too will change process, while still clinging tenaciously to the changeless authority of Scripture, the changeless Lord we serve, the immutables of our faith in Christ, and our passionate desire to serve Him. Our ability to change the way we think and the way we "do business" may be our best way to secure the future of our treasured "unchangeables."

To all those who helped to make Scripture Press what it became, thank you. And to those who work hard today to secure a future for both Scripture Press Curriculum and Victor Books (under the Cook umbrella) and SP Ministries (under its own umbrella), thank you. Both are in God's hands and we pray for His guidance for the future as He has guided the past.

It is important for you, the reader, to read this book in its entirety, to see the whole story. As you do, remember, the story continues beyond the last page, and each of us can be a prayer participant in that continuing story which reaches to the ends of the earth for the glory of the Lord.

V. Gilbert Beers
President, SP Ministries
June 1, 1998

Preface

Writing this book has stirred up more than a half century of memories for me. Coworkers of the early years have been brought to mind once again, and I have enjoyed "visits" with countless other SP employees down through the years. I wish I could have mentioned each and every employee in this account. For news of people, I depended largely on items published in our company house organs, first *Press Proof,* then *Spotlight*. I'm sure I missed some newsworthy items that could have made the book, and I apologize to employees who do not find their names in these pages. Some items jumped out at me, and others didn't.

Selection of photographs proved difficult. I wish many more employees could have been pictured, both those in leadership positions and those from the ranks. At first, we planned to use only 30 or so photos, then we more than doubled that number; but even then, we wished we could have included many more. To picture as many people as possible, I selected group photos.

I would have liked to have used many more group photos, such as those that appear in an employee photo directory of the '70s that I ran across in the SPM Archives. For those who have the opportunity to visit SPM headquarters, this directory is included with items in the Appendix, which, as stated earlier, is in the Archives with the "official copy" of this book.

Prologue: A Short History of the Sunday School

The vision of Victor E. Cory that led to his establishing Scripture Press can be best appreciated by turning back the pages of time and getting a clear picture of how the modern Sunday School movement started. The following is adapted from Clarence H. Benson's History of Christian Education *published in 1943 by Moody Press and* The Sunday School in Action *by Dr. Benson, published in 1932 by The Bible Institute Colportage Association.*

More than 14 centuries before Robert Raikes began teaching children in the slum district of Gloucester, England in 1780, schools of a similar character were organized in upper Egypt, in Armenia, and elsewhere in the East. But Raikes is credited with making the Sunday School a worldwide movement.

A reformer and a philanthropist, Raikes had a deep concern for children. When a resident complained to him of the bedlam created by the rough and rowdy children of the Gloucester slums, he refused to condemn the reprehensible laxity of the parents through his weekly newspaper, or demand additional policemen from authorities. Instead he rented a room in the most congested district and gathered a group of these "miserable little wretches" for both secular instruction and a knowledge of God and the Bible.

There were no public schools in that day in Europe. Education was a privilege of the upper classes. Children, many of whom worked six long days in factories, generally were as ignorant of the fundamentals of education as of the Bible. Raikes had to teach them to read before they could ever read the Bible. He had all but given up instructing prisoners at Gloucester; it seemed fruitless to try to teach and reform these adults. Thus his thoughts turned toward neglected children.

But Raikes' contemporaries—church leaders included—considered his plan for educating the "little savages" a wild and futile effort. Nevertheless, he persisted. He rewarded with pennies the faithful few who came regularly, and imposed no other requirements than asking that the children have clean hands and faces and combed hair.

Out of his own pocket he provided four teachers to instruct in reading, writing, arithmetic, good morals, and religion. They conducted classes from 10 a.m. to noon and from 2 until 5 in the afternoon. He paid the teachers the equivalent of 25 cents a Sunday, adequate pay for that day.

Teachers faced many difficulties and discouragements, but eventually Robert Raikes proved that "the little vermin could be made to learn." Order improved and numbers increased. The first rooms soon became inadequate, so he opened school after school to accommodate children seeking admission.

Publicity, finally

Raikes gave publicity to his enterprise in his weekly periodical, but not until 1783, three years after the start, when his experiment had proved successful. Other papers in Great Britain published accounts of the origin and progress of the first Sunday School. It is said that through the means of the press, the knowledge and nature of Sunday Schools were "diffused with the rapidity of lightning throughout the world."

Yet at first many church leaders opposed the movement. To them, it was sacrilegious to teach children on Sunday, especially reading and writing. But despite ecclesiastical opposition, the Sunday School got the support of many influential individuals. The Earls of Ducie and Salisbury gave it their approval. John Newton, poet William Cowper, and theologian

Thomas Scott backed the movement heartily. Ladies of fashion volunteered to teach. The Queen herself gave fresh impetus to the new movement by placing on it the stamp of royal favor. Sending for Robert Raikes, she learned from his own lips the story of his work. Thus Sunday School teaching came not only to be reputable but fashionable among the better classes of English people.

Raikes reached some 400,000 children

Raikes lived to see the success of his ragged school, and when he died in 1811, Sunday Schools were scattered throughout England and reached some 400,000 children. As a proof of his love for children, each child who attended his funeral received a plum cake and a shilling, in accordance with his will. During more than 30 years of his life, Robert Raikes had given freely of his time, talents, and money to a movement destined to transform moral conditions in England and to help shape the destiny of America.

Two contemporaries had much to do with the success of the Sunday School movement: philanthropist William Fox and John Wesley, founder of the Methodist Church. Fox, a prosperous London merchant, born on the same day and month in 1736 as was Raikes, had a vision of a great moral and religious transformation if every poor person in Great Britain could read the Bible. In his business journeys throughout England, he often found hamlets and villages where the poor were entirely without Bibles. Even when presented with a copy, not one in 20 could read. His friends gave him little encouragement. They thought that only by legislation by Parliament could these people be taught to read.

But Fox gathered a group of influential Christians and presented the urgent need of an organization that would provide the common people with sufficient education to enable them to read the Bible. About this time the success of Robert Raikes' Sunday Schools attracted the attention of Fox. He saw immediately that Raikes' plan of using Sunday rather than weekdays for instruction could best accomplish his purpose.

On September 7, 1785, Fox launched the Sunday School Society to organize and support Sunday Schools. A donation of 10 guineas a year gave individuals lifetime memberships, and Fox interested many philanthropists in his project. The Society supplied Bibles, Testaments, and spelling books for use in the schools and paid the salary of teachers. Within 20 years, 2,542 schools with a total enrollment of 226,945 pupils had been established, and the Society had furnished 219,410 spelling books, 50,126 copies of the New Testament, and 7,213 copies of the Bible.

John Wesley takes an active interest

Though most clergymen in Britain and America were either hostile or indifferent to the movement, John Wesley took an active interest and encouraged people to volunteer to teach in the Sunday Schools. He supposedly once said that the Sunday School of that day was "one of the noblest specimens of charity which has been set on foot in England since the days of William the Conqueror" and it seems that "it will be one great means of reviving religion throughout the nation." Wesley urged itinerant preachers to spend an hour a week with children, to talk with them in their homes, and to pray earnestly for them. His chief reason for this solicitude related to the revival then under way. He asked, "If religion is not extended to the children, what will be the outcome? If family religion be neglected—if care be not taken with the rising generation—will not the present revival of religion in a short time die away?"

The Methodist Church owes much to the Sunday School for its success. This is particularly true in North America. W.E.H. Leckey, in his review of the methods and influence of the Wesleyan movement, says, "Methodists appear to have preached especially to children."

On July 13, 1803, William Brodie Gurney helped to influence the founding of the London Sunday School Union, whose chief purpose was to improve Sunday Schools and promote some system in religious education. It appropriated large sums for establishing schools, as well as publishing such helpful literature as *A Plan for Forming Sunday Schools, A Guide to Teachers,* and *A Reading Primer.* The formation of new schools, and aid in housing and equipping them, were a large part of the Union's activities. The abandonment of paid teachers, which had constituted such a large portion of the expense of the Sunday School Society, enabled the London Sunday School Union to focus on preparation and publication of periodicals.

"The beginning of popular education"

The Sunday School movement in Great Britain was, according to one historian, "the beginning of popular education." Leckey also refers to "the establishment of Sunday Schools [as] an important step [in the line of] a revived interest in education. Not only was the Sunday School the beginning of the English system of public school education, but indirectly it was responsible for the formation of the British and Foreign Bible Society and the Religious Tract Society. The ability of the common people of England to read multiplied the demands for Bibles and Christian literature, which was the direct occasion for the organization of these two ministries whose activities became worldwide.

While the Sunday School originated in Great Britain, it achieved its greatest growth and development in America. In 1785, two years after Britain had declared the 13 original Colonies a free and independent nation, the first Sunday School was started by William Elliott in his home in Accomac County, Virginia. The state-supported schools of New England and the parochial schools of the central Colonies had not penetrated into the southern states. Elliott set aside each Sunday evening to instruct his own children and the slaves on his plantation. Neighboring children were invited and attended. Negroes were taught but at separate hours. As rapidly as possible, the pupils were prepared to read the Bible, which was the object of Elliott's school. The Scriptures were read, explained, and much of it memorized by teachers and pupils. About 1818 the school became affiliated with his church and, known as the Oak Grove Sunday School, it was still in existence well into the 1990s.

The second Sunday School, expressly for the instruction of slaves, was established by Francis Asbury in 1786 in the home of Thomas Crenshaw of Hanover County, Virginia. Asbury, who later was made bishop of the Methodist Church, was a great admirer of John Wesley, and being in regular communication with him, learned from him the success of the Sunday Schools in England.

The Methodist Conference in Charleston, South Carolina gave official recognition to the Sunday School as the best means for instructing poor children who were unable to read, by the following resolution, adopted in 1790:

> Let us labor as the heart and soul of one man to establish

> Sunday Schools in or near the places of public worship. Let persons be appointed by bishops, elders, deacons, or preachers to teach all that will attend and have capacity to learn, from 6 o'clock in the morning until 10, and from 2 o'clock in the afternoon until 6, where it does not interfere with public worship. Be it further resolved that the council should compile a proper schoolbook to teach them learning and piety.

These early efforts lacked great success but helped spread the movement northward until Sunday Schools became popular in the Northeast.

A Mr. Collier of Brown University opened a Sunday School in Pawtucket, Rhode Island, in 1791. He was assisted by Samuel Slater, an Englishman who founded the American cotton industry in 1790 in Pawtucket. In 1796 he established a Sunday School for the workers of the Almy and Brown 72-spindle mill which he ran. A Sunday School was opened in Broadway Baptist Church, Baltimore, in 1804, making it the first and oldest denominational school in the United States.

The first Sunday School in the state of New York was organized at Stockbridge in the home of an Indian woman, a sister of the Rev. Samson Occom, a distinguished Indian preacher.

In 1809 Pittsburgh, Pennsylvania was only a village but large enough for the formation of a society whose purpose was "the suppression of vice, reformation of manners, and the propagation of useful knowledge." For carrying out this program, a school for religious instruction on Sundays was recommended, and the first Sunday School of Pennsylvania was organized on August 22, 1809. Two hundred and forty children and adults attended the first session.

In 1809 Hannah Hill and Joanna Prince organized a Sunday School in Beverly, Massachusetts after hearing of the success of Raikes' school in England. The first Sunday School in Delaware was opened in Wilmington as a result of a visit by a Mrs. Sharpe, wife of a pastor, to the Charles Street Baptist Sunday School in Boston.

Well into the 1900s, Philadelphia was recognized as having the largest number of Sunday Schools of any city in the United States, though surpassed in population by New York and Chicago. The first movement for Sunday School organization began with the formation of the First-Day or Sabbath School Society. Among distinguished citizens of Philadelphia involved were the Rev. William White, the Episcopal bishop of Pennsylvania, and Dr. Benjamin Rush, whose reputation as a physician was worldwide. The preamble of their constitution, adopted by this Society on January 11, 1791, declared:

> That the first day of the week called Sunday, a day which ought to be devoted to religious improvements, being employed to the worst of purposes, depravity of morals and manners, it is therefore the opinion of sundry persons that the establishment of first-day or Sunday Schools in this city would be of essential advantage to the rising generation.

From March 1791 to January 1800, nearly $4,000 was spent by the Sabbath School Society for the support of its schools. During these nine years, 2,127 pupils were admitted for instruction, the average attendance being about 180; the average expense was about $2.25 a year for each pupil. This was more than the expenses of the schools that employed volunteer teachers, and 40 cents more than the public schools that were in session five days a week. The Society used student monitors to assist teachers.

Sabbath School societies formed

The achievements of the Philadelphia Sabbath School Society led to similar organizations in other cities. Unions for the promotion of Sunday School were organized in such cities as New York and Boston, in 1816.

But not until the organization of the Philadelphia Sunday and Adult School Union in 1817 were the wants of Sunday Schools truly supplied. This ministry made an impact in its first year. Its first annual report showed that it had taken care of 43 schools, 565 teachers, and 5,970 pupils. By 1824 the number of teachers and pupils assisted totaled some 57,000, scattered throughout 17 of the 24 states in the Union.

From this movement came the American Sunday School Union, whose purposes as stated in its constitution were "to concentrate the efforts of Sabbath School societies in the different sections of our country; to strengthen the hands of friends of religious instruction on the Lord's Day; to disseminate useful information, circulate moral and religious publications in every part of the land, and to endeavor to plant a Sunday School wherever there is a population."

Thus was started a movement which was destined to play a large part not only in the nationwide promotion of the Sunday School, but in laying the moral and religious foundations of the sparsely settled portions of the new Republic. The American Sunday School Union entered upon a nationwide work with vision and system and enthusiasm. The organization sought people qualified to introduce better principles and methods of instruction, with sufficient magnetism and force of address to inspire a deeper and wider interest in the cause at the very centers of population. Some of the leading educators gave their services.

The endeavors of Arthur Tappan

In 1830 Arthur Tappan proposed forming a Sabbath School within two years in every town in the Mississippi valley—actually, all of the country west of the Alleghenies to the Rocky Mountains, and from Michigan to Louisiana. In this area, estimated at 1.3 million square miles, his plan was to reach many of the 4 million people living there, one-tenth of them children and youth.

Funds were raised through large gatherings in Philadelphia, Boston, Washington, and Charleston. The most momentous meeting was held in Washington. A United States senator presided. The clerk of the House of Representatives acted as secretary. Daniel Webster and Francis Scott Key were among the prominent speakers. The meeting was reported in newspapers as "one of the most important ever held in the country."

This launched a far-reaching missionary effort. In one year 17,000 reportedly made public confessions of faith in Christ, and foundations were laid for a multitude of new churches. One minister and missionary who served this ministry for 20 years reported that 50 churches had grown out of Sunday Schools he and his associates had organized. Another missionary estimated that "eight-tenths of the churches in the valley of the Mississippi organized in the previous 15 years had grown out of Sunday Schools."

From 1824 to 1874, 61,299 schools came into existence with some 407,000 teachers and approximately 2,651,000 pupils. The amount expended in missionary operation during that period totaled more than $2,133,000, of which about $517,000 was for literature.

Stephen Paxon, missionary extraordinary

If a hall of fame should ever be originated for the world's great missionaries, one niche would surely be reserved for Stephen Paxson. In the mid 1800s, at his little daughter's invitation, he went to Sunday School with her in the small village of Winchester, Illinois. He came to Christ, and became a missionary under the American Sunday School Union. The Union paid him a dollar a day, considerably less than he had made as a hatter. Unable to afford the upkeep of his home in the village, Paxson took his family by covered wagon into the wilderness of Pike County, where a rude log cabin became his missionary headquarters.

He went out despite severe handicaps. A crippled ankle gave him considerable pain. He stammered so badly that as a boy he had been nicknamed Stuttering Steve. His schoolteacher had neglected him, and he learned to read by spelling out the letters on sign boards.

Paxson first traveled over much of Illinois, and was away from home for sometimes weeks and even months. He visited pioneer homes, talked with people about their need for a Sunday School, and urged them to organize one. He traveled by horseback. When his first horse became disabled after traveling for several years, the Congregational Church of Pittsfield, Illinois took an offering to buy him "a missionary horse." The new mount was named Robert Raikes and became one of the best-known animals in the country. For over a quarter of a century, Robert Raikes carried his master more than 100,000 miles. So well did the horse learn the habits of Stephen Paxson that it is said he would never pass a child on the road without stopping, and would always turn in when he came to a church or schoolhouse. When the horse was retired, a New Yorker sent $100 so Paxson could purchase a new mount, which he called Robert Raikes, Junior.

Paxson's efforts resulted in the organization of some 1,300 Sunday Schools with more than 83,000 members, and encouraged and aided about 1,750 other schools. It is said that no one ever equalled his record of organizing 47 Sunday Schools in 40 consecutive days. A city daily in New York reported: "Stephen Paxson made an address in which his aristocratic auditors were so deeply interested that they wept and smiled alternately, never heeding mistakes in grammar or rhetorical discrepancies."

Paxson had an opportunity to help promote a different kind of enterprise, but refused. He pointed to a record of 50,000 pupils gathered into Sunday Schools and said, "I would not alter the record nor change the investment."

National Sunday School conventions spring up

In time, national and international Sunday School conventions sprang up, the first on May 23, 1832 in Philadelphia. By the time the fourth convention convened in Newark, New Jersey on April 28, 1869 it had become international in character. The chief subject of that gathering was the promotion of teacher training. The convention disapproved of the idea that the Sunday School was in any sense a substitute for family or pulpit instruction. According to *The Sunday School Times,* "Never before had so many Sunday School leaders of the land been brought face to face. Taken as a whole, it was the most memorable Sunday School gathering ever assembled in the United States, if not in the world."

From 1790 to 1815 the catechism, with few exceptions, constituted a Sunday School curriculum. This was largely because there was no other course of Bible study in print. In 1816, with the formation of the American Bible Society, Bibles could be purchased at reasonable costs, and as a result the Bible moved nearer to the center of the curriculum. Memorization of Scripture became an accepted method of learning.

The period from 1840 to 1872 in the history of the American Sunday School curriculum is generally referred to as "the babel period," a time of great confusion, for there was no unity of teaching material or any systematic plan of instruction. During this period both the catechism and the Bible memory work gave way to a variety of teaching materials. The American Sunday School Union launched a plan for study of up to 20 Bible verses a week, the first step toward uniformity of instruction. Some schools had pupils memorize a verse a day, to prepare them for Sunday's instruction.

Denominations awaken

Denominations began to awaken to the need for courses of study in which denominational teaching could be included in Sunday study. Almost all of the lesson materials of this period took the form of question books. However, the questions didn't enable pupils to master the context, and application of the lessons to the lives of pupils was almost totally lacking. In addition, the words and concepts used were for the most part too difficult. Individual lessons did not have definite aims, and the primary purpose appears to have been to cover so much material and pour factual knowledge into heads. Something was greatly needed to systematize and unify the instruction of the Sunday School.

It was in 1869 that the first explanatory book was added to the question book series, giving answers to the questions of the other books. But just prior to that, in 1866, Chicagoans John H. Vincent and B.F. Jacobs took important steps toward unifying a lesson system. Vincent, a Methodist minister working with the Sunday School Union, began publishing *The Sunday School Teacher*. The first issue contained a newly conceived lesson series titled "A New System of Sunday School Study." The Vincent system was the world's first with analytical and illustrative helps for teachers and lesson helps for pupils. It was at once adopted by many schools.

When the Rev. Edward Eggleston became editor of the *Chicago Teacher,* he elaborated and extended the lessons. Though his paper was rapidly leading the way toward national uniformity, Eggleston himself strenuously combated the idea as inconsistent with the graded principle. At the Fourth National Sunday School Convention in 1869 (the movement was begun by leaders in the American Sunday School Union and the Presbyterain General Assembly in 1832), B.F. Jacobs championed a plan of uniformity that got the vote of three-fourths of superintendents attending the gathering. This eventually led to a committee to prepare a list of lessons for the following year. At the Fifth National Convention in 1872 the plan of uniformity became a reality and found instant favor at home and abroad.

By 1890 some 11 million were committed to uniform lessons, and this number was increased to 15 million at the beginning of the new century and to 17 million five years later. But despite their popularity, uniform lessons did not provide comprehensive, consecutive, and complete knowledge of the Bible. They constituted a brief outline study rather than a complete curriculum. Lutheran and Episcopal Churches were the first to prepare a system of graded lessons for their own Sunday Schools.

The Lutheran series emphasized loyalty to the doctrines of the Church and made a special effort to create a distinct sectarian consciousness. Each text began with New Testament material, and concluded the latter half of the year with lessons from the Old Testament. Though Bible narratives were largely employed as material for the children's texts, selections from the poetic, prophetic, and doctrinal portions of Scripture were chosen for older pupils.

The writers of the Episcopal Christian Nurture Series made much of correlated readings, drills, and notebook work in connection with the teacher's textbook. The series was graded on a one-year basis, beginning in kindergarten with four-year-olds, and providing a separate course for each grade to the end of high school.

Independent pioneers introduce graded lessons

Independent pioneers also entered the picture even before the denominations had begun to break into the solid flanks of Sunday Schools that protected and preserved uniform lessons. One was Dr. William R. Harper, a distinguished Bible scholar. While president of the University of Chicago, he planned a graded series for his Sunday School. His materials were first mimeographed, to be tested and published only after a year's use. When perfected, the lessons were widely used by schools of many denominations.

The Rev. Erastus Blakeslee, who had served as an army officer in the Civil War, hitchhiked on Dr. Harper's work and created the Blakeslee six-year course. It found its way into many schools of nearly all denominations and was popular both in the United States and abroad. After Blakeslee's death in 1910, Charles Scribner's Sons published his lessons, which became known as the Completely Graded Series. Despite some weaknesses, the uniform system borrowed ideas from the Blakeslee curriculum and editors of the International Graded Lessons also adopted some of its characteristics.

The International Graded Series grew out of a movement

spearheaded by Mrs. J. Woodbridge Barnes, an outstanding Primary leader, who asked leaders, "What do we wish our children to know about the Bible before they are 12 years of age?" After the question of graded lessons was debated by leaders of the International Sunday School Association in 1908, work began on these lessons. They were built on the closely graded plan, and patterned after the public schools, having a separate unit of study for each grade or year. Four leading denominational houses—Congregational, Methodist Episcopal North, Methodist Episcopal South, and Presbyterian— formed a syndicate for the joint publication of these lessons. The first lessons were introduced in 1910 and the series was completed by 1914.

But many became concerned when the writers for the syndicate set forth in the lesson helps their liberal views, which eliminated the miraculous and raised questions as to their belief in the supernatural origin and character of the Bible. After an investigation, the Northern Presbyterians withdrew from the syndicate.

In 1914 efforts were begun to improve uniform lessons, and in 1918 the International Improved Uniform Lessons hit the market. In the first cycle of this series (1918-1926), 202 lessons were taken from the New Testament, compared with 105 from the Old Testament, and 60 percent of the former were chosen from the Gospels. Though the Gospels were used repeatedly, not a single paragraph was taken from 14 books of the Bible, and only 15 percent from 17 other books.

Further changes were made, and experience-centered curriculums, influenced by liberal educators John Dewey, Ashley Horace Thorndike, and William Heard Kilpatrick, began to pour off the presses. This curriculum emphasized and substituted methodology at the expense of Bible content. Many people concluded that the lessons were as unsatisfactory as the so-called improved lessons. According to one evangelical leader, this "ethical cultural curriculum" could not be distinguished from the humanism of Compte or Adler.

Clarence Benson and his students

As a result of the crisis in Christian education that these inferior curriculums caused, some students who were enrolled in the Christian education classes at Moody Bible Institute, Chicago, began a project that would bring a superior product on the scene. In 1925, under the direction of Dr. Clarence H. Benson, curriculum-making classes began a critical examination of all existing curriculums.

Students would then plan and write a model course of study for the Sunday School that would provide comprehensive, consecutive, and complete Bible instruction. In the preparation of this All-Bible Graded Series of lessons, Benson and his students laid down certain fundamental facts as guiding principles:

A. *As the chief educational agency of the church, the Sunday School should center its instruction in the Bible.* Extra-biblical subject matter—modern missions, temperance, Bible geography, and church history—should be left to such auxiliaries as Vacation Bible School and Week Day Church School.

B. *All Scripture is profitable for instruction.* The Bible is a literary unit. It tells the human story. Every book, every chapter, and every verse contribute to the progress of the narrative. There is no superfluous material. No course in Bible study, therefore, is complete unless in one way or another it includes the study of every chapter in the Bible.

C. *Lessons should be adapted to the capacity of pupils.* Educators generally agree that the graded principle must be adopted in the Sunday School if pupils are to gain any comprehensive knowledge of the Bible. The Word of God contains moral and spiritual truths which can be adapted to the understanding and needs of an individual from infancy to old age. But it is not difficult to see that lessons which are written for adults are neither interesting nor educational for children. Dr. G. Campbell Morgan, in his book *The Child and the Bible,* says:

> If the Bible is to be taught, the one supreme necessity must ever be that we remember the child's interest must be held. The old idea of an international lesson which is graded to meet all in the Sunday School is utterly wrong.

D. *Bible instruction can be made personal and practical.* Modern educators have made a mistake in thinking that expressional methods can be improved by changing the content of the lesson. The Bible is the changeless book for a changing age, and the Scriptures can be applied to meet the needs of each individual. It is not the content of the lesson so much as the preparation and training of teachers that determines whether pupils will apply the instruction to their own lives. There is no question that better trained teachers will mean not only better acquisition of the truth by pupils but above all, better appropriation and application.

E. *Bible instruction should parallel religious observance.* We have sufficient Bible authority (Ex. 13:14) to recognize that the time to impart instruction is when a child's interest and curiosity is aroused. As in secular instruction, historical facts are best impressed when associated with the observance of a national holiday. In like manner, Bible truths will be remembered when connected with Christmas, Easter, and other Christian days.

F. *Bible instruction should be adapted to department organization and public school divisions.* The All-Bible Graded Series provides for the Sunday School a complete course in Bible to parallel the 12 years of secular instruction received in grade and high school. The four departments of its instruction correspond to the public school divisions as follows:

Primary Department	Grades 1-3
Junior Department	Grades 4-6
Intermediate Department	Junior High School
Senior Department	Senior High School

The uniform lesson for each department is preferable to the closely graded plan, not only because it makes possible a program of worship in harmony with the theme of instruction, but also because of the opportunities provided of correlating the Sunday School lessons with the topics of discussion in the Christian Endeavor Societies and other expressional agencies.

(1) PRIMARY DEPARTMENT

Since Beginners classes for ages 4 and 5 prepare children for the systematic study which will begin at the time children start first grade, a 12-year Bible course should start with the Primary Department. In the three years that children spend in the Primary Department, lesson material should contain a wide range of Bible stories to enable them to learn about God's love and care, and their duties to God and His creatures. Here the teacher is the central figure, and his/her life and example will constitute the greatest lesson that can be taught.

(2) Junior Department

Pupils now take up the narrative of the Old and New Testaments in chronological order. Bible history is predominant. The Bible itself becomes the central figure, pupils using it as their text. Pupils familiarize themselves with the Bible's arrangement by books, chapters, and verses, as well as the content of its narratives.

(3) Intermediate Department

Since pupils of this age group respond readily to evangelistic effort, the sacrificial work of Christ on the cross should constitute the central teaching, and primary attention should be given to decision and church membership.

Since Intermediate pupils are now entering junior high school and taking up science as a subject, Christian evidences should be introduced to counteract the teaching of evolution, as well as to awaken an interest in the Bible as a whole.

Since in early adolescence pupils gather knowledge en masse rather than detailed information, lessons should provide Bible surveys during the thirteenth and fourteenth years. Thus, even if a boy or girl should drop out of Sunday School during this period, we will have provided them with a knowledge of the entire Bible and afforded them a taste of, if not quickened their interest in, the unexplored portions of the Bible.

(4) Senior Department

Having now received nine years of graded instruction, adolescents entering senior high school should look forward to completing study of the entire Bible in the three remaining years in the Senior Department.

The first year could be most profitably spent in the study of doctrine. Most of the material for these lessons should be taken from the Epistles, some of which until this time have been too difficult for pupils to understand.

The second year should be devoted to a study of the poetical books. The natural theology which abounds in Job and Psalms is peculiarly fitting for a pupil's deepening love of nature, which now characterizes the soul of adolescents. In like manner, the lessons in Proverbs are of great assistance at this time of life, when youths are passing through their moral and spiritual struggles. Ecclesiastes was likely written for this very hour of worldly allurement, when material things loom large upon the horizon and spiritual things are little appreciated.

The last year should be devoted to studies in the prophetical books. In the Bible proofs with which pupils are already familiar, they discover that prophecy was one of the outstanding evidences of the infallibility of God's Word, and with this knowledge acquired, pupils may likely become interested in this vast unknown and unexplored portion of Scripture.

Such a curriculum, graded by department from the sixth to the seventeenth year, would not only unfold the Bible in systematic order, but would provide growing boys and girls with as adequate a knowledge of the Book of books as they receive on any secular subject.

* * *

In the early 1930s God was preparing a man who had once worked for the Moody Colportage Association to publish the All-Bible Graded Series. His name: Victor E. Cory. It would be a great step of faith that would impact not only Sunday Schools in the United States but also in Canada and Great Britain—and the lessons would also be translated by faithful workers for use in other countries.

CHAPTER 1

Aunt Jennie's Valentine Party

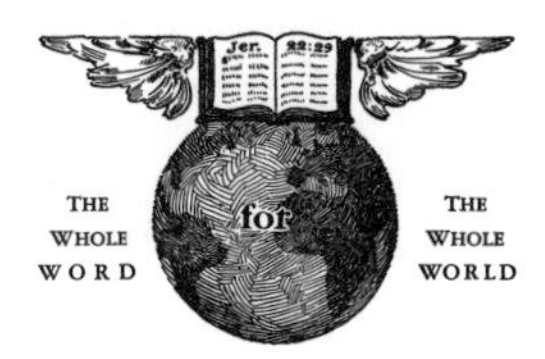

The year 1920 was an eventful time on the national scene. Women's hemlines were rising and were astonishingly nearer the knee than the ankle. More importantly, Secretary of State Bainbridge Colby signed the papers certifying ratification of the 19th Amendment to the U.S. Constitution, giving women the right to vote. Terrorists were even at work that year, for a time bomb killed 30 people and injured 300 others on Wall Street in New York. Prohibition went into effect in January, and by mid-June physicians in Chicago had written more than 300,000 spurious prescriptions for whiskey for patients, to treat everything from stomach cramps to insomnia. Baseball made big headlines during the summer when the Boston Red Sox sold Babe Ruth to the Yankees for $125,000 and when eight Chicago White Sox players were indicted on charges of conspiring with gamblers to fix the 1919 World Series. And in November, Warren G. Harding, an Ohio newspaper publisher, was elected president and Calvin Coolidge became vice president.

President Warren G. Harding

A meeting by divine appointment

One evening in Chicago that same year, 1920, a group of young people gathered in the Chocolate Shop not far from North Shore Church, Wilson Avenue at Sheridan Road, for refreshments. Bernice (rhymes with *furnace*) Tucker, a senior at the University of Chicago, dug into her hot fudge sundae.

She was being closely observed by the young man seated directly across from her. He was Victor Cory, who had popped into the church one Sunday some weeks ago to get out of the rain. The warm welcome he got triggered his becoming a regular at church functions, particularly the Christian Endeavor youth meetings and other activities.[1]

As the young people enjoyed their ice cream and sodas, someone started a game that hilariously described different persons in their church with one word. To Bernice, herself a relatively newcomer, this was more than a game—it was an interesting way of getting acquainted with other church people.

Suddenly, Vic leaned toward her and teasingly asked, "What word would you use to describe me?"

"Fickle!" she blurted out without hesitation.

A stunned look swept the young man's face. "Fic-fickle?" he stammered. "But you don't even know me. Why, wh—?"

"The group was breaking up, and I made it a point to see that another young man escorted me home," Bernice later wrote. "Vic didn't know, of course, that the girls in our youth group had laughingly told me that he would be asking me for a date—'for,' they cautioned, 'he always dates the latest newcomer.' And at once I decided I'd play hard to get. Who was *Victor Cory,* anyway?

"Actually, I was too busy to get involved, for I was using every spare minute to study during my senior year at the University of Chicago. Even so this young man began to make a deep impression on me. I learned that he was an electrical engineer, a recent graduate of Case Tech in Cleveland and a former student engineer in the Officer's Training Program during World War I."

A strong hand on her arm

Soon it was Halloween and the North Shore Church Christian Endeavor group was wending its way, weirdly enough, through a cemetery at midnight, returning from a party. Suddenly, Bernice felt a strong hand take her arm. "Somehow I wasn't averse to Victor's persuasiveness then," she wrote, "for it was a spooky experience walking among the grave markers at that witching hour. We had a good time, and Victor saw me to my door. And as predicted by the girls, he asked for a date, and I agreed to go out with him."

From then on, Bernice admitted she was flattered by his evident enjoyment of her company, and soon she was enjoying this eager young man. Up till then, none of the young men she had dated, nor Bernice, had been the least bit serious. Marriage, for her, was on the far-off horizon. After all, she was preparing to be a high school English teacher, an ambition she had cherished from grade school days. Her father, Lloyd B. Tucker, her well-loved confidant, had encouraged her for years to study hard and keep well at the head of her classes so that she would be no ordinary teacher, but one well informed and as capable as possible. She felt she had no place in her program for imminent romance!

But Victor, being six years older than Bernice, was obviously serious. He was unhappy when, after her graduation from the university, she accepted an offer to teach in a township high school in central Illinois. "However, that nine months of separation—with but few brief get-togethers—was good for both of us," Bernice continued. "Psychologically, it was good to communicate our deepest affections via paper and ink."

"The green ink man"

In the little town where she was a schoolmarm, where everybody knew everyone else's business, Victor was known as "the green ink man." The postmaster became so used to his green ink missives that when Victor addressed one of his letters special delivery to "The Queen of the Universe," Bernice promptly received it.

Victor and Bernice were both young Christians by this time. They called themselves spiritual twins because they both came to Christ at a memorable Valentine party they had attended at her Aunt Jennie Rader's home. [She was a sister of Bernice's mother, Frances Tucker. Aunt Jennie's husband, Lyell Rader, was a brother of the widely known evangelist Paul Rader.] The party that Valentine's Day in 1920 had all the trimmings of a typical sweethearts' party, with the room decorated with red hearts and a valentine box covered with red-and-

Aunt Jennie Rader

white crepe paper into which the young people dropped valentines as they arrived. But Aunt Jennie's party was to be *very* different!

Her warm personality attracted the young people of North Shore Church. They enjoyed coming to her cozy cottage on Devon Avenue near Lake Michigan to pop corn and have good times with her three lively sons and daughter [Lyell, Paul, Daniel, and Frances].

"Hearts-and-love" Bible verses

As the party progressed, Aunt Jennie invited the group to sit around her dining table, close to a glowing potbellied stove. With a twinkle in her eye, she announced, "It being Valentine's night, I thought it would be appropriate to read some Bible verses relating to hearts and love. As you know, the Bible has a great deal to say about both hearts and love."

The low-hanging center light glowed brightly as Aunt Jennie read "heart" and "love" verses from her Bible. Without doubt she had her niece in mind, for Bernice was not living "the separated life" and didn't even know the Lord. Bernice winced as Aunt Jennie read, "All things are lawful unto me, but all things are not expedient. . . . [they] edify not" (1 Cor. 6:12; 10:23).

But it was 1 John 2:15 that caused Bernice most concern: "Love not the world, neither the things that are in the world. If any man love the world, the love of the Father is not in him."

"Aunt Jennie," Bernice interrupted, "that verse simply is not true!"

"Why do you say that?"

"I know it's not true, because I love the world and I love the Father, too."

Bernice was most sincere. She was honestly puzzled, just as she recently had been in Sunday School when her teacher, Mrs. Johnson, had said, "You cannot serve God and mammon."

Aunt Jennie looked at her niece searchingly, the light above her Bible spotlighting her earnest face. "Bernice, can you imagine a woman loving a man enough to want to marry him and be a true helpmeet to him, the kind of wife that God intends she should be—a helper in every respect—and at the same time *wanting* another man?"

The illustration hit home. "Aunt Jennie, if you're right, then

I'm willing to jump the fence tonight." For weeks deep down inside, Bernice had felt she was straddling a spiritual fence. It was her way of saying that she was receiving the Lord Jesus Christ into her heart.

Aunt Jennie, who had been praying for this all day, gave Bernice a big hug. Then the party continued.

Later, Bernice talked with the Savior. "Lord Jesus, if You're everything that my aunt Jennie thinks You are, and everything Mrs. Johnson and our pastor think You are, then please show me, because I'm from Missouri." This was certainly an unconventional prayer, but the Lord heard. And that Valentine evening He gave Bernice Tucker a brand-new heart.

I've 'jumped the fence' too!"

Next morning, Sunday, as Bernice walked into Sunday School, Vic approached, waving a New Testament. "I've 'jumped the fence' too!" he exclaimed. "I read my Testament till 2 o'clock this morning, and the Lord has convinced me that I also needed to ask Christ into my heart."

Soon Bernice returned to her teaching job in Charleston, Illinois. Vic remained behind, absolutely enmeshed in church activities and, as a result, grew as a Christian.

Bernice, on the other hand, received little or no spiritual food in the church she attended, and her only avenue of service was teaching a Sunday School class of teen-age girls.

"I was a poor Bible teacher," she admitted. "I knew so little of the Word of God, and I was not faithfully reading it daily or praying with my former earnestness. I was what the wise writer of Proverbs calls a 'backslider in heart . . . filled with [my] own ways' (14:14). Also I found it hard to keep turning down the increasingly tantalizing invitations of one of the town's most eligible bachelors, who had taken a liking to me. After all, I argued, Vic and I weren't engaged, and Liz, the math teacher, would have been highly elated if Alex had paid similar attention to her."

In late October, seven months after Aunt Jennie's valentine party, Vic noticed a change in Bernice. They were attending a University of Illinois football game. "Somehow, Bernice, you aren't the same girl who left Chicago."

"What on earth do you mean?" Anger surged within. What right did he have to pass judgment on her! Later he pulled out his Testament and read what sounded like a scorching indictment. He felt she had not made a real break with the world. He did not like the pleasure-seeking crowd she ran with, the worldly people who lived in the house where she roomed. Then, rubbing salt into her wounds, he bowed his head and prayed for her—"as if I were a Skid Row bum," Bernice recalled.

"Much as I dreaded it, I took Vic's advice and moved out of the cheery, comfortable house in which I was rooming, clear across town to a somber, 'safer' room. It almost created a town scandal when I left the frivolous atmosphere of our most worldly minded teachers and lived with a married couple. The Paynes, my new 'landlords,' were a steadying influence, and Marie Payne helped me get back on my Bible-reading track."

Thus, Bernice learned early in her Christian experience the subtle influences of environment and the need to shun associations that drew her away from her Lord and destroyed her appetite for His Word. "The Lord," she later revealed, "more than compensated for what I, at first, had looked on as a 'sacrifice.' I felt relieved to be rid of tumultuous temptations and was glad for the increasing joy and satisfaction I experienced in my new surroundings."

Engaged at last

Suddenly it was Christmas—and home she went for the holidays. "By this time my topsy-turvy heart was willing to accept Victor's urging to become engaged," she continued. "Thus our romantic Aunt Jennie's announcement party for my sister Ruth and her fiance, Kenneth Mullins, turned out to be a double announcement party. I had no ring, as Ruth did, but my cousin Frances promptly made one for me, from some tinsel on the tree. What a happy party we had, with our family and friends!"

Bernice's heart was in Chicago as she finished her high school teaching job that she so much enjoyed. The days from January to June were busy and full of anticipation, punctuated by more meaningful letters from her "green ink man."

Vic and Bernice were married on June 16, 1922 in a simple wedding in their beloved church. It was attended only by their immediate family and relatives. Actually they couldn't afford both a big church wedding and a honeymoon. So they chose the latter.

Victor and Bernice started their married life at a breakneck pace. Victor was president of their Christian Endeavor Society and led the group to sing on the church steps Sunday nights to attract passers-by, and conducted evangelistic meetings on a street corner near the church. Led by Vic, they visited hospitals and homes for the elderly, passing out tracts there and on the streets.

In 1923 they welcomed their first son, Lloyd, and in ensuing years, sons Paul, Dan, and Phil.

A challenge for Vic

In 1924 Vic, now a testing engineer for Commonwealth Edison Company, went to the Lord in prayer after Paul Rader challenged him, "Why don't you quit and get into the Lord's work?"

An invitation came to become manager of the Tabernacle Publishing Company, and he left Commonwealth Edison (now ComEd) to try his hand at publishing. Later he worked for a time at Hope Publishing Company. Then, in the late '20s, burning his electrical engineering bridges behind him, Vic became assistant manager of the Moody Colportage Association, forerunner of Moody Press, the publishing arm of Moody Bible Institute, Chicago. The Lord had led him a step closer to a venture that would impact Sunday Schools across America and in many countries abroad, for here he became a close friend of Clarence H. Benson, director of Christian Education courses at the Institute.

Vic Cory (straw hat) armed with Gospel tracts with group gathered for a street meeting at Devon and Western, Chicago, probably 1921.

---

[1] Adapted largely from "Aunt Jennie's Valentine Party" by James R. Adair, *Power for Living*, February 14, 1965.

Just Who Were the Corys—and Clarence H. Benson?

VICTOR E. CORY: An electrical engineer from Ohio

TO HELP CELEBRATE the boss' 63rd birthday, Scripture Press employees on July 31, 1956 enjoyed a Ralph Edwards' type program titled "This Is Your Life, Victor E. Cory." The script read as follows, with some details added:

> Victor Edwin Cory, you were born in North Baltimore, Ohio, on July 30, 1893. Your father, Orrin James Cory, was county supervisor of schools in Tiffin, Ohio, where you moved with your family in your very early years. Your mother, Mary Ellen Cory, had been a schoolteacher. So, you come from pedagogical stock. You were the older of two boys, your brother Russell coming along four years after you were born.
>
> Oddly enough, Mr. Cory, even when in grade school, you were connected with the publishing business—you were a news carrier—and you were a life member of The National Newsboys Association. I wonder if you remember what the card motto said. It went like this: "He does not approve of swearing, lying, stealing, gambling, drinking intoxicating liquors, or smoking cigarettes. . . ."
>
> Yes, those were exciting years for you as a boy, deliver-

ing the Tiffin daily newspaper.

As you went on to graduate from Tiffin High School in 1911, you were indeed a handsome fellow, with a full head of hair and a smile that made the girls of that day swoon.

Mr. Cory, you continued your climb up the publishing ladder as you went on to Heidelberg College in Tiffin. You became business manager of the *Ki-lick-a-lick,* the college's newspaper. It was your first real publishing venture, and you loved that work.

After you got your B.S. degree from Heidelberg, you got a fellowship to Case University, and electrical engineering became your first love, and for a time publishing was forgotten. At Case you proved that you were living by the code of your newsboy's card, when you, with your brother, Russell, joined a fraternity. Things got rough, and you moved out of the frat house; drinking, gambling, and such things were not for you, even before you met the Lord. During this period, you played your clarinet in a trio.

Vic Cory in Tiffin days.

At Case, where you got your second B.S. degree, you wore Uncle Sam's uniform, as it was during World War I. By the time you were out of Case, the war was over. And you began to search for work.

Sometime during college days, you had worked for the Weather Bureau in Detroit, but this hadn't appealed to you. So, with your brother Russell and some college pals, you hit out for Chicago, a city of opportunity. You arrived in the summer of 1919. All of you landed jobs and roomed together near the lakefront, in the vicinity of Wilson Avenue and Sheridan Road.

It was this same summer, Mr. Cory, that a sudden summer thunderstorm proved to be the spiritual turning point in your life. You and your brother and friends were so-called good boys, believed in going to church, and on this particular Sunday you were on your way to a church of your denominational persuasion. But before you got there, rain began to pour. To keep from becoming drenched, you and your pals ducked into the nearest building—North Shore

> Church! God had His man at the door, John Long, the friendly head usher, who made you feel at home. Following the service, he introduced you to some other young people, and you were invited to a social that week. Being a boy in a strange city, you were delighted, and soon you were entrenched at North Shore Church.

[The "This Is Your Life" presentation went on to give details mentioned in chapter 1 of this book.] The presentation continued:

> Now about this same time, Mr. Cory, a lot was happening in the life of a certain young woman named Bernice Tucker. [After her sophomore year of college studies at the University of Denver], she returned to Chicago in the summer of 1919 and began attending North Shore Church at the invitation of her Aunt Jennie Rader. God had done great things for the Rader family, and Aunt Jennie was to have a great influence on both Bernice and you. Evangelist Paul Rader had been instrumental in bringing to the Lord his older brother, Lyell, and his wife and their family. Lyell's wife was Bernice's Aunt Jennie. So, when Aunt Jennie invited Bernice and her mother and father and two sisters to North Shore Church, it was with a real motive.
>
> At North Shore Church several people played a part in reaching both you and Bernice for Christ. There was Pastor Paul Riley Allen, a man who had been a liberal minister but had found the Lord in a real way; then your Sunday School teacher, A.M. Johnson, a millionaire who loved the Lord, and his wife, Mrs. Johnson, who was Bernice's teacher.
>
> It seems you were never formally introduced to Bernice; you were both members of the same youth group, and you, Victor Cory, at first thought Bernice Tucker was only a kid and paid little attention to her. You were a college graduate with two degrees and weren't interested in a mere schoolgirl. But one Sunday afternoon at a Christian Endeavor meeting, Dr. Hibbard, a young dentist, introduced Bernice as a senior at the University of Chicago [she went to the U of Chicago for her freshman and senior years and to the U of Denver her sophomore and junior years] and gave her a bit of a buildup, and you, Mr. Cory, pricked up your ears.

After she described you as "Fickle!" at the Dutch chocolate shop on Broadway, you began to date Bernice to prove you weren't fickle. The two of you had good times with the North Shore group—swimming, hiking, partying, praying.

But where love develops, there often is disappointment for someone else—and that was the case with your girlfriend. For in your college days, you had courted a girl from Western Reserve. For Christmas 1919 you gave her a string of beads; you gave Bernice a box of candy. But two Christmases later, things had changed; you gave Bernice a diamond ring, and, of course, the Western Reserve girl got nothing!

[The script continued with the account of Aunt Jennie's Valentine party, resulting in both Bernice and Vic "jumping the fence" to a relationship with Christ.]

Victor Cory, you and Bernice were married in a quiet ceremony on June 16, 1922 at North Shore Church, and very appropriately, in one of the Sunday School rooms. From the first, you wore seven-league boots of faith, and you meant business for the Lord. At that time you were president of the Christian Endeavor at the church, with an attendance of about 100. On holidays you would lead a group in blanketing communities with tracts and Gospels of John.

The Cory Family Brass Quartet: Paul, Lloyd, Dan, and Dad, plus little Phil.

There were Gospel meetings on street corners. Four nights a week you and your new bride would board a streetcar and go to street meetings. You looked like immigrants, you with a folding organ and a chair, and Bernice with tracts and Gospels of John. Two nights a week you held forth at Lincoln and Giddings, and two nights at Wilson and Kenmore.

Even when Lloyd, your first son, came along, Bernice and you would give your testimonies as you rolled Lloyd in a baby carriage. Later, when you had four sons, three of them, Lloyd, Paul, and Dan, joined you in The Cory Family Brass Quartet. You played in missions, churches, street meetings, and even a penitentiary.

At the time of your marriage, Mr. Cory, you worked for

Commonwealth Edison Company as one of their nine testing engineers in Chicago. Your business life wound around volts, amperes, generators, and transformers, as your son, Lloyd, once put it. One day, when you were in a substation, a worker on a nearby elevated line dropped his crowbar across the third rail. Immediately the substation looked and sounded like the grand finale of a July 4th fireworks demonstration, except that it was all indoors. You, Vic Cory, dived through the nearest window, which probably saved your life. All you had to show for the mishap was a small piece of molten metal which imbedded itself in a lens of your glasses.

About 1925, Paul Rader, pastor-evangelist of the Chicago Gospel Tabernacle, challenged you (you played your clarinet in Rader's band). He asked you to work in a Sunday boys club. You replied that you would like to but that you often had to work on Sundays. "Why don't you get out of that work and get into *God's* work?" Rader retorted.

The idea of leaving your electrical profession shocked you, but you prayed about it. Soon you became manager of Tabernacle Publishing Company. A.M. Johnson, president of American Life Insurance Company, who was your Sunday School teacher at North Shore Church, had bought up numerous copyrights of songs and had established that publishing firm. Rader, under whose ministry Johnson had come to the Lord, had encouraged him to buy up "blood" songs, Second Coming songs, and other favorites of that day.

As you have remarked, you then didn't know the difference between a telegram and a bill of lading and you learned the business of publishing songbooks from those who worked under you.

The year 1927 found you at the Bible Institute Colportage Association, where you served as assistant manager. You became acquainted with Clarence Benson, and he called you "Mr. Syntax," because you did such a good job editing his books. Then came the Great Depression, and you were out of a job.

[The script went on to chronicle events that led to the founding of Scripture Press, including moves that led in time to 800 North Clark Street, where the "This Is Your Life" presentation was made.]

Helped start Sunday School movements

In addition to founding Scripture Press with his wife, Bernice, Vic Cory helped start the Greater Chicago Sunday School Association and was one of the main founders of the National Sunday School Association. In 1958 he received an LL.D. degree from Wheaton College in recognition of his contribution to the cause of Christian education. Eunice Fischer, instrumental in helping start Scripture Press with her letter written to Dr. Gray of Moody Bible Institute (see chapter 4), congratulated Dr. Cory with a long list of things he did not have to do to receive his doctorate (Appendix): For example, he didn't have to spend a day in the college library, type out a term paper, pay a board bill.

The first Board of Directors of the Greater Chicago Sunday School Association, 1940. Vic Cory and G. Otto Underwood, a Moody Bible Insitute graduate and employed by MBI, worked out the polan for GCSSA. Front row: C.V. Egemeier, editor of *The Sunday School Promoter*, executive secreatry of the board; Gene Saulnier (Bernice Cory's sister), part-time office secretary; and Underwood, the first chairman. Second row: Bill Johnston, superintendent of Maquette Manor Baptist Sunday School; Kenneth Brouwer, superintendent of North Shore Sunday School; Vic Cory, superintendent of North Side Gospel Center Sunday School; Ed James, general superintendent of Moody Church Sunday School; and Carl Stone, superintendent of Cicero Bible Church Sunday School. The first convention was held in 1940.

Though his heart was always in Scripture Press, he served on the boards of at least 11 other evangelical Christian organizations, among them both of the mentioned Sunday School associations, Evangelical Teacher Training Association, Pacific Garden Mission, Lightbearers, Child Evangelism, Winona Lake Corporation, and the Great Commission Prayer League.

Dr. Cory would not take any credit for his remarkable achievements. One of his characteristic remarks was, "The Lord had a job to be done, and I just happened to be standing around where He could use me."

He enjoyed pithy sayings

Vic Cory, known for his smile, bald head, and whistle as he walked the halls of Scripture Press, appreciated the Book of Proverbs and enjoyed collecting pithy sayings similar to those he read in his Bible. He scribbled many on scraps of paper while hearing messages from such men of God as Jack Wyrtzen, Lindsay Glegg, Torrey Johnson, Bob Cook, Alan Redpath, and his pastor, Malcolm Cronk. He did not usually indicate the sources in his notes; so no credit is given for any of the following quotations from his files:

> Bond slaves don't make decisions; they accept decisions.

"A failure is not someone who makes mistakes but someone who refuses to learn from them."

"The difference between an honorable and a prudent man: The former deplores a discreditable act even when it has worked for his benefit [but not necessarily so for the prudent man]. 'Whatever works is good' has led more men into the devil's camp than any other slogan."

"Why do sincerity and stupidity so often go hand in hand?"

"We usually admire the dramatic when we think we are admiring the courageous. In other words, we respect the window washer when actually he is safer than the pedestrians 15 stories below."

"We are to grow in faith to increase our faithfulness."

"Noah did what he did because he believed what he believed."

"Find out what God says; believe it and behave it."

"The man who wholly follows God will follow the man God appoints."

"So much trouble in Christian circles comes from strife over methods and procedures."

"We must sacrifice differences of opinion to unity of principle."

"Be careful you don't start something when you try to stop something."

"The smartest person is not the quickest one to see through a thing but to see things through."

"Important words: 'I am proud of you' and 'What is your opinion?'"

"To men who follow Him, God gives not only a vision of unlimited horizons, but a strong back and a determined mind to push on toward those horizons. As always, the horizons are ever moving ahead of them—ever out of reach—yet God's man strides on!"

"You don't have to have a high coefficient of gullibility to be a Christian."

"Let's eliminate the gadgetry and get on with the dynamics of the Sunday School—for times like these."

"The world is looking for somebody. God is looking for a nobody."

"Live a moment at a time—and that moment for God."

> Raise our sights on the value of a soul, the power of the Word, and the value and importance of teaching the Word of God. We must not be salesmen for Jesus but sales managers.

Cory also enjoyed jotting down humorous bits and pieces, among them:

> A lot of men miss their wives' cooking—every chance they get.
>
> An undertaker's problem: How not to look happy at a $10,000 funeral.
>
> Personnel supervisor: "What previous experience have you had and what work have you done?" Applicant: "I was a secretary. All I had to do was look like a girl, think like a man, act like a lady, and work like a horse."

And the Scripture Press president also had his views relating to readable lessons:

> Lowering the fog index usually means: Keep sentences short. Prefer simple to complex. Prefer familiar to unfamiliar. Avoid unnecessary words. Put action in your verbs. Write the way you talk. Use terms your reader can picture. Tie in with your reader's experiences. Make full use of variety. Write to express, not impress.

And he had this formula for writing letters of apology:

> If you want a letter of apology to have impact . . . to sound sincere and be effective: Keep it short and sweet. The letter should do four things:
>
> 1. Show the recipient that you appreciate the way he feels.
> 2. Take all the blame you possibly can.
> 3. Tell him you're sorry.
> 4. Show him what you are going to do to make amends.

A man of The Book

Lastly, as you would expect, Vic Cory—man of The Book that he was—memorized Scripture passages and made various notations of verses that had impacted him.

Especially at times when evil forces seemed to be trying to disrupt the ministry of Scripture Press, he would go to 2 Chronicles 20. He would pray in the words of verse 12: "O our God, . . . we have no might against this great company that cometh against us; neither know we what to do, but our eyes are upon Thee." And then he would remind God that he believed the promise to King Jehoshaphat: "Thus saith the Lord . . . , 'Be not afraid nor dismayed by reason of this great multitude; for the battle is not yours, but God's. . . . Ye shall not need to fight in this battle. Set yourselves, stand ye still, and see the salvation of the Lord with you. . . . Fear not, nor be dismayed; tomorrow go out against them, for the Lord will be with you' " (vv. 15, 17).

Vic Cory's favorite New Testament chapter was John 11, the raising of Lazarus. In praying, he would quote Jesus' words, "This . . . is . . . for the glory of God, that the Son might be glorified thereby" (11:4, KJV).

His favorite song was "God Leads His Dear Children Along." He loved its message, son Lloyd recalls.

He marked other favorite Scriptures in his Bible, copied verses on cards and note paper, and even filled entire sheets with passages from the Word—such as:

> "Ascribe ye greatness unto our God" (Deuteronomy 32:3, a verse he had painted on the wall of the lobby of the Wheaton offices of Scripture Press).
>
> "Ask of Me, and I shall give thee the heathen for thine inheritance, and the uttermost parts of the earth for thy possession" (Psalm 2:8).
>
> "That I may publish with the voice of thanksgiving, and tell of all Thy wondrous works" (Psalm 26:7).
>
> "I am crucified with Christ; nevertheless I live; yet not I, but Christ liveth in me: and the life which I now live in the flesh I live by the faith of the Son of God, who loved me, and gave Himself for me" (Galatians 2:20).

* * *

As Victor Cory searched the Scriptures and strengthened his faith through the Word, his wife and business partner, Bernice, also feasted on her Bible.

BERNICE T. CORY: Editor in Chief

Bernice Tucker Cory was born June 26, 1899, in Denver, Colorado, the daughter of Lloyd Byron and Frances Campbell Tucker. She received a Ph.B. from University of Chicago on June 15, 1920. As previously mentioned, she spent her sophomore and junior years at University of Denver, and while at Denver she earned partial tuition by assisting professors in the departments of Psychology, Education, and English.

After graduation, she taught for a year at Oakland High School near Charleston, Illinois, teaching Junior and Senior English, French, Public Speaking, and Physical and Commercial Geography.

In 1920, Bernice Tucker met and fell in love with a young electrical engineer, Victor Cory. And as previously recounted, it was on Valentine's Day, at a party planned by Bernice's Aunt Jennie for the young people of the Sunday School they attended, that both Bernice and Victor received Christ as their Savior.

In a paper written about 1960, she gave the following information about Aunt Jennie and went on to tell of the encounter with Christ that she and Vic had:

> Paul Rader led his brother Lyell to Christ. Lyell married my mother's sister, Aunt Jennie. When they started to interest us in Christianity, we thought they had gone off the deep end. We both were reared in Methodist churches and felt that all good people went to heaven. We were determined that my aunt and uncle weren't going to influence us! But the Lord worked otherwise. We are very grateful to Aunt Jennie for all she did for us in bringing us to the Lord.
>
> Mrs. A.M. Johnson, being my Sunday School teacher and knowing the separated life problems so well, was a wonderful person to come into my life at that time. I was impressed that she, with all of her wealth, didn't care about any of it compared with her faith in the Lord. She became a really earnest Bible teacher when she was saved. Her parlor was furnished with pretty drapes and nice furniture, and it made a real home away from home for girls working in the city. We never missed the Monday night class there or Mrs. Johnson's Sunday School lessons. It was through these means and my aunt's working on us at other times that we came to know the Lord.

After the Valentine party, Victor and I walked home. He asked, "Aren't you going to the movies with me tomorrow night?"

I replied, "No, I am not. I am going to try to think." I prayed that night, "If Christ is everything Mrs. Johnson thinks you are and my Aunt Jennie thinks You are, You have to show me, because I am from Missouri." I thought, "If it does not work, I can easily go back to what I was. I will just see."

The next morning in Sunday School, Victor came toward me waving his Testament. "I jumped the fence, too," he said. He had gone home and read his Testament until 2 a.m. and made his stand at the same time I did.

Dr. J.C. O'Hair, pastor of North Shore Church, had been a modernist before he was converted under the ministry of Paul Rader. He was not powerful and didn't indoctrinate people in the Word as Paul Rader did. But I loved that church. We literally prayed Scripture Press into existence at that church. It was O'Hair's preaching that got me into the Bible. I never went to a Bible institute or took a Bible institute course in college. Mr. O'Hair gave me a love for the Word of God. I learned a lot of Scripture by hearing him say it over and over again.

"Blessed Quietness": favorite song

From the outset of their married life, the Corys were active in Christian work. They worked in the Sunday School, in Christian Endeavor, and during the first few years held street corner meetings on an average of four nights a week. While bringing up four sons, Lloyd, Paul, Daniel, and Philip, she said her favorite song was "Blessed Quietness."

Bernice Cory taught Sunday School classes regularly, beginning in 1920. Thus her writing bore the sure touch of one who had learned in the school of experience.

A plumpish woman whose long stride always seemed to make her appear in a hurry, Bernice often spoke at Sunday School Conventions, conferences, and seminars, as well as at Mother-Daughter banquets, missionary meetings, and other Christian gatherings. She addressed Sunday School gatherings in England and Scandinavia, and traveled extensively throughout the world (Europe, the Near East, Far East, and South

America) in the interest of Sunday School work.

On her travels she kept extensive logs written in a clear, legible style. In a small red notebook, she recorded a mid-'30s trip to Georgia and North Carolina with with details, such as:

> It was already dark when we started out for Atlanta, which was the next town, and we were dreadfully tired. We had a pretty good supper at the Melba Cafeteria and then went to the Salvation Army home to try to locate Frances. We found the home dark and locked, and I was very disappointed; but as we were trying to get in, the night watchman, a garrulous old man, approached and wanted to know what we wanted. I asked him if he knew Mrs. Longino and indeed he did! When he found that my cousin married Commissioner Damon's daughter, 'twas the "open sesame" signal. He escorted me through the side door to the third floor, where a hilarious party was in progress. It was the annual Christmas party, but held mainly for Salvation Army youngsters and a merry group it was. I met Mrs. Damon and found out all the Rader news. Frances and Frank are in Lakeland, Florida—some 600 miles south of here, so we'll not be able to see her. . . . We stayed for most of the party, saw a magician's act, and had a pretty good time. As we had no place yet to lay our weary heads, we left before it was over.
>
> The Commissioner presented us with a lovely box of candy, and then we began to comb the streets for a tourist home. Unlike the small towns which abound in such places, Atlanta has practically none. So we finally found an inexpensive hotel on Peachtree Street—Hotel Byron. Paid $1.50 and got a room and bath, such as it was! It was a dump, and it saddened my spirits to have to stay there, but I was so tired that I could have slept on a stove poker. We both got baths, however, and slept well, even though the sheets were split and the blankets needed a good bath. We thought we had a private bath, but after we were in bed found that the next room was being occupied and the bath between was our joint property pro tem!

On the trip Bernice kept a running record of such expenses as:

Henderson, Ky., 5 gals. of gas. 68
Blue Ridge, Ga., 5 gals 1.08
Dinner. 1.00
Lunch. 40
Room 1.00
Cabin 1.26

Like other travelers of that era, the Corys enjoyed the popular Burma Shave signs strung out along highways. She recorded some of the messages:

- Lather was not used by Daniel Boone. He lived 100 years too soon.
- Have pity on the mighty Caesars. They pulled each whisker out with tweezers.
- Beneath this stone lies Elmer Gush. He was tickled to death by his shaving brush.
- Every day we do our part to make your face a work of art.

She edited, wrote, and supervised

From the beginning of Scripture Press, Bernice Cory edited Bible-teaching materials. She authored perhaps 200 books and Sunday School manuals, and personally edited all Scripture Press Sunday School and Vacation Bible School materials from October 1934 until 1948, when her son Lloyd joined the staff. He began as editorial production manager, working with printers and artists. Later he became assistant editorial division director, and after her death, Editorial vice president. He was an English major at Wheaton College, graduating after serving in the infantry in the Pacific during World War II.

Bernice Cory in October 1947 at 800 North Clark working with her assistants, (l. to r.) Barbara Hendry, Ruth Camp Reid, and Ruth McNaughton. Photo on wall: Dr. James M. Gray.

As editor in chief, Bernice Cory supervised the work of 20 people who wrote, edited, and prepared for printing the All-Bible materials used by people belonging to more than 70 denominations, on every continent on the globe.

When asked what she considered her most significant contribution to Christian life and thought, she replied, "I have tried to make the Word of God clear, understandable, and attractive to boys and girls and teachers of all ages through (1) careful and prayerful Bible study and (2) a variety of nonprojected visual aids. The Lord has graciously blessed the Gospelgraph which I originated. This is a visual aid designed for the flannelboard. Its purpose is to clarify Bible doctrines and relate those truths to practical everyday living through analogies used in the Scriptures — sowing-reaping, for example, and analogies such as paths, highways, feet, shoes, etc."

Bernice Cory received an honorary Litt.D degree from Biola College (now Biola University) in 1959.

She never slackened her pace, but kept a demanding work schedule that frequently involved 10 or 12 hours a day at the office. She was especially happy after she finished a Cradle Roll course about 1950 that included separate letters to parents and a how-to manual. In the letters, she presented pictures of a baby's physical and emotional development from birth to 2 years of age and encouraged parents to grow in grace and set godly examples for their children.

When asked in 1950 concerning her vision and burden for years to come, Mrs. Cory replied, "To pass on to consecrated, talented youth (especially young men) in Bible Institutes, Colleges, etc.: (1) the unlimited possibilities in the field of Christian education; (2) the worldwide missionary aspect of Sunday School lesson writing; (3) the joy of being used of God to spread the Gospel through the printed page.

She added that her goals included:

> "To inform and inspire pastors concerning the importance of the Sunday School in their overall ministry: (1)The fact that the Sunday School is the only organization within the church that reaches the entire family; (2) the importance of training preschoolers—the Cradle Roll and Nursery departments of the Sunday School—in Christian character building; (3) the value of the church-home link—ministries which the Cradle Roll and Home Department can provide; (4) to turn out more and ever-better teaching materials for all age-groups, as God gives us wisdom, strength, and ability (not to mention helpers); and (5) to recruit a godly, Bible-loving, educated, editorial staff."[2]

DR. CLARENCE H. BENSON: He too had a vision

Dr. Clarence H. Benson entered history at a crucial time for the historic Christian faith. Nationalism, evolution, and theological liberalism were advancing like a flood tide, sweeping away many established citadels of truth. The faith of millions was being threatened. Whole denominations, schools, and many homes were hurrying to the brink of total abandonment of the Word of God. Into this darkening picture came the quiet, hardworking man whom God chose to use against the advance of educational error.

Unlike the reformers of the Sixteenth Century who opposed established error, Dr. Benson was on the scene when the departures were being made. Controversy arose as extra-biblical material was introduced into the widely used International Graded Series of Sunday School curriculum.

By 1917 the Religious Education Association sought to introduce their experience-centered, Deweyan philosophy into the curriculum of the national Sunday School convention. This was a blow to conservatives who resolutely resisted both the graded system and experience-centered lessons because of their neglect of the Scriptures that accompanied these developments. Thus there was no provision for the conservatives in the Sunday School. Furthermore, teacher training received a near death blow when the conservative Advanced Training Course was changed to the Leadership Training Course by the liberals, and the curriculum was revised to eliminate evangelism, missions and adequate Bible study. Because of these factors, American Sunday Schools plunged to a new low, and from 1922 until 1945 there was no organization known as a Sunday School association. "For such a time as this," the Lord gave Clarence H. Benson to His Church.

Dr. Clarence H. Benson, under whose direction the All-Bible curriculum began.

Born into a missionary family

Clarence Benson was born in a manse in August 1879. His father was a preacher-missionary; his grandfather and great-grandfather were Moravian missionaries to the Indians. His father was a pioneer builder of churches and he started 16 young men, including his own son, in the ministry. His family was sturdy, industrious, and purposeful and their educational interests and pursuits were above average.

Though young Benson early learned the meaning and value of work, he was also trained in cultural and aesthetic things by his devout mother. She cultivated his interest in nature, particularly astronomy, in which he later majored at college. He became an enthusiastic pianist and vocalist after his mother introduced him to music. His conversion cannot be dated, since his trust in Christ was in the midst of a warm Christian atmosphere and training, which he had throughout his entire youth.

During his youth Clarence Benson came under the loving guidance of a Sunday School teacher (name unknown) who counseled and encouraged him even after he left home for college. Benson studied at the University of Minnesota and Macalester College, majoring in astronomy and at the same time, pursuing journalistic interests. While at Macalester he played halfback on the varsity football team. He was fond of yachting, and in later years played volleyball regularly in order to keep physically fit. He graduated from Princeton Theological Seminary in 1908.

Benson's first ministry consisted of two country churches in eastern New York. In August 1908 he was ordained, and in September he married Rena Pearl Clark, whom he had met at a Christian Endeavor convention in Minnesota. An earnest Christian, his wife encouraged, supported, and shared Benson's ministry throughout his lifetime.

During subsequent years he served five different pastorates in New York and Pennsylvania until, in 1919, he was called and he went to the pastorate of the Union Church of Kobe, Japan. After three years of successful and varied ministry abroad, Benson returned to the United States.

Following much soul-searching, Clarence Benson accepted an invitation from Dr. James M. Gray to join the teaching staff of the Moody Bible Institute. Though he little realized it at the time, this was the beginning of his destined ministry as a Christian educator to that school, to the Sunday School, to the Church, and to the world.

In 1924 the Moody Bible Institute inaugurated its Religious Education course, later named Christian Education, and Benson was made its director. He was described by his colleagues and students as "visionary though practical, friendly, thorough, and possessing an excellent sense of humor." He spent much of his time working with individuals. This was true of his home life, too. He was an understanding husband and a sympathetic, wise father who sacrificed much to build a lifelong fellowship with his two sons.

The work of Clarence Benson

As a pastor, Clarence Benson was an eminent success. He was always close to his people through extensive visitation. He was keenly aware of the needs of youth and was tireless in his work for them. He maintained a thoroughly biblical pulpit ministry which always increased his congregation. He advocated the personal responsibility of each member to witness regularly, have a family altar, give systematically and proportionately to the church and missions. He believed in the publicity of church activities, lay leadership, cottage prayer meetings, personal evangelism, and strong Sunday Schools. He preached and practiced a godly harmony of human effort and the ministry of the Spirit.

As an author, Benson had an early interest and was active in periodical journalism. For 15 years he was an associate editor of *Moody Monthly.* He founded and was editor-in-chief of *The Church School Promoter* magazine, later called *Sunday School Promoter* (see Appendix for the May 1943 issue that contains a biographical sketch of Benson). He contributed regularly to *The Sunday School Times.* He is best known, however, for his many books: *The Greatness and Grace of God;* two on astronomy—*The Earth, the Theatre of the Universe and Immensity;* six on Christian Education—*A Popular History of Christian Education, Techniques of a Working Church, The Christian Teacher, An Introduction to Child Study, The Church at Work, The Sunday School in Action.* He wrote extensively for the curriculum of the All-Bible Graded Series and also for the Evangelical Teacher Training Association.

In his writing ministry Benson's slogan became "The whole Word for the whole world." His slogan as a teacher became "Teaching teachers to teach others to teach." He had a background in secular education which helped prepare him to teach pedagogy later on. His first Sunday School teaching experience was in his teens. At Moody Bible Institute he taught Child Study, Pedagogy, Sunday School Administration, History of Religious Education, Teacher Training, Curriculum

Making, and Practice Teaching.

In most courses he used the lecture method exclusively, probably due to his background of preaching. One student accused him of being cold and mechanical, boring, being bound to his notes and having annoying nervous mannerisms. If this was true, his defects only served to heighten the marvel of his impact on those he taught.

Benson was unquestionably sincere and vitally enthusiastic regarding Christian education. As a promoter of Christian education, Clarence Benson has indirectly affected the lives of millions of boys and girls and adults through his curriculum making, teacher training courses, and national Sunday School conventions. In the face of the avalanche moving toward Dewey's secular philosophy in education, Benson wrote, "Modern educationalists have made a mistake in thinking that expressional methods can be improved by changing the content of the lesson. The Bible is the changeless Book for the changing age and the Scriptures can be applied to meet the needs of the individual."

He and his students wrote a completely graded, biblical curriculum for the Sunday School. They rejected the closely graded approach, favoring departmentally graded lessons. They wrote lessons to force the teachers and pupils to use their Bibles. The curriculum included all the Scriptures in one way or another and not just 35 percent as the Uniform lessons did, or 65 percent, as previous graded lessons did.

In 1932, Victor Cory and Clarence Benson teamed up with several other educators to establish Scripture Press for the purpose of publishing the All-Bible Graded Series, though the first lessons were not published until October 1934. By 1956 there were 2,918,000 boys and girls who were reached with Scripture Press Sunday School materials.

In 1930 representatives of five Bible Institutes gathered under the inspiration of Benson to discuss the desperate need for teacher training among conservatives who would not join the liberal International Council of Religious Education for such training. They consequently organized the International Institute Council of Christian Education, later named the Evangelical Teacher Training Association. Since that time there have been over 20,000 graduates from their standard course and these trained teachers have effectively instructed countless numbers of Sunday School pupils.

In 1939 Benson was appointed chairman of a new lesson committee in the Administrative Board of the National Association of Evangelicals. To meet the need for those who insisted on uniform lessons, he worked with others on the Uniform Bible Lesson Series which was adopted by many denominations and publishers. These lessons were used by over 3 million pupils. Out of this work grew the National Sunday School Association which held its first convention in 1946 in Chicago. For years the national conventions grew in numbers, enthusiasm, and productivity. This was the fulfillment of a long-held dream of Dr. Benson's.

When he died in 1954, Clarence Benson's ministry had reached out and touched at least indirectly most evangelicals in America.[3]

---

[1] "The Story of Scripture Press" told by Bernice Cory, O Box, SP Ministries Archives.

[2] Biography on disk in SP Ministries Archives.

[3] Details related to Clarence Benson are from a brief biography in the SP Ministries Archives from Scripture Press Publications, Ltd. (Canada). Attached to that copy is a note from Dr. John Unger (Ontario Bible College) to Lana Bills (president) dated 6/7/91 in which he states, "Enclosed is some old historic bits of information I used in doing my doctoral research." There is no indication of who wrote the article or when.

CHAPTER 3

A Letter to Dr. Gray

About the time Herbert Hoover became president in 1929, Eunice Fischer, a young Sunday School worker who had for a short time been a student at Moody Bible Institute and who had studied under Clarence H. Benson, wrote a letter to MBI president Dr. James M. Gray. In essence, it read as follows:

> Only dire necessity bids me take up your time with my problem. No doubt you have heard of the appalling need for Sunday School literature before this, Dr. Gray. Dr. Benson said a year ago that Moody Bible Institute had been vaguely considering getting out fundamental Christian literature to meet the need in hundreds of dissatisfied churches. Is this not possible? Why should conferences and evangelistic campaigns always take precedence? These evangelistic endeavors among adults are needed. But how about the children? If the Catholic Church can say, "Give me the child until he is seven, then he may go where he likes" (and psychology proves the truth of this), do we not need to teach the Bible to those little ones entrusted to us, many of whose parents never even come to church but who would be reached by "the little child leading them"?
>
> I am not presuming to advise. I am merely laying the need before you as best I can. How can the Church expect or hope for a revival with such a neglect?[1]

Years after writing her letter to Dr. Gray, Eunice Fischer worked for SP as a convention speaker and editor.

With her letter, she sent Dr. Gray samples of four kinds of teaching materials being widely used in Sunday Schools. At the time she was superintendent of a department that included about 100 pupils through age 9, and 8 or 10 teachers. Now living in Rich Hill, Missouri, Miss Fischer, recalls that she "felt responsible for the curriculum and was dissatisfied" with what the teachers used, "the best" available in that day, according to Benson. "I wanted Dr. Gray to see with his own eyes what Sunday School teachers had to use," she continues.

After reading Miss Fisher's letter and examining the sample materials, Dr. Gray, with whom consistency was a jewel, called together Clarence Benson, William Norton, manager of the Moody Colportage Association, and Mr. Gaylord, Colportage treasurer and business manager of the Institute. Dr. Gray read the letter and passed around the sample materials and asked, "What can be done to meet this problem?"

Seeking to get the facts before the group, Benson spoke up. "My students, all college graduates, have been working with me on a 12-year curriculum extending from Primary through Seniors. For seven years these classes have worked intensively on materials for various age levels, and now the work is just about complete, with themes and Scripture references covering all the Bible and embodying the latest principles of pedagogy. If published, this curriculum could meet a great need in the Sunday Schools across the land."

Turning to Mr. Norton and Mr. Gaylord, Dr. Gray asked, "Could the Colportage publish the lesson material that Mr. Benson and his students have prepared?" The men explained it would require a lot of study and, therefore, no immediate answer could be given. Some weeks later the Colportage Association gave a definite no. It would be too costly. The Colportage couldn't afford getting into the business of publishing Sunday School lessons and marketing them to churches across America.

Miss Fischer remembers that, "after Moody declined, Dr. Benson wrote me and thanked me, 'for the great service you have rendered the Sunday School.'" Dr. Gray wrote, a note to her, ending "Keep on praying!"

Victor Cory, out of a job

It was probably a wise move for the Colportage Association,

for though the future looked bright when Hoover became president in 1929, his administration had hardly begun when the country suffered the worst business crash in its history. That fall, on October 29, the stock market crashed as desperate speculators sold 16,400,000 shares of stock. By year's end the country was in a deep depression. The government estimated that the crash had cost investors $40 billion. Millions of persons had lost every cent they owned. Banks failed, factories shut down, stores closed, and almost every business seemed paralyzed. In 1930 some 6 million Americans were out of work. Desperate men sold apples on street corners, many ate in "soup kitchens," and thousands lived in clumps of shacks called "Hoovervilles."

The Colportage Association lost money deposited in a bank that failed and had to retrench. There could be no new books; hence, no editorial work and no advertising. As a result, in 1930 the Colportage reluctantly released its manager, Victor Cory. He found himself looking to the Lord for the next step in his life—and a source of income to keep bread on the table for his growing family.

Lloyd Cory, the Corys' eldest son, comments: "I remember when Dad got fired. I think I was in second grade. Our family talked and prayed about everything around the kitchen table in our house in Chicago. I didn't know enough to be worried. Anyhow, nearly everybody we knew was poor during the Depression, so we four boys were happy. Dad's bank closed, and he lost all of his inheritance money, $18,000 from his father. Things got tough. The family got just one quart of milk a day, for all four boys—and the milkman paid for it till Dad could get a job. All the family soon wore cardboard in the bottoms of their worn-out shoes. But disappointment became a stepping stone. . . ."

Mrs. Cowman bounces in with hope

God sent Mrs. Charles E. Cowman, whose best-selling books, *Streams in the Desert* and *Springs in the Valley,* books that Vic had edited, to bring him hope. By appointment, they met in the 830 building of the Institute. She "came bouncing across the room with a lively step and beaming," Vic later wrote.[2] "I have tried to pray for you a score of times, but I simply couldn't," was Lettie Cowman's greeting.

His face, long and sad-sack looking when she approached, got even longer and sadder. He felt he had lost a good friend.

"I have tried to pray for you but no sooner would I start when the Lord would tell me, 'I know all about it, and I have already answered every prayer you could ask for the Corys,'" she continued. "There are wonderful things ahead, even though it may be necessary to go through a tunnel before the sunshine appears at the other end."

Vic's countenance brightened. Many verses, such as abound in Mrs. Cowman's books, came to mind, including this King James Version verse that had become one of his favorites, "And the Lord, He it is that doth go before thee. He will be with thee, He will not fail thee, neither forsake thee; fear not, neither be dismayed" (Deut. 31:8). By the time she and Vic parted, he was sharing "the unbounded joy and confidence felt in the heart of that great soul, Mrs. Charles E. Cowman."

Things did happen indeed. Mr. Benson still longed for the day when his 12-year curriculum would be available for America's Sunday Schools. After the Colportage Association declined to publish the lessons, Vic and Mr. Benson from time to time shared thoughts about getting the material published. Vic made it known that he would somehow start a business to get the lessons published. Harry Saulnier (later to become superintendent of Pacific Garden Mission), who had married Bernice's sister Gene, was leery of the idea. He asked, "Why don't you just get out some Gospel tracts? You can't buck International lessons—people are used to them. Why are you putting all your eggs in one basket?"

Bernice answered for Vic: "But, Harry, we believe God is leading us and we have only one egg!"

A giant step of faith

Soon Vic took a giant step of faith. Using borrowed money from a partner, he opened a printing plant sometime in 1931, put up a sign, The Scripture Press, Inc., Publishers & Printers. The firm's letterhead, with a touch of red under the word *Scripture,* gave the address as 829 Orleans Street, Chicago, Ill. The telephone number listed was DELaware 3082 and the slogan was proudly displayed, "Called into existence by the need for more Bible in the Bible schools of America." The proprietor of the print shop firmly believed God had given him the name

The Scripture Press and the slogan. The plant had three presses, a cutter, a stitcher, and a number of cases of type.

Son Lloyd remembers: "The plant was just south of where the Cabrini-Green projects are today, four blocks west of Clark Street and just north of Chicago Avenue. I recall as a little kid visiting there and seeing two presses running at once."

An agreement was signed in 1932 with Benson stipulating the working terms to supply teaching materials. He guaranteed to produce 12 completely edited quarterly units in exchange for "royalty of one-half (1/2¢) per copy on all Teacher's and Pupil's Manuals actually sold." In return for the copyright privileges of the compendium of the All-Bible Graded Series published in January 1933, the booklet of specimen pages printed in May 1933, and the Simplified Six-Point Record System, the publisher agreed to pay Benson $232.75, $210.75, and $25, respectively. Reimbursement for this was to come from profits occurring from the sale of the new Sunday School material

While Benson and his small staff prepared materials, The Scripture Press did commercial printing, particularly for Christian organizations. Initial products were stationery and envelopes. Printed boldly across the stationery was 1 Corinthians 15:57—"But thanks be to God, which giveth us the victory through our Lord Jesus Christ"—and on the envelope, "'And this is eternal life, that they might know Thee the only true God, and Jesus Christ, whom Thou hast sent' (John 17:3)."

Another product The Scripture Press offered was a printed circular intended to serve advertising needs. A customer's first wholesale order on circulars meant a thousand free circulars, and a trade discount offered 50 percent off orders totaling more than $50.

The little printing firm also published booklets that were sold to bookstores, churches, and schools. One of the first booklets was *The Church and the Great Tribulation* by William R. Newell. Booklets sold for 20 cents, with a 40 percent discount to dealers. SP printed a quarter of a million copies of the Gospel of John and sold more than 80,000 copies within the first three months of its first printing. For up to 500 copies, the trade price was 1.5 cents each with discounts offered on higher numbers. This was possible since much of the money for art, type, plates, etc., was donated. Gospels were imprinted for an additional charge on orders of more than 1,000.

All in the family

Vic took on the job of editing the lessons. Working in their home on the North Side at 4851 Saint Anthony Court (later renamed North Hamilton Avenue), the entire family pitched in to assemble advertising pieces that went out to churches. Lloyd, being oldest, got 11 cents an hour; Paul, 9 cents; and Dan, 8 cents. Phil was too young to participate. Lloyd remembers brother Paul asking, "Dad, why are all these guys named Rev.?" (He pronounced it "reev.") Items to be mailed were weighed on a homemade scale rigged up by Dad (see Appendix, "Historical Briefs").

Cory home in Chicago where it all started.

Soon "we printed the first compendium containing the themes and Scripture references for the 12-year course," according to Vic Cory's account. "By dint of much hard work, the first lesson for each department was written, set in type, and saw publication light in the form of a 32-page booklet. We mailed these around to friendly churches, and [I] carried a pile of them under [my] arm to conventions, conferences, Sunday School teachers' meetings, and everywhere anyone was found who could be interested enough to listen to a sales talk. The printing plant was quite impressive—to us anyway. To keep it going, however, we did all kinds of printing jobs for churches, institutions, and business firms. For a while, we printed most of the tracts used by the Colportage Association."

An entry penned on January 3, 1933 by Vic Cory on a letterhead with 1 Corinthians 15:58 ("Be ye steadfast, unmovable, always abounding in the work of the Lord, forasmuch as ye know that your labor is not in vain in the Lord") gives insight into the step of faith he was taking:

> This is the first day of work at The Scripture Press for the new year. Charlie, our foreman, was home sick with the flu. Our force was quite depleted, only Walter, Esther [Van Fleet, who worked as the Corys' housekeeper and also at SP on occasion], Willard, and I being on hand.
>
> I suggested to Norm Karsten my going to see Mr. Norton regarding our printing of the Moody Colportage

Library. He said it would be inadvisable as no change is being made now. We here are unitedly praying for this large job, averaging about $500 per month for the year for presswork only. We believe we should have it rather than a group of godless men working in a godless organization. Moreover our prices should be lower because of our smaller size and our particular knowledge of the work. We are praying that Holy Spirit wisdom might guide Norm and Mr. Norton in making their decision.

Mr. Benson was well pleased with final proofs on the Compendium. Mr. Vallee of the Sales Dept. of the Hall Printing Co. came in to visit. I told him we didn't have much work ahead but we were "trusting the Lord."

A check for almost $100 came this morning from Mrs. Cowman. Among the bills paid was one for electros and my own home gas bill (today being the last day without penalty). Praise Him!

The first annual meeting of stockholders was held on January 16, 1933, according to the minutes of the corporation. Previously, on October 3, 1932, stockholders had signed the initial subscription agreement at $10 a share—Vic Cory, 99 shares; Lloyd B. Tucker, 50; and Harry G. Saulnier, 1. The state of Illinois issued the certificate of incorporation on October 10, 1932.

"God Answers Prayer"

One day a petty thief stole a purse from the office during the noon hour. To avoid a repetition, the SP pressman rigged up a number of almost invisible wires running from the outer door to pulleys over various spots in the office and plant. On one of the pulleys directly over the large press he tied a ten-inch wooden spool. When someone opened the door, this spool slowly descended to a point just clearing the pressman's face. He then knew someone was coming in the door. In the middle of the bindery, he tied an old coffee pot, and when the door opened, the pot descended among those seated eating lunch. Another wire ran into the inner office, and from time to time a sign dropped down declaring "God Answers Prayer."

"Call unto Me, and I will answer thee, and show thee great and mighty things" (Jeremiah 33:3, KJV).

Many times, Cory wrote, the sign would descend as he was talking with some visitor. Or it would happen during a prayer meeting and "perhaps even as our foreman would be using his favorite prayer expression, 'Lord, make me lower than the linoleum.'" It was always a surprise, "but we somehow felt that our Lord would cause that outside door to be opened at some very auspicious times," the printer asserted. The prayer motto was later framed for display in the third-floor lobby at 800 North Clark Street.

"Come and get the presses"

The Depression worsened, and commercial printing almost declined to a vanishing point. By mid-1933 the rumble of presses had all but ceased. The kindhearted landlord died and the new owner raised the rent. It became impossible to pay the rent and at the same time meet the payments on the printing equipment. So on September 27, 1933, Vic picked up the phone and called the manufacturer, "Better come and get your presses. We're through."

It was a sad day when he moved his effects—an old black desk given in payment for some printing by a dentist, an old typewriter that Vic had used in college, some books, and scratch pads. He set up an office in a spare bedroom in his home on St. Anthony Court. But far from being defeated, he continued correspondence with prospects for the ABGS curriculum and kept on visiting every Sunday School convention and conference he could manage to attend.

One early letter from 829 Orleans Street read in part:

> WHY NOT MORE BIBLE FOR YOUR BIBLE SCHOOL?
> Since time immemorial the three fields of religious instruction have been the home, the school, and the Church. But there never was a time in the history of America when there was less Bible taught in the home and in the school than today. One would suppose that . . . the Church would make special effort. But instead, most of the Protestant denominations, in recent years, substitute methodology for Bible. And the Bibleless training course and the Bibleless Sunday School lessons have resulted . . . disastrously to the Church . . . experiencing marked loss in accessions to membership and in gifts to benevolences.

> The All-Bible Graded Series puts the Bible into the Bible School! A comparison of Bible material utilized by (perhaps you can list here the material you are now using) fully explains why, in response to hundreds of requests, the All-Bible Graded Series was called into existence. Since the Bible is what America needs, why not put more Bible into the Bible School? . . .
>
> We now send you herewith our new booklet of specimen pages, giving a complete lesson from each of the teacher's and pupil's manuals for the Junior, Intermediate, and Senior Departments. . . . Despite the fact that this series is not being prepared for profit, we will need to publish a first edition of no less than 30,000 in order to offer the manuals at a lower price than most present lesson material. This new price of 10 cents each for the 32-page pupils' manuals will no doubt lower your present expenses. The 80-page teachers' manuals are 25 cents. . . .
>
> The order for YOUR Sunday School is very necessary to bring into existence for this October the ALL-BIBLE GRADED SERIES of Sunday School lessons.

There was much prayer behind this and other advertising pieces—by the Corys and others. Women at North Shore Church met in a home each week and prayed for the ministry. Bernice Cory was a member of the prayer band, and asked the group to pray particularly that a certain quota of users could be reached, to justify the publication for the October 1933 quarter. "How these dear saints of the Lord prayed for the quota," Vic commented. But their prayer wasn't to be answered for 1933, for by July 1 only 46 Sunday Schools had committed to use the ABGS lessons (see Appendix). More groundwork had to be laid. God's timing would be a year later.

Comments by leaders served to keep the Corys' spirits up. Letters such as from the Rev. E.H. Murdoch, minister, Darlington Congregational Church, Pawtucket, Rhode Island brought encouragement. In part the May 17, 1933 letter read:

> I cannot conceive of anything more efficient and appropriate for our Church Schools. Have hoped for something like this for years. Have recommended them to our Church School, and they have decided to regrade our School and use these

helps. I also showed the book of sample lessons I received from you to another Sunday School teacher in Providence yesterday, and she is going to bring the matter before the school where she is a teacher. The school has an enrollment of 600. I shall do all I can to advertise these lessons for you.

Prayer in a time of great despair

This was the year 1933. Under the dark clouds that mirrored the despair of the nation, Franklin D. Roosevelt, as he was sworn in as president in March, had asserted, "The only thing we have to fear is fear itself." Across the Atlantic, Hitler had become chancellor of Germany and in March had grabbed dictatorial power. The National Recovery Act went into action on all fronts in the U.S. in August. And, according to a report, fewer people were attending church: they were staying home to hear radio sermons by Harry Emerson Fosdick, the liberal minister of Riverside Church in New York City.

As the new year began—1934, when lessons would actually be shipped out to Sunday Schools—Vic Cory remarked, "We are impelled to pray and pray and pray. God has so mightily brought us to this point—through prayer. Our continued intercession for the bringing of Bible truth to many thousands of children in our Sunday Schools will be heard—and answered."

Scripture Press was about to begin its God-appointed mission, that, after four revisions from 1968 to 1971, would be put in these words in 1989:

> "Called by God and committed to produce excellent Bible-based, life-related curriculum, books, and Christian education products that will be used to reach and teach people for Christ."

---

[1] 1948 banquet script, "People and Providences" (see Appendix).

[2] Most details in this account are from a paper titled "Scripture Press Historical Survey" prepared by Victor E. Cory, October 19, 1948, combined with details from various employee banquet program scripts (see Appendix).

A New Beginning

1933–1935

THE YEAR 1933 marked Chicago's centennial of Chicago, and the Century of Progress Exposition opened on a strip of reclaimed land about six miles long and 600 feet wide along Lake Michigan. Despite the severe depression, the fair, with its emphasis on science and industry, proved a financial success. But Vic Cory had other things on his mind. On September 27, 1933, he mailed a letter in response to an advertisement in the *Chicago Tribune.* It read:

> Your ad interests me as there might be a possibility of an arrangement being worked out to our mutual advantage.
>
> Our firm has been obliged to discontinue its printing operations because of inability to come up to the excessive terms of a new lease submitted by the new owners of the building. We have a number of booklets to be regularly published, as well as some other work coming in between times. We have valuable contacts, most of them being with Christian organizations. On checking up the other day, we found that our credit losses for the past year for this class of work was less than 1/4 of 1%. Relations are most pleasant and indicate a good future. As for my own activity, I am looking for opportunity to place this work, as well as a new work which I believe I can secure.

> More could be said, but in a personal interview there can be brought out the information we both seek. I will be glad to meet you. Call or write.

This letter found in the SP Ministries Archives reveals how desperate Cory (often hereafter VEC, as many called him) was to keep his dream alive to publish Clarence Benson's All-Bible Graded Series of Sunday School lessons and to stay in the printing business. But nothing was to come of this cry for help.

Consecutive entries in his diary about this time indicate that VEC was much in prayer about the matter:

> Friday, November 24, 1933—Am praying that Mr. Benson may yet give us the teacher training manual; that I might get down to bedrock in Christ.
>
> Sunday, November 26, 1933—During S.S. read the old Book and had a prayer meeting back in the church boiler room. His promises are precious.
>
> Monday, November 27, 1933—A rather dull day. I seem to be bound and restrained, like an animal pacing back and forth in a cage. I feel no urge to follow up the newspaper want ads or other clues. Yet we are in need in many ways. But His promises do ring true! We can do nothing but cling to them. God would teach us lessons during these days. We want to profit by them.
>
> Tuesday, November 28, 1933—Another dull day but waiting on Him—or rather on Him to whip *us* into shape, to permit Himself to work through us.

An "angel" to the rescue

In his 1948 "Historical Survey," VEC mentions William R. Thomas in connection with Paul Guiness and Stacey Wood, who came to Wheaton College and "were all wrapped up in getting out *His Triumph,* a Gospel of John for use on college campuses. Every Saturday," he wrote, "I met with them at the office of the American Bible Society, where dear old Dr. McLaughlin was offering to help them. Originally, we were to have printed this in our own plant, but this now being non-existent, I brought into these meetings William R. Thomas, vice president of Geographical Publishing Company (the firm printed *Wizard of Oz* books) and an earnest Christian who I thought could very well print the book."

Thomas soon showed that he was more interested in the vision of these young men and the use to which the Gospel of John was to be put than in the printing of the book itself. One Saturday it dawned on VEC that maybe Mr. Thomas would be the instrument of the Lord in publishing the ABGS project.

"The next Monday found me in his office," VEC continued. "He told me to draw up my plan for publishing this series, the costs of the necessary advertising and promotion. It took another day or so for me to get these figures and have my plan all drawn up in a six-page contract."

VEC figured $1,400 would be needed to cover the maintenance of an office and a continuous advertising program through magazine space and by direct mail for period of 11 months. Another $1,600 would be required to pay the first printing bill—a total of $3,000. He included an estimated sales forecast with all costs and even a schedule for the repayment of the cash advance.

"There were a lot of 'whereases,' 'parties of the first and second part' and 'to wits," VEC recalled, "but Mr. Thomas overlooked all of this, turned to the last page, and asked, 'Is this where I sign?' He never even read the contract I had spent so much time drawing up! Very seldom have I been so complimented and been shown such trust and confidence.

"Mr. Thomas said, 'I just happened to have that much money loose in the bank at that time.' But I did say our Lord knew all about that. In our old office, the door would surely have opened, and there would have come down before us our old motto, 'God answers prayer.'"

The contract with Thomas actually called for an advance of $1,538, given over a period of 11 months. The money was used to promote the new curriculum and pay VEC's nominal salary, a mere $25 a week. Another aspect of the agreement stipulated that "for the first three years and as long as money is owed to Mr. Thomas for finance or printing costs, The Scripture Press agrees to order printing of all quarterlies or manuals from or through Mr. Thomas." The contract specified that SP would repay Thomas the principal plus interest in increments of $100, which happened long before the suggested date.[1]

An agreement involving Thomas, Benson, and SP stipulated that if enough orders did not arrive by May 1, 1934, the contracts between the parties would be cancelled. On March

5, 1937, after the venture proved successful, a new contract was drafted, assuring Scripture Press the exclusive rights to publication and guaranteeing the lessons would be ready four months prior to the publication date and raising the payment for writers to $10 a lesson.[2]

First employee saw no future

While still working out of his home on St. Anthony Court, VEC hired SP's first employee. She was a typist just out of school, working two days a week at $2 a day. After a short time she left, saying she saw no future in the business.[3]

Of those days, Lloyd Cory comments, "SP was born and bathed in much prayer. Dad was loaded with zeal and faith. He watched and prayed while he drove his '29 Chevy, believing, 'The God of heaven will give us success.'"

VEC's Chevy took him wherever he could find people to tell about the forthcoming Sunday School materials—to churches, homes, business offices, and Sunday School conventions. And, as Lloyd said, he prayed as he went.

A new address

Time came when VEC began looking for office space outside the Cory home. Larger quarters were needed, and also Mrs. Benson didn't like the St. Anthony Court address for a business called Scripture Press—to her it sounded too Catholic. She was much more pleased with the new address, 741 North LaSalle Street, where VEC set up office in January 1934 on the second floor of what was then a rooming house, in a room 10' × 10 1/2'. Equipment included his old black desk, a few tablets of paper, resource books, and the old "educated typewriter," as he called it, that he had used in college.[4]

Lloyd comments: "My father wrote ads and keyed them in magazines by using different addresses [741, 743, 745, on to almost 800]. Some east coast visitors figured out that SP was in the middle of Chicago Avenue! There were no coffee breaks in those days. The place closed down for the 1936 Soap Box Derby. I had built and raced in the 'Spirit of '36' and took second in the whole city (there were about 500 entries). Back at 741 a sign announced: 'Gone to the races.'"

Actually, according to VEC's "Historical Sketch," it was a pastor replying to an ad carrying the address as 767 North

LaSalle who determined 767 would be in the middle of the Chicago Avenue streetcar tracks. "Thereafter," he wrote, "we began using other keys for our ads, such as the more simple Dept. BTFSPLK or Desk 27 POX."

At the 1953 SP annual banquet, a chorale sang about the many addresses listed on North LaSalle:

> Oh where, oh where is that office
> I've heard so much about?
> According to this address, it's here without a doubt!
> But there's no building at all here—
> Why I'm on a streetcar track!
> Scripture Press, where, oh where, are you?
> Please bring your office back!

While the company did not get enough promises of orders to produce lesson manuals for the fall of 1933, God kept hopes alive for 1934. Beginning in January 1934, SP advertised in every issue of *Moody Monthly* magazine. Small ads challenged: "Why not teach the whole Bible?" and "Why neglect prophecy?" Inquiries increased as teachers considered the proposed products. Finally bona fide orders began arriving at 741 North LaSalle—741 orders, they counted at one point, believe it or not, matching their address number! An ad later told the rest of the story. Sold Out!

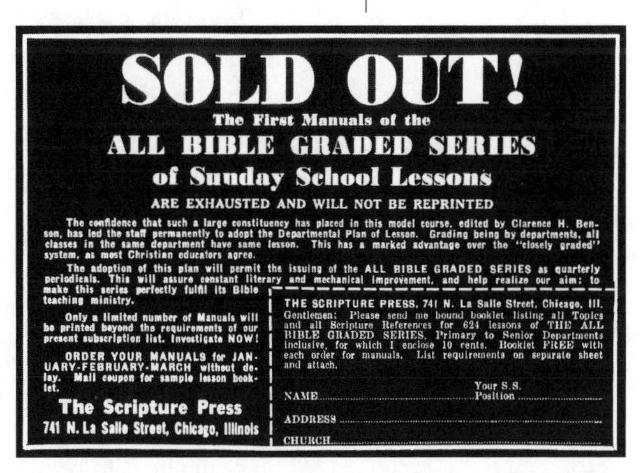

Bad news—GOOD NEWS! 1934

Meantime, lesson writers continued to write (see Appendix for a list of "product firsts" and dates they were produced).VEC kept the evangelical world informed, reminding that never before had such a talented and suitably equipped group of college- and university-trained Christian Ed majors been assembled to prepare the lessons—the students of Clarence Benson at Moody Bible Institute. In his "Historical Sketch," VEC listed them:

•Mary and Lois LeBar prepared the Beginner and Primary lessons, though the materials of these two departments were not ready for distribution until 1935 and 1938, respectively.

•Frances Poundstone and Gladys McElroy wrote the Junior lessons.

•Julia Cole, Millie Whisler (she later married Oscar Lowry), and Natalie Morris (she later became Mrs. Roland Agers) wrote Intermediate lessons. When Julia Cole was called as a missionary to India, Scripture Press hired Frances Poundstone in 1939 to write Intermediate lessons at $10 a lesson, according to a letter written by VEC. "We believe you will be a help for all eternity to 40,000 or 50,000 boys and girls and teachers in the Intermediate Department of our Sunday Schools," he wrote in closing.

•Miss Nettie M. Cox worked as Benson's most valued editorial assistant.

Typesetting began. "[We carefully scanned] long galleys of proofs . . . in order that 'Calvary' would not be spelled 'cavalry,' etc.," VEC recalled. He brought proofs home, and he and Bernice worked together checking them. "That is how the team started," he added. "This work was done at night, and, in fact, many was the hour we munched crackers, as noisily as possible, to keep from falling asleep while intoning page after page."

In those early days, Bernice Cory (often BTC hereafter; through the years many employees were often referred to by their initials) devised a speedy method of proofreading. Instead of saying 'comma' or 'period,' she tapped her pencil once for a comma and hit her fist on the table for a period, Jim Adair recalls.

Bernice wrote about beginning the work at home:

> I can still remember the day in 1934 when Victor and I pored over first galley proofs on the new Sunday School lessons that we were about to publish. We had great fun laying the proofs out on the dining room table, and Victor taught me how to proofread them. I remember reading Dr. Benson's galley proofs. I asked one night, "Vic, are these lessons supposed to be only for Presbyterians?"
>
> "No, any group," Vic replied.
>
> But it seemed he had the Westminster Catechism in every lesson! So it was, change a little bit here and a little bit there. Even though the writers were college graduates, they had never written for publication. The girls made a lot of mistakes in grammar and doctrine. One writer particularly,

> who had a year at McCormick Theological Seminary, used liberal terminology. I knew she was as fundamentally conservative as we were, but anyone reading her lessons would think she was modernistically inclined. I had just called Victor's attention to that and to her grammar, punctuation, and doctrine and theology. The proofs would be black with corrections. Finally he said, "I think you ought to look at all these manuscripts before they go to the printer; it costs more to have them set in type after proofs are corrected."

Bernice found herself having to do more work outside of home. She prayed earnestly that the Lord would send her a housekeeper, because the woman who came in from time to time "couldn't speak the King's English and the older boys were copying her."

In 1984 Esther Van Fleet Post wrote about coming to Chicago:

> It was during the Depression, and I had just left a teaching position near Detroit. I had wanted to attend Moody Institute for years. So either it was faith or nerve that took me to Chicago with very little money and no promise of work. For days I walked the streets until finally I got a place in a boarding house. I was very unhappy there and prayed for something else. But on arrival in Chicago, I enrolled at Moody. Through the instrumentality of 10 different persons with whom I'd had correspondence, I got in touch with the Corys. I found out they knew every one of those 10 people! I fell in love with [Mrs. Cory] at first sight and with . . . three-year-old Philip whom she was holding. . . . I [started at $5 a week and] lived with the Corys for 17 wonderful years. She and I became like sisters. . . . The first day I was with them I worked in the home. The second day [Mr. Cory] carted me off in their old Chevy "Ebenezer" to the office, up a flight of stairs in an old apartment building on LaSalle Street. As Mrs. Cory was editor, she went to the office when it was time to prepare for the next issue of lessons while I stayed at home with the boys. Then the thing was reversed; I went to the office, she stayed home.
>
> Many was the night she and I stayed up till midnight proofreading. I'd been a commercial teacher, so occasionally I wrote letters or took some dictation.
>
> Over a period of years [Bernice once said] one thing

led to another, and I got to writing lessons. The thing that started me was Miss Cole's melancholy slant for Junior Highs. She must have had some experience in her life that made her speak constantly of taking up the cross daily and dying to self. It is OK to put that into lessons but too sad and melancholy for Junior Highs. Because of that, I would write lessons just to counteract some of the lugubrious tone in her lessons. Miss Cole eventually went to India as a missionary. For a while Dr. Rebecca Price wrote Junior High lessons for us, six for teachers and one or two for pupils.

I learned about printing the hard way. Old gruff printers taught me such things as how to figure run-arounds on a page, about excelsior pica and other matters relating to type, page layout make-up.

Praying and searching well into the night

There were times that after proofreading and editing VEC would start praying and searching for ideas to use in the mailing pieces that he called broadsides. At the 1953 banquet a chorale gleefully sang about his nocturnal work:

The boss is writing the copy,
Working till after dawn.
He's drinking gallons of coffee,
But yet he has to yawn.
The milkman's bottles are clicking,
The sun's rays are piercing the gloom—
VEC puts down his pencil—
Now watch the sales curve zoom!

Actually, according to a correction BTC penciled in on a copy of the banquet script, VEC didn't really drink coffee to stay awake; he munched crackers. He was likely too keyed up to go to sleep. Whatever, it was said VEC believed that advertising copy written in the predawn hours packed the most wallop.

Churches reach out for lesson manuals

Orders rolled in and, according to BTC in her remarks in 1952, one of the biggest questions they faced was how large their first print order should be. "Many times," she said, "after we had decided on 32,000, we asked ourselves, 'Wasn't that a bit too high? How could we ever expect to sell 32,000?'"

She recounted that by 1937 the number was more than 64,000 and "throughout the country in a growing number of churches men and women with a real love for the Lord Jesus Christ were beginning to see the need for Sunday School lessons presenting the whole Bible in all of its truth and beauty and its glorious story of salvation to the boys and girls in their Sunday Schools."

"By the end of another three years another 100,000 had been added," she recalled, "so that now Scripture Press lessons were reaching over 300,000 boys and girls. But it wasn't easy. On every hand we were confronted by obstacles. We were scorned by modernistic pastors, barred from some Sunday School conventions, and castigated by entire denominations which had lost their love for the Lord Jesus Christ [or never had true love for Him]. When we didn't dare to look around us for encouragement, we were forced to look upward. And our God was always faithful. He led the way ever upward."

In the very early days, VEC hired a secretary, just out of high school and rather timid. She wasn't sure she would be worth the $5 a week offered her. "Jean Clymer did have a remarkable memory, however, so we had no need of looking things up," VEC recorded in his "Historical Sketch." "She knew the names and addresses of the Sunday Schools and their secretaries and treasurers. Furthermore, she knew the zones and express rates in each case. Only until the work had grown to reach many hundreds of schools was her memory overtaxed. One day she told us that she guessed we had better look them up in the files.

"How did we carry on all this business in our small room?" VEC continued. "We partly solved the problem by moving the manuals, the shipping supplies, and any other excess properties out into the hallway during the daytime. When ready to close up for the night, we would simply move the stuff back into the room, managing somehow to push the door shut. What did we use for a shipping room scale? The bathroom scale from 4851 served the purpose for many years."

The first shipping table consisted of three doors VEC brought from home that he hinged together, with a shelf and a one-legged table attached. When the orders were too much for half a girl (Jean) to handle, Arnold (Doc) Langhauser came as a part-time worker to join several other part-timers. He had time in between other jobs to lend both hands, and would work feverishly with his black derby pulled down over his ears, a speedy shipper if there ever was one.

A banquet chorale sang about it in these terms:

Three doors were fastened together,
Making the shipping room.
He shipped on a one-legged table,
Morning and afternoon.
A bathroom scale weighed our parcels,
A cigar box held each stamp.
Working in his big black derby
Was Doc, our shipping champ!

At first SP bought Beginner and Primary material from Standard Publishing Company. "Our purchases started to climb, and our advertising and correspondence must have impressed the Standard people," according to VEC. "They decided to visit us. They drove up in front of the place in a cab, looked up and down for the 741 number, and with some trepidation began to climb the rooming house stairs to our quarters. They came to the entrance of the quarters of The Scripture Press Incorporated and looked in on the scope of all its operations and were speechless. It seemed minutes before they were able to say 'Hello.' To think that such a highbrow front could be put on by such lowbrows in such a lowbrow place!

A need for more office space

"The 10' × 10 1/2' room really became crowded. We needed another helper and had to specify that she could not be very tall or take up much room otherwise. There came to us one of Mr. Benson's recent graduates, Laura Odelberg, as a secretary. Jean, the typist, had become the part-time shipping room force. We really needed more room. We prayed," VEC continued.

"Suddenly one day we heard that the people occupying the two rooms next to ours were moving. We applied for that additional space and got it. One of these rooms had served as a dining room and the other as a kitchen. This allowed for expansion. The kitchen became the new shipping room. We found that the kitchen stove worked too and starting with making coffee, we soon were cooking all kinds of things. Laura was especially proficient in making Swedish meatballs. We all knew when it was lunchtime. This made it hard to get rid of customers and visitors.

"During these days the Lord was very precious, and we felt ourselves in His training school. Money was scarce—almost nonexistent—yet the Lord taught us the ABCs of stewardship. We would ask the Lord for some of the simplest and most intimate things. We asked Him to change people's minds, people with whom we had dealings. We prayed for teachers' meetings, boards, and other groups where our lessons were up for consideration. We asked for victory where it was clearly a case of Bible teaching or Bibleless teaching. We prayed for the writers headed by Dr. Benson. They came over and prayed with us once a week. We prayed for the printers and for our advertising. We prayed for our printing runs, how many manuals we should print.

"Once we had 10,000 broadsides and order blanks all ready to mail, but no money for postage. The test was that we actually had sufficient money in the bank, but it was earmarked to pay other bills not then due and, therefore, was untouchable for this purpose. We piled the broadsides and order blanks in the middle of the room and in simple faith prayed that the money be sent in. We knew the Lord wanted those advertising pieces to reach Sunday Schools. Certainly, He was more interested in them than we were. The pile of broadsides was in the way. We frequently stumbled over them. That would simply remind us to pray even more.

"In four or five days, a printing order came from Mrs. Cowman calling for a reprint of some circulars for which we had the plates. We sent the job out to a printer and found that our margin was $100, the amount needed to pay the postage on that pile of broadsides. Furthermore, the order and her check had been mailed on the very day we started praying about it. That is just a simple incident, but there were hundreds like it.

"We had promised the Lord [earlier] before we opened up at Orleans that we would begin each day with prayer, a practice we continued. The days of 1933 and 1934 were days when intercession was made that was no doubt answered years later.

"Our staff at 741 also included Lloyd B. Tucker, Bernice's father, who [with Bernice's mother, had moved in with us when he lost his job] kept the books and made our bank deposits. We simply couldn't have gotten along without him. He also doubled up in shipping, and how he could write collection letters! In those days, our correspondence was quite direct, to the point, and very effective. Something like, 'Please give me the name of a good lawyer in your town, for I think I'll have to sue you unless you pay up.'

"The time came," VEC continued, "when the three rooms were filled up with desks, typewriters, people, and corrugated paper [good for kneeling on during prayer time]. One day in [January?] 1936 I needed a haircut and asked the barber in the shop at 800 North Clark Street if he knew of some vacant space in the neighborhood. He said, 'Wait a minute,' and in a few seconds there stood by my side the manager of the 800 North Clark Street building to tell me about some space he had for rent. I looked it over, but it was far too much space for us. It would have been big enough for an organization of 20 to 25 people! However, we signed up for the space at $60 a month, and the day came when we moved into the 750 square feet area."

BTC flatly said, "My husband is balmy to think we can occupy this much space." But in time she was to be thankful for her husband's foresight. [5]

---

[1] "Memorandum of Agreement" between Cory and Thomas found in S Box in SP Ministries Archives, dated December 1933. Also referred to in chapter 2 of "Dissertation Presented to the Faculty of Temple Baptist Theological Seminary" by Clayton Jacob Hunt, Jr., August 1984. (See Big Box A for folder of correspondence between Vic Cory and Thomas.)

[2] Contract between Cory and Benson found in S Box and mentioned also in Hunt dissertation, chapter 2

[3] Mentioned in various papers, including banquet program scripts.

[4] Mentioned in various banquet program scripts.

[5] Ibid.

A New Home at 800 North Clark Street

1936—1948

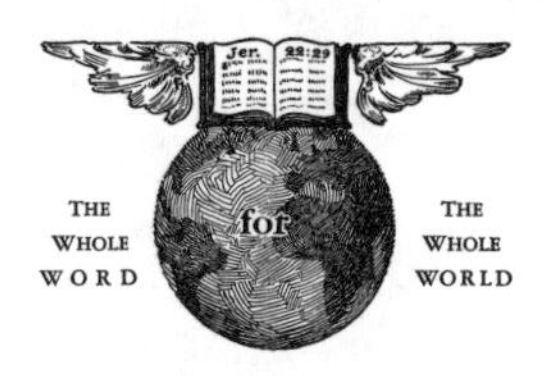

THE YEAR WAS 1936. In March, Hitler's troops entered the Rhineland, violating the treaties of Versailles and Locarno. In June, Italy conquered Ethiopia. In August, Jesse Owens won four gold medals in the Olympics in Berlin. In November, Franklin D. Roosevelt was elected to the second of his four terms.

President Franklin D. Roosevelt

And in January 1936, VEC's faith told him he was in no way "balmy" when he signed a lease for space in the Chicago-Clark building at 800 North Clark Street, on the northwest corner of Chicago Avenue and Clark (see brochure in Appendix). The North LaSalle rooms were simply too small for this fast-growing organization. Truckers came a few days later and moved the furniture to the new quarters, and "we all carried the small items in our arms . . . [in] about two trips apiece," according to the 1953 banquet script. (The first board meeting at the new location was held on January 20, 1936.)

Chicago-Clark Building (800 North Clark Street) as seen from Chicago Avenue, home of SP, 1937-1947.

It was a move VEC believed God had made possible. Here, in this old six-story building, he could have two legitimate addresses: 800 North Clark Street and 100 West Chicago

Avenue (he used the Chicago Avenue address in a hip-pocket business he called Grace Publications that published William R. Newell's books). He had a partition built across the room and included one window on each side. One room was the shipping room and the other, office space.

What hath God wrought! In December 1938, four and a half years after SP began, employees and family rejoiced at the fact All-Bible Graded Lessons were touching the lives of 200,000 boys and girls and teachers. Identified are: Mary LeBar (forefront left, glasses), Paul, Dan, and Lloyd Cory (forefront right, Gene Saulnier (behind Paul), Vic and Bernice Cory, William R. Thomas, Clarence H. Benson (right to left, in front of poster), Mr. and Mrs. Lloyd B. Tucker, Bernice Cory's parents (in front of Mr. Thomas); Lois LeBar (far right).

Before nailing boards together for a shipping room table, VEC and workers temporarily tacked them together into smaller tables, and the growing company had an open house banquet. Including all the staff, their relatives, the writers, and their relatives and other friends, 45 people were present. This was the first of many annual banquets, that in ensuing years were held on the premises and other places, including hotels, the Logan Square Masonic Temple, the Furniture Mart at 666 North Lake Shore Drive, the Elmhurst Country Club, and St. Andrews Country Club.

Within a year or so, with more workers hired to handle the mounting number of orders from Sunday Schools across America, the space that had seemed too large was not enough. "The 750-square-foot space was actually crowded with the properties and personnel of Scripture Press Incorporated," according to VEC's "Historical Sketch." "Next to us was the office of a publisher of secular magazines. We needed his space. We asked the Lord for it. We believed the Lord would give it to us.

"One Saturday afternoon I walked into the next office," VEC continued. "The editor and owner were there, and before I could say anything, the editor asked, 'I wonder if you'd care to sublease my space. There is another suite of rooms around the corner I would much rather have.' To myself, I just said, 'Thank You, Lord,' and to him I said, 'I believe it could be arranged.'

"We took over this space but only room by room as we needed it. Soon we had acquired the entire space. A little later we found we needed a store or display room. [Alex Koval was the first manager of the SP store, probably begun in 1941; see Appendix for history of the SP bookstore.] Then came the need for more space by every department of the work, and one by one, offices became mysteriously vacant in our pathway. The shipping room, however, was packed against the wall. Shippers' groans became prayers. One day a legal paper was posted in the elevator to the effect that the firm [evidently, the Franklin Publishing Company] on the floor below was in bankruptcy. We surely hope we will never be held responsible for that, but we did appreciate the space. [One of its employees, Mildred Vaters, got a job with SP after that firm closed.]

"We needed more space and still more space on both floors and people had a mysterious urge to move elsewhere or else they went out of business. To many of our friends with whom we did business, it was uncanny, but we knew all the time that God answers prayer."

The October 1946 issue of *Press Proof,* the company newsletter, detailed the growth at 800 North Clark as follows:

> With "Prayer Changes Things" as the motto from the beginning, SP began to shoo the rest of the firms off the sixth, then the fifth floor of the Chicago-Clark Building. The Editorial and Art Departments, then the store occupied the corner which is now Ruth Mead's domain. Members of the Art Department may be inclined to hop around a bit, for their room used to be a tap dancing studio. The Shipping Department transferred to the fifth floor, and the rest was gobbled up by SP, room by room. Advertising took the last office in May 1945.
>
> Besides space, products grew to include not only ABGS

Sunday School lessons, but also the Vacation School series, Nursery course, *Power* and *My Counsellor* take-home papers, Suede-graphs and Gospel-graphs. [See Appendix for a list showing when products were introduced.] About 85 full-timers answer the call to prayer each morning at 8:15. SP still counts Dr. Benson and the Moody Bible Institute as co-laborers.

Steak for shippers

When at the beginning of a quarter, the shipping room crew seemingly could send out only about 25 mail bags of orders a day, VEC gave the workers a challenge: If by "dint of great effort, you can reach 60 bags a day of parcel post, I'll treat you to a steak dinner!" The crew soon reached the 60-bag mark and, true to his word, the boss dug down into his pocket, went to the meat market, and put on a delicious steak fry in a public park for the 20 or so workers.

Then, since he felt these boys had more know-how, he promised another steak dinner if they shipped out as many as 75 bags in a day. Ditto. Another steak dinner. Steak fries followed in ensuing quarters as the crew reached 90 bags, and then 100. In his "Historical Sketch," VEC humorously commented, "We weren't quite sure but that some bags were held over from the day before or that shipments normally sent express were sent parcel post, but anyway, there were 100 bags that went to the post office that night. That was the best steak fry of all, but it was the last one, for steak became extinct the following quarter."

A new printing press

Gladys Siegfried [later, Halleen] was the contact person to meet salesmen, according to Cory's report, and one day in 1939 a personable salesman with a little mustache persuaded her that "we needed to buy one of his gadgets, a small office-style Multilith printing press" [Gladys remembers otherwise: she says she had nothing to do with buying the press but was drafted to run it]. For some time she was the only one who could run it after the salesman showed her how. Several of the other employees tried to operate it but couldn't feed it properly. Gladys explained, "You gotta have rhythm." Hank Holmbo came along then. He had rhythm and became an expert printer.

Then in March 1941, Emil Hudacek came on the scene, and from then on he did the multilithing in an expanded printing department that eventually consisted of three small presses. Emil's coming was in itself an answer to prayer, the Corys believed. BTC had given a talk at Emil's church, using Romans 8:28 as her text. Bringing BTC home that evening, Emil's mother mentioned that her son Emil had just graduated from high school, knew printing, and needed a job.

On arriving home, BTC thought of Romans 8:28—"All things work together for good. . . ." She phoned VEC at the office. He quickly sent a telegram, which, oddly enough, arrived at the Hudacek home about 3 a.m. A sleepy-eyed Emil showed up at work that morning and worked for Scripture Press for many years, until the firm began sending all of its printing to outside printers.

A heated battle among Presbyterians

Miss Ursella Cook (later of Evangelical Teacher Training Association) liked SP lesson manuals so well that she used them in her Sunday School in Pittsburgh, Pennsylvania, showed them to her pastor, won approval, and then visited the office of the United Presbyterian Board. Dr. Milligan, manager of the U.P. Board of Publications, looked over the teaching materials, and saw something that the U.P. literature did not have. He boarded a train for Chicago to see Scripture Press and to offer Clarence Benson congratulations for the new course and to seek arrangements for its use by United Presbyterians.

At the next U.P. general assembly in Akron, Ohio, Dr. Milligan brought the recommendation that their own graded literature be discarded in favor of the All-Bible Graded Series. After a heated battle, ABGS got approval. In Akron, the morning after the assembly session, Dr. Milligan was found dead in his hotel room, apparently the victim of a heart attack. His last effort was in behalf of the ABGS teaching materials. The "heated battle" the previous day may have been too much for him.

ABGS to Shanghai

As BTC worked into the night, as she often did, the bright beam from the rotating beacon atop the Palmolive Building would sweep over her desk at regular intervals. It would remind her: "Just as surely as that great light is illuminating a tremendous, dark area of this city, someday our lessons will sweep around this darkened world and reveal the Lord Jesus, the Light of the world." Already she knew the Lord was leading toward that goal.

An American missionary, Lucy Conover, had been in Shanghai on behalf of Sunday School work. Her conviction was that effective Sunday School work should be carried on with high efficiency and deep spirituality and a working knowledge of the Bible. She organized the Sunday School Promotion League of Shanghai, made up principally of local Christian leaders. Many large Sunday Schools in Shanghai and other cities were part of the league. It was one of the most remarkable pieces of Christian work in that area of the world. The organization stressed teacher training classes with experienced leaders. Only the best of Bible lessons would be used. Of all the material available in the world, Miss Conover chose the ABGS for translation and publication and was given permission to proceed.

The translation of the Primary and Junior lessons was made and typeset and books printed. The entire three-year cycle had been printed and was in use when Japan made an all-out attack on China in 1936. After China was plunged into war, workers buried the type and plates underground. After the Japanese turned elsewhere and laid plans to attack Pearl Harbor, publication was resumed and the lessons were in use for many years.

By 1948 ABGS materials had been translated, in addition to Chinese, into Polish, German, and Spanish, according to the June 1948 *Press Proof.* The fact that lessons had been translated into Polish caught the attention of Julia, the cleaning woman and commentator each evening on her various aches and pains, her daughter, and "that woman on the fourth floor" at 800 North Clark. One evening she was passing the time in President Cory's office, when she suddenly spied a Polish edition of an All-Bible Graded Series lesson manual on Cory's desk. Grabbing it up with great delight, she exclaimed, "I can read it! See, it's in my language!" And she went on jabbering at great length while looking over the manual. It was the work of two missionaries before the beginning of World War II and there was little hope of any wide distribution in Communist Poland.

SP takes on a Sunday School magazine

In the late '30s Benson and Cory discussed the possibility of publishing a Sunday School magazine on methods, a magazine with inspirational messages and with news of Sunday School activities all over the U.S. The first issue of *The Church School Promoter,* later called *The Sunday School Promoter,* was dated April 1939. Benson was listed as the editor, with C.V. (Chris) Egemeier assisting him. But making it a success proved no easy task as the team struggled to raise its circulation to a sustaining figure. Four similar magazines on methods had tried and had failed.

In the early '40s, while riding the commuter train from Wheaton to Chicago, VEC ran across Robert A. Walker, editor of a new magazine called *His,* published by InterVarsity Fellowship. VEC told him about his struggling magazine, and after a number of conversations in ensuing months, he asked Walker to take over the direction of the publication.

Robert Walker took over *The Church School Promoter* that in time developed into *Sunday* magazine and later *Christian Life.* He served as SP's director of marketing from 1945 to 1954. He has continued his association with SP as a board member, with over 50 years of service to the company.

Walker agreed but insisted on changing the name, pointing out that the current name *Sunday School Promoter* had limited appeal. They agreed to shorten the name simply to *Sunday*. "I was rather naive," Walker recalls, "and said I would be willing to take the magazine over for a period of five years and be responsible for its indebtedness, which today would be a couple of hundred thousand dollars. I didn't have any great plans—only to change the name and clean up some of the editorial content and make it more palatable. At the end of the five years, the magazine would be mine if I could pay off the indebtedness. Vic had one other stipulation, that I would serve part time as the marketing manager of Scripture Press, because he had no one in that capacity."

Walker accepted the offer. He eventually gained control of the magazine, and *Sunday* eventually absorbed *The Way* magazine and in 1947 took over the subscription list and equipment of *Christian Life and Times,* a Clyde Dennis/Good News publication (edited by Charles Lampman), and in 1948 the magazine became *Christian Life* with a circulation of almost 40,000. Bob Walker served from 1945 to 1954 as director of Marketing for Scripture Press. In 1945 he was elected a member and director of Scripture Press Foundation.

Typewriters go to war

After the Japanese plunged the United States into World War II in December 1941, Scripture Press faced hardships. "The war, with its alphabetical boards covering all phases of labor and materials, was upon us," according to Cory. "Many of our employees had brothers, husbands, and sons on various battle fronts, so there was much prayer for them in our morning devotions. We eventually sent three typewriters off to war. The government asked for a voluntary offer of about 10 percent of the typewriters of business firms, and we sent three of our best. We received from the War Manpower Commission a letter of essentiality, which helped us in some ways."

There were times when Cory and his employees literally went to their knees to pray for enough paper for printing lesson manuals, and lo and behold, a carload of paper would show up. When firms were being granted paper based on the amount used prior to rationing, SP told its customers:

> It is hoped that publishers of text material for Sunday Schools will not be so drastically affected as others which have purely commercial ventures. Besides serving as morale builders in a time of national crisis, All-Bible lessons are preparing the current young generation to play a strong part in the post-war rebuilding era.

Once there was a need for cork for a handwork project that would teach children a valuable Bible truth. Cork was a military commodity, and its purchase by a private company required government approval. "You'll never get cork," a fellow worker told Louise Rodman, who handled purchasing for Scripture Press during the war years. "The government just won't grant Scripture Press a priority."

The comment sent Louise to praying only harder. "Lord, I know You can supply that cork. But if You don't, I'm going to take it as in indication that I should leave the company. Because, if I can't get the needed material, I shouldn't be in this job." Louise kept knocking at Uncle Sam's door. The government granted the request for cork, and the Bible activity became a reality. Louise's faith was strengthened, and she served Scripture Press a total of 37 years, retiring as employment manager.[3]

Shortages brought challenges to Sunday Schools. In one of SP's 1943 Intermediate Teacher manuals, the matter of gasoline rationing was addressed as follows:

> Some say that Sunday Schools will benefit, and that is our confident expectation. As a matter of record, Sunday School attendance reached its highest peak before the horseless buggy became such a common vehicle of transportation and began to take folk out of town on Sundays, away from Sunday School and church. Were this new restriction to bring back the old days of bigger Sunday School attendance, it would be a blessing in disguise.
>
> Whatever happens, the whole situation at the moment is a challenge to you, teacher—definitely a challenge. Aside from your daily occupation to earn a living, your Sunday School work should have first claim to enough gasoline from your four gallons-or-so ration to enable you to carry on. If you can ride streetcars or buses, there is even less reason for diminishing your effort to reach Young America. Press on!

Developing an appreciation of good art

"A development of our Art Department and the appreciation of art at Scripture Press came from small beginnings," according to VEC. "Way back, almost at the beginning, we heard of Joe Barcanic, and we took material to be illustrated to his home, way out west of Harlem Avenue. His was about the only house in the block, so we trudged through the snow of the prairies many a time to drop and leave material with him, and later picked up some beautiful artwork.

"We needed more art and persuaded Joe to give us his afternoons while still working on his regular job in the mornings. But we needed more pictures and still more, so that finally Joe came to us full time. [Barcanic gave the take-home paper *Power* a professional touch to get the publication started in 1943.]

"Then along came Faith McNaughton and others [including, over the years, such art directors as DeWitt Whistler Jayne, Frank Dietz, Vic Erickson, Ben Wood, Carl Lindgren, and Sam

Postlewaite]. Joe Barcanic had a hard time selling the rest of us on more advanced art layout and typography. We just didn't appreciate it. Thereupon, he arranged for a series of eight or nine lectures and demonstrations from one of the leading artists and type designers in the Midwest, Don May. These sessions were held at Scripture Press and were attended by about 35 people from our firm, Moody Press, Good News, and several advertising agencies. Much of it went over our heads, but all of us acquired a new appreciation of art and design in our publications. From that time on, we believe we have been in the forefront in that respect among evangelical publishers.

"Any account of our stay at 800 North Clark would be incomplete without something said about Julia, the cleaning lady," VEC's "Historical Sketch" continued. "She was both valuable and voluble [she loved to stand and talk with anyone she encountered, especially those who worked after hours, and had no thought that she was interrupting]. She got acquainted easily and the better acquainted, the more sociable she became. But we all liked her." [And not to be forgotten, the elevator operator, Julius, who took us up and down on the slow-moving, creaky elevator, was almost equally sociable, and was a fixture at 800 North Clark.]

VEC makes lemonade

At 800 North Clark, SP had no lunchroom facilities. Employees either went down to the ground floor and patronized Thompson's Restaurant or crossed the street to another eatery.

Jim Adair recalls that VEC went to Thompson's one morning with a lemon and proceeded to "borrow" sugar and water from the restaurant to make himself lemonade.

He was always frugal, too much so for some employees who felt that he should pay higher wages. But he made it clear why wages weren't higher: SP employees were working on a "missionary margin"; profits were being plowed back into the company in order to reach out more effectively and farther with Bible-based teaching materials.

The Editorial Department at 800 North Clark had cozy little quarters right off the elevator. The big difficulty was that, while editors tried to concentrate on something in the Gospels or the Epistles, all the conversation of those waiting at the elevator and people talking in the hallway hit their ears.

One day, while busily engaged in preparing lessons, the editors smelled smoke, and, checking, discovered a fire. Campy [Ruth Camp, now Reid] with great coolness hustled down to the Printing Department for Emil. "Now," VEC recounted, "Emil had been used to fires from the heaters on his presses; so, grabbing his extinguisher, he hustled down and just as coolly and as calmly as any professional fireman would, he gave the burning stuff a few shots of his chemical, and with one jump, the editors were out of the office. Employees laughed over that incident many times."

SP becomes a foundation

On May 9, 1945, The Scripture Press Incorporated was organized as Scripture Press Foundation. According to the minutes, it was the Members' [Victor E. Cory, Bernice T. Cory, and Harry G. Saulnier] "purpose to donate to it all of the capital stock of The Scripture Press, Inc. (TSPI), so that the stock and eventually the property of that corporation would be permanently and exclusively devoted to the nonprofit religious purposes described in the charter of this corporation."

At the organizing meeting of the Foundation directors the same day, "it was reported to the Board that there was being contributed to this corporation all of the shares of stock of TSPI and that it was contemplated that, as soon as might reasonably be, the business and assets of TSPI might be turned over to this corporation in complete liquidation of TSPI. It was intended that this corporation should thereafter carry out the development and distribution of religious literature, and the organization of religious movements, particularly relating to Sunday Schools, as an objective in itself, and not as a business for profit."[1]

Memo to the president

In mid-1946, VEC was bubbling and fired off a memo to Bob Walker, head of sales, according to *Press Proof* for August 1946: "Here's a marvelous opportunity, Bob!" He told of a lead he had that could put the company's products into a major denomination. But the bubble burst. The memo with the hot tip came back to the president's desk with the notation: "When we can be sure of inventories," Walker stated, "and can 'error-lessly' and promptly handle the present big volume so as to keep our customers happy, then we're ready to make a drive—and not until!"

Walker's response set the wheels moving for a reorganization of Scripture Press departments (see organizational chart, Appendix). Its major effect was the creation of the new Production Division. With Lloyd Siegfried, Gladys' brother, as its director, it matched Editorial, Sales, and Finance. An office for "inventory control" was set up in the southwest corner of the fifth-floor shipping room. Elinor Pearce was given the responsibility of caring for customers' interests, in addition to her regular duties in assembling orders for catalog sales. "Out of stock" notices, substitutions, split shipments, and refund notices were to be handled through "inventory control."

The *Press Proof* news item relating to the change concluded with: "That drive Mr. Walker bargained for won't be launched in a day or even for several weeks. But V.E. Cory is figuring on making his Sales Department head eat his words someday in the future."

Paul Langdon named SP controller

In September 1946, according to a *Press Proof* announcement, Paul R. Langdon, former director of finance for United States Railroad Retirement Board headquartered at 844 Rush Street, was named controller of Scripture Press Foundation. The controller's chair had been vacant since David L. Reiff left SP in June for a job in Spokane, Washington. Langdon, a CPA from Columbus, Ohio, would, according to the news item, be in charge of procedures and control the budget.

The November 1946 issue of *Press Proof* announced the long-awaited news that government approval had been given for SP to operate as a tax-free corporation (application to become a tax-exempt foundation had been made in May 1945):

"Since May 1945, when Scripture Press was declared a corporation not for profit, efforts have been under way to wind up affairs with the IRS. Final steps were taken by Controller Paul R. Langdon during a recent visit to Washington, where the SP controller spoke with officials, later sending sample publications as evidence that the company is in substance a missionary organization, doing its work in the Sunday School field.

"Taxes paid since May 1945 will be refunded and will go toward operation and expansion of the publishing house, as will all 'profits' under the new set-up. Besides federal income tax, this includes Social Security taxes which have been paid by the corporation.

"The nonprofit plan is not new to Scripture Press. Since the organization's beginning 12 years ago, profits have been plowed back into the work to finance operations and pay for present equipment. Under the new ruling, the government books say that no one 'owns' Scripture Press. All employees and executives are associates in reaching and training a half million boys and girls, young people, and older people for Christ and the Church.

"Although employees will no longer be under Social Security, Controller Langdon explained that contemplated legislation in Congress during the next year or two should provide benefits for all workers, including those in nonprofit organizations. Too, he said that Scripture Press is investigating a pension system. A system will probably be adopted and go into effect within the next few months."

[In 1947 SPF established a pension plan. Employees paid 2 percent of yearly base earnings. As of June 1971, cost of the plan was paid entirely by the company.]

In regard to Scripture Press' becoming a nonprofit organization, Glenn Ingram, Sr., whose firm, Glenn Ingram & Company, audited Scripture Press books, made the following comments in a book manuscript he prepared in relation to his life and work:

> With the beginning of World War II, federal income taxes became more of a problem and for the first time, formally, Mr. Cory came to me for advice and counsel. It didn't take long to see that some tax planning was necessary and in order. The pattern of their gifts had been such that a major portion were in excess of the limitations upon contributions deductible by corporations for income tax purposes. Something had to be done, and it seemed that the indicated solution was a charitable (religious) trust. Mr. and Mrs. Cory were adamant that in excess of a reasonable wage for their services, they wanted to turn everything back into the WORK—even to the extent that in the event of their deaths they did not want their children nor their children's nominees to receive anything from the residue.

> The Trust, as recommended by [attorney] Herman Fischer, with whom we worked, provided that the Corys, during their lifetimes, would be paid living salaries and that the balance of all income derived from the Trust would be retained for the advancement of the work. All title to properties in which Mr. and Mrs. Cory had interests were contributed to the Foundation entirely without consideration. Mr. Fischer then obtained a clearance by the Internal Revenue Service as to the Trust being nontaxable and also that no tax returns need be filed by it. Thus began an era when the operations of the Foundation prospered; the funds remaining after proper salaries being devoted to the buying of real estate in Wheaton. . . . .[4]

An attempted takeover?

After Paul Langdon had been in office for several months, the Corys became concerned that he wanted to move up and take over as president. "The attempted coup, if that is what it really was, happened about a year and a half after my arrival at SP in July 1945," recalls Jim Adair. "It's all hazy in my mind. Being new and perhaps a bit naive, I hardly knew what was going on. Some of the employees in managerial positions backed Langdon, the controller."

Gladys Siegfried Halleen recalled in 1997 that, to her recollection, Langdon made a demand of the Corys to upgrade the salary structure and employee benefits program. It all sounded good to a number of employees, and they signed what seemed to them a Langdon-produced "petition" to improve employee salaries and benefits. Gladys Halleen said, though she signed the paper, she never had a copy of it, and did not feel that it any way threatened VEC's position. At that time the company operated on VEC' s "missionary margin," as previously mentioned. The Cory plan called for employees not to expect wages that were paid in the secular business world. SP was a missionary enterprise, the boss often stressed. But the Corys believed Langdon had his eye on the presidency, and so did their family.

From a family viewpoint, Lloyd Cory remembers: "According to Dad, Langdon conned some of SP's best people, and others, until they joined his dastardly scheme. One day, during the height of this thing, Paul, Dan, and I (all college students) went to the office. Paul and Dan wanted to [do Langdon bodily harm], but Dad calmed them down, saying the Lord would take care of the matter. And He did."

The uprising culminated in an emotional prayer meeting in a large room of the Palmer House, as Adair remembers it, with the Corys and repentant employees praying together, many in tears. Employees pledged their loyalty to the Corys, all was forgiven, and the SP ship began again to sail in smooth seas.

A message to employees from the boss

In February 1947, VEC addressed employees in *Press Proof* as follows:

> When difficulties arise in such a Christian organization as Scripture Press, it is time to stop and take stock. We should ask ourselves: 'Have I been allowing the Holy Spirit to LIVE in me? Or are there times when I, in my way, try to deal with the details of daily business?'
>
> Here are some verses the observation of which will keep us in fellowship with each other and with our Lord:
>
>> But if we walk in the light, as He is in the light, we have fellowship one with another, and the blood of Jesus Christ His Son cleanseth us from all sin (1 John 1:7).
>>
>> If we say that we have no sin, we deceive ourselves, and the truth is not in us (1 John 1:8).
>>
>> If we confess our sins, He is faithful and just to forgive us our sins, and to cleanse us from all unrighteousness (1 John 1:9).
>
> Scripture Press is a Christian organization, but God wants it to be more than nominally Christian. He wants it to be a Holy Spirit led group of believers. From the Book of Acts we can get a few suggestions. Beginning with the first chapter and throughout the book, we see how the Holy Spirit gives power, the Holy Spirit gives utterance, the Holy Spirit gives boldness, the Holy Spirit demands purity, the Holy Spirit directs cooperation, the Holy Spirit directs organization, the Holy Spirit forces expansion in some cases and forbids it in others (Acts 16:6-7), the Holy Spirit gives direction, the Holy Spirit breaks down barriers.

For enlightening books on the Holy Spirit, read Ruth Paxson's *Life on the Highest Plane* and volumes by Andrew Murray, F.B. Meyer, and A.B. Simpson. It's one thing to be a Christian with the Holy Spirit dwelling in the heart and another to be Spirit-filled.

Paul Langdon, of course, was quickly out. He returned from Columbus in April 1947 for a visit and to wind up business affairs. Several SP employees met with him at the Lawson Y for dinner, giving him a belated send-off. Accountant George Sharpe made a presentation of a gift.

"Years later Dad visited Langdon in Ohio," Lloyd recalls. "By that time Langdon was a complete cripple, in such bad shape that Dad felt sorry for him." Apparently all was forgiven. Paul Langdon died some years later.

A new controller, R.A. Ginter

Enter R.A. Ginter on April 21, 1947. He took over as controller and quickly became an authority figure at Scripture Press. [His portrait hangs in the Heritage Room of Scripture Press Ministries, along with those of the Corys, Clarence Benson, Lloyd Tucker, William R. Thomas, Wilfred Frykman, David Hall, and Gilbert Beers.] A 1927 graduate of the University of Illinois, Ginter had served as controller of such organizations as Stewart-Warner and Walk-Over Shoe Stores. He was member of Northbrook Presbyterian Church and reportedly turned down more lucrative jobs to put his talents to work for the Lord at SP.

The Boss welcomes R.A. Ginter as SP's new controller in 1947. It was the only time RAG was caught with his eyes closed.

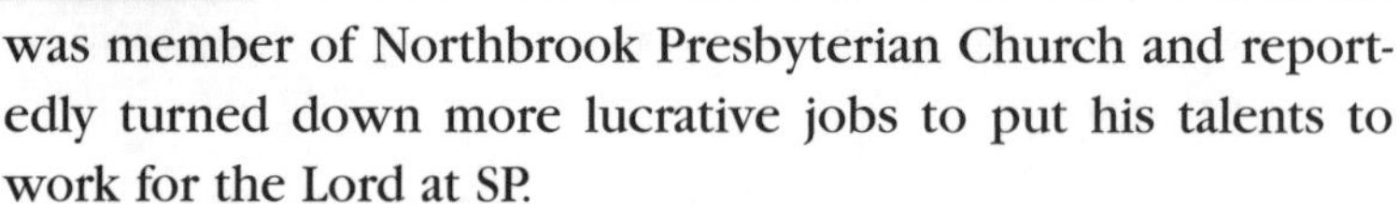

Ruddy complexioned and with receding hair, Mr. Ginter, as everyone from the president on down called him, dressed impeccably, was all business, spoke in even tones, and was greatly respected. He kept a watchful eye throughout the organization and was a finance man down to the penny. Lloyd Cory remembers Ginter picking up a pop bottle on the floor beside Lloyd's desk and saying, "Young man, don't you know this bottle cost us two cents?" Adair recalls Ginter did not believe in criticizing an employee unless there had been prior compliments about his/her work. "You can't take cash out of the cash register unless you've put some in," he reminded.

Ginter soon announced benefit changes for employees, though, according to *Press Proof* for May 1947, the board of directors and officers of Scripture Press Foundation had been considering a generous and comprehensive program. The article announced:

"Each male employee between the ages of 25 and 55, and each female employee between the ages of 28 and 55 who has had three or more years of service will be eligible to participate in the benefit program. Monthly retirement benefits will begin for females at age 60 and for males at age 65. The monthly income will be one percent of the average monthly salary for each year of service up to a maximum of 25 percent."

Also employees who could pass a satisfactory physical examination would be provided an insurance death benefit 100 times the employee's monthly income. For those who were uninsurable, the income was to be provided through a straight annuity contract without insurance benefits and would have continued protection under a new liberal group insurance program, replacing the old one.

The amount of group life, sickness, and accident benefits were announced as follows:

Weekly Salary	Life Insurance	Weekly Accident & Sickness Benefits
under $50	$1,000	$15
$50 to $60	$1,000	$20
$60 to $80	$1,500	$20
$80 to $100	$2,000	$30
$100 or over	$2,500	$40

SP on the grow at 800 North Clark

"Meanwhile," VEC's account continued, "we kept up our march of progress, taking over room after room until we had taken over everything on the fifth and sixth floor, and a lot of space in the basement. The building owned by an eastern insurance company was sold to one John Gomberg, who wasn't too bad to get along with.

"Evidently, he couldn't make payments, so the building was resold to Eli Herman, a fat, hard-nosed lawyer. He wouldn't do a thing in the way of upkeep, and at times leaks in the roof drenched desks and correspondence and discolored the ceilings. Many times, too, we came in to work and there was no heat. Protests were of no avail. Mr. Herman just didn't seem to like us. Then one day we received a legal court order to vacate the premises within 10 days! Herman had a good legal argument, but VEC's attorneys from Herman Fischer's office had better arguments, and the case was thrown out of court. However, it was just one more thing to keep us looking to the Lord.

"Mr. Herman, the building owner, wasn't through, however, for before the lease expired, he told us the rent would be doubled," VEC wrote. "We simply took that as our marching orders from the Lord."

It would be a number of months before the Lord revealed the next building where the management team of Scripture Press would find suitable office space.

---

[1] Details not otherwise noted in this chapter are from various historical sketches, banquet program scripts, and items appearing in copies of *Press Proof*, the company newsletter.

[2] *The Wheaton Leader,* February 14, 1957 (archives box, BTC #1).

[3] Archives Box BTC #1.

[4] See Appendix this chapter, "Summary of Minutes for Members & Directors/Trustees of Scripture Press Foundation/Ministries" 1945-1996.

[5] Archives O Box, folder 15.

CHAPTER 6

800 North Clark Street Potpourri

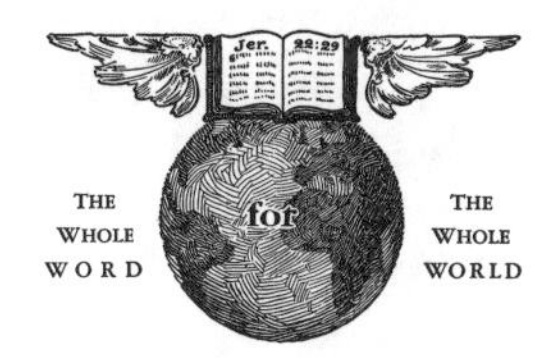

As Stalin, Roosevelt, and Churchhill conferred abroad on war matters, the difficult years of the early '40s saw gas rationing keep most people who weren't in the military closer to home, and people were learning to drink their coffee without sugar. In 1942 at the University of Chicago, a group of physicists led by Enrico Fermi achieved the first controlled nuclear chain reaction, opening the way to both the atomic bomb and nuclear energy. In early 1945, Allied troops closed in on the Germans, Hitler committed suicide on April 30, and the free world, along with SPers, celebrated May 8 as V-E (Victory in Europe) Day. Then, following the atomic bombing of Hiroshima and Nagasaki, SP employees offered thanks to God for the end of the horrible war as they viewed the parade on Michigan Avenue that followed V-J (Victory Over Japan) Day in early September.

The Big Three talk it over.

Meanwhile, at 800 North Clark Street in Chicago, Scripture Press was growing "like topsy," as Bernice Cory often said. A company banquet script put it in these terms:

> Vacation Bible Schools were gaining popularity in the late, '30s. There was only one fundamental course on the market and since it was strongly denominational, it was not usable among all groups. Teachers were having a difficult

time planning their own lessons and handwork projects and were clamoring for a prepared course. We presented Junior and Intermediate lessons in 1939 and the following year added the Primary and Beginner lessons. And thus we launched the Superior Summer School Series of lessons, later called the All-Bible Vacation School lessons.

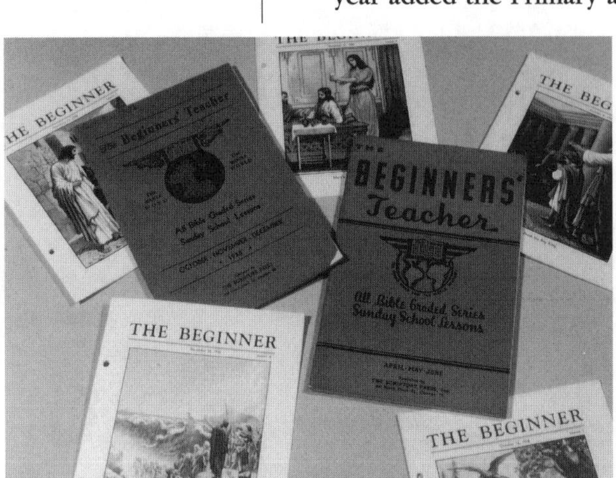

Early lesson materials for tots.

Pastors and teachers wrote of their appreciation of the courses—and their criticisms too. One teacher gave such helpful criticism that we hired her as a writer. In those days, if you made a suggestion, you might find yourself with a job!

New products were coming out every year. An efficiency expert warned, "You're having your babies too close together!"

In 1941, the first Junior visual aids appeared. They were printed in only one color on oaktag stock, and were packaged in uninteresting-looking brown envelopes, but they were eagerly purchased and enthusiastically used. Two years later, "Christian Living" appeared—the first of a long line of Gospel-graphs that taught spiritual truths.

That same year, 1943, Laurin Zorn dreamed up a brand new kind of Sunday School paper for teenagers and adults—one that pupils would not leave in their seats. Titled *Power,* it featured Christianity in action, showing real people who live for Christ. It sold so well that Zorn designed a similar paper for 9- to 13-year-olds, *My Counsellor* [later, *Counselor*].

Then, Zorn needed a full-time editor to take over. An ad brought only one reply of consequence, so we hired him. Young David used only one stone to kill the giant, but he had five carefully selected stones to choose from. We had only one logical choice. But it turned out that Jim Adair was God's man for the job.

In a few years we multiplied our staff nearly eight times—from 18 to 142. We opened a retail store and began convention activities.

Everyone worked hard, but even though we added new personnel, the work seemed always a step or two ahead of us. A couple of efficiency experts convinced us that our work methods were not the best and that our efficiency could be improved about 100 percent.

For several weeks they snooped, pried, and stared at our every move. We had to fill out forms showing what we did every day, how we did it, and the time spent on each job. It seemed as though it took longer to fill out the forms than it did to do the work! But when the experts evaluated the setup, many of their recommendations were incredibly helpful. Work flowed more smoothly, bottlenecks were eliminated, more work was done in less time.

A chorale sang about the experience with the efficiency experts, probably from the George S. May Company.

Oh, the experts came and they asked my name
And said, "What do you do here all the day?"
They gave me a sheet to fill out neat
To show them what I do here and the way.

Woe is me! Now they'll see
That I don't earn all my pay.
So I guess I must work harder
Or my boss will yell much louder,

Till I get much more work done every day.
Then they checked their chart and they liked my part
But showed a better way to do the work.
It was easier, too, for me to do,
No more did jobs-to-do on my desk lurk.

Happy day! Bigger pay!
And new benefits are great:
Blue Cross and life insurance,
Pension plan and health insurance.
Yes, Scripture Press with me does surely rate!

The first employee publication

The first house organ, titled *Name It,* a four-pager, hit employees' desks at 800 North Clark in August 1946. Five silver dollars were offered to the employee submitting the best name. The winning name, SPI *(Scripture Press Informer)* came from Everette Schoenthal, a seminary trained shipper, but editorial staffers decided on *Press Proof.* They explained the name related to the final proofs of a publication and tied in with "proof that there's plenty being done for the Lord."

ABVS sales encouraging

The August issue also carried the exciting news relating to All-Bible Vacation School materials. Shippers had mailed out 550,000 manuals, representing about 135,000 more boys and girls reached in 1946 than the previous year. Typical of the many letters lauding the materials was the following, from Mrs. Angelo Venditti of Ilasco, Ralls County, Missouri:

> We just closed a two-week DVBS. It was wonderful. I taught the Intermediates. I had 19, from 12 to 19 years old. I liked the way your days are planned, and the straightforward message in your lessons. Most of our materials take us away from our Bibles instead of making us search our Bibles for the truths we need to know. I just think it is grand. I highly recommend your material to anyone.

Walker begins CWI

The September 1946 issue told of "Professor Walker" tutoring "450 Christian writers." The previous year, in October, he had announced the "Beginning Christian Writer" correspondence course "for hopeful but inexperienced Christian journalists." In a year's time enrollment leaped from a dozen students to 450. Christened "Sunday Magazine School of Religious Journalism," the ministry had changed its name to "Christian Writers' Institute." Walker announced a new course for Christian workers authored by Donald Hoke, "young author and pastor." Editor Walker, the news item stated, was writing a fiction course.

The same issue proclaimed that nearly 425,000 ABGS manuals were in shippers' hands by August 16 and began hitting the mails three days later. Soon, the article mentioned, 90,000 issues of *Power* and almost 60,000 issues of *My Counsellor* would be en route to customers.

Also announced: "Mary and Lois LeBar, SP Primary and Beginner material authors, have moved to New York for a year to put in some licks on Christian education doctorates."

And: "Report is that V.E. Cory has confiscated copies of the current *Coronet.* Lead article for the month is 'How to Get a Husband.' [Too many single women were marrying and leaving.]"

About this time "Scripture Press" became the trade name of Scripture Press Foundation. Letterheads began carrying the following line: "A Nonprofit Organization for the Distribution of Sunday School and Related Bible Teaching Material."

And this word in 1946 likely irked many workers below supervisory level: "Employees are asked to use the pay phone for all outgoing personal calls . . . except by individuals in positions of section chiefs and up. This, it was explained, is a move to keep phones open for important business calls. On incoming calls, the switchboard operator will ask if the call is personal or business. If personal, the caller will be asked to talk during the lunch hour on the pay phone, and the employee will be given a report. Of course, in cases of emergency all regulations will be waived."

On December 10, 1946, men and women met separately for "straight talk" in connection with "office attitudes." Paul Langdon addressed the men, and Clara Sander, women. The same month SP leased a Linotype machine "to do all typesetting for *Press Proof* and some on manuals and instruction sheets on visual aids." And a song sung by Ruth Camp, Louise Rodman, and Barbara Hendry introduced "Clean-up Week":

Clean up right
Clean up bright.
Scripture Press will shine 'ere long;
Clean up right
Clean up bright
Happy little clean-up song.

The way it was then

Lloyd Cory remembers:

•Most writers in those early days hated to be edited, but their copy really needed it: convoluted sentences, poor grammar and spelling (no spell-checks on typewriters!), often weak or erroneous Bible content. If we had published their stuff they way it came in, as they wanted us to, SP never would have survived.

•We had no carpets (except in the president's office), no piped-in music, no Scotch tape, no postage machines, no calculators, no copying machine, no air conditioning, no electric typewriters, no computers, no ballpoint or fibertip pens.

•Unlike in later years, everybody had to go to chapel (except two or three in the cashier's cage, who opened the mail, to have work ready for others).

•Some things we had then that we didn't have in later years: water cooler; a long, compartmentalized cigar box full of stamps ($1.00 to $1.25 for 40-inch cartons to the west coast); dirt blowing in through the windows; completely open office concept, except for the top four or five people; Sunday School papers from Standard Publishing in Cincinnati delivered in big wooden boxes (not on skids); Pepsi and hamburgers; fast-growing sales (no real inflation factor then); prayer on our knees (on semi-spongy corrugated boxes); more working and less talking; more overtime pay, pop in bottles, and free coffee.

Jim Adair recalls:

•When I arrived in July 1945 to begin my job as associate editor of SP's relatively new Sunday School take-home paper *Power,* one of the first employees to befriend me was E. Clara Sander, a straight, quick-moving, prim and proper former employee of Scott-Foresman. Of German descent, she enjoyed talking about the struggles of her beloved father in the early years of her life in Chicago. She was a stickler for proper grammar, apparently as outlined in Scott-Foresman textbooks. She pointed out to me that *fewer* refers to numbers, *less* to quantity: *Fewer* (not less) than 100 people; Tom felt *less* tension a day later. Miss Sander, as I called her for a long time, was a lifelong friend and asked me to oversee arrangements for the funeral of her sister and also her own funeral.

•Andy Jessen, SP's advertising man who created a series of scare advertisements to promote our teaching materials, was quick to invite me into his home in Itasca for a weekend and introduced me to Wisconsin's Door County. He came into my office just before Labor Day 1945 and invited me to go to Washington Island. I thought it was a few miles away perhaps somewhere nearby in Lake Michigan. The Island, at the tip end of Door County, became one of my favorite vacation spots, and the area still beckons my wife and me to this day. About a year after I got acquainted with Andy, he left for another job but continued to produce SP advertising; then a year or so later he was back at SP.

•In my early days interviewing story subjects for *Power,* I used a wire recorder. The thin wire, which preceded tape, at times would become tangled, worse than a fishing line. I recall interviewing an editor at *Coronet* magazine and losing much of the interview when the wire became hopelessly entangled.

• For dictating letters, we first used a Dictaphone with wax cylinders and later a dictating machine with little green plastic disks.

•Florence Beabout, a Wheaton College grad who edited *My Counsellor* and later went to Japan as a career missionary, had, as did Clara Sander, strict ideas regarding grammar. She insisted, for example, in the following construction, it should be, "Elijah's praying fire down from heaven," instead of "Elijah praying fire down...." I inserted the apostrophe in a final proof, and the apostrophe was inadvertently set as a comma by the typesetter. The printed product was rendered: "Elijah, spraying fire down from heaven."

•About a dozen male employees had company memberships at nearby Lawson YMCA and kept fit playing handball. Other male employees could work out for a dollar, payable by VEC. Bob Walker lifted weights and kept his Charles Atlas look.

•For lunch, managerial workers and some others visited various restaurants: Isabelle's, Yonkers, Ricketts, the Lawson Y, and McCormick YWCA.

•The Chicago campus of Northwestern University was about a mile east and some employees took night courses there. And, of course, Moody Bible Institute was a block west, and employees studied there.

•From time to time Bev Shea, briefcase in hand, visited Bob Walker at 800 North Clark. Bob had worked part time as an assistant to Herbert J. Taylor, president of Club Aluminum Products Company which sponsored Bev on "Club Time," a 15-minute ABC network radio broadcast that began with Bev's deep voice ringing out, "Singing I go along life's road, praising the Lord, praising the Lord . . . ," followed by favorite songs and hymns. Bob served as script writer for that program.

Chapel services appreciated

In November 1946, according to *Press Proof*, employees spoke of the greatest blessings they had received from devotions:

•George Sharpe (Accounting): "The greatest blessing I received from our devotional meetings could hardly be pointed to one single phase. I enjoy them all. One phase, however, that does give me a thrill is when we hear reports of answered prayer. It is further evidence that His promises are secure, and also that our daily effort in prayer is not in vain. Yes, God answers prayer!"

•Bernice Bosman (Indexing): "The message Mr. Fred Beard of Good News brought was inspiring. It got one to asking, 'Lord, is it I?' Am I like Judas, a hindrance to the Lord's work, or am I doing my part to help others know and love Him? As the Lord knew what was in the heart of Judas, He also knows the intents of our hearts."

•Astrid Norager (Filing): "The outstanding devotional period dates back to the Gospel-graph 'Sowing and Reaping,' given by Mrs. Cory. It was a real challenge to me as a Sunday School teacher."

"Pressing Toward the Goal"

The 12th anniversary banquet held in November 1946 at Logan Square Masonic Temple, 2451 N. Kedzie, attracted 160 persons and featured skits, musical numbers, games, and speeches. Bob Walker presented the challenge of the future, in keeping with the theme, "Pressing Toward the Goal." Paul Langdon served as toastmaster. VEC gave the inside story of "Scripture Press and How We Grew" in a flannelgraph demonstration. Menu and place arrangements were handled by Lucy Wood (Order Clerical). Others on the banquet committee: Barbara Hendry (Editorial), chairman; Louise Rodman (Order Clerical) and Astrid Norager (Filing), program; Elinor Pearce (Inventory Control) and Ruth Sander (Catalog Sales), decorations; and Helen Wachtel (Art) and Emil Hudacek (Printing), promotion.

On December 24, 1946 employees enjoyed a grab-bag party, planned by Bernice Cory. Management permitted employees to knock off work at 3 p.m. for the party. Grab-bag gifts were not to exceed 25¢. Features of the program included skits, a devotional period, and refreshments.

Predictions for 1947

The January 1947 *Press Proof* asserted, "If the Lord tarries, this year will mark an important milestone in SP history." The lead article went on as follows:

> The outlook for the year shows 156,000 pieces of mail coming in, meaning nearly 130,000 orders. Total sales may reach a million dollars as some 350,000 parcel-post packages go out at a mailing cost of $32,593.62. This does not include permit and special mailing matter.
>
> Dick Hess [the office mail carrier] probably will make 1,561 visits to each office during the year, and Helen Warren and other switchies expect to handle 120,000 phone calls of all kinds, inside and out.
>
> Quentin Young hopes to procure a stitcher for the bindery within six months, besides an ice cream machine with 10¢ cups, for hot weather, and a Coca-Cola machine. Young and Lloyd Siegfried probably will use a bottle of Anacin a month while moving pegs several thousand times on some 1,000 jobs.
>
> Emil Hudacek and gang will apply 600 pounds of ink to 102,000 reams of paper. Gladys Siegfried and associates will sell some 35,000 yards of flannel to be used to teach the Word of God, plus four more yards to make a black night-gown for a Kentucky woman, and at least 16 yards for baby clothes. Too, during the period, Marie Starnes, John Fish, and others expect to ring up sales for nearly 20,000 customers in the bookstore.
>
> The 4,784,000 copies of *Power* will present the Gospel story with 16,848,000,000 words, and, if the 3,356,000 copies of *My Counsellor* were placed end to end, the line would stretch from Chicago to Knoxville, Tenn. If all copies of the 12 numbers of *Sunday* magazine were laid end to end, the last one would be in Zion, Ill. The 2,272,000 SP publications, of all types, will be read by some 700,000 persons.
>
> To accomplish this, and hundreds of other things, the more than 100 employees will attend devotions for a total of eight days, eat 74,880 candy bars, guzzle 5,000 bottles of pop, drink more than 2,080 gallons of water. Artist Helen Wachtel, after work, twice weekly will feel 200,000 pulse beats as a nurse's aid at Cook County Hospital, and artist Ed

Pike will plow through 10 classics from the library shelf. And *Press Proof* will appear 11 more times in 1947, if this hasn't proved fatal.

Three employees revealed their New Year's resolutions for 1947 as follows:

Ruth Camp (Editorial): To reduce. I am always planning to and never do.

Jolena Stockebrand (Publication Sales): To wear track shoes to keep up with Miss Sander.

Dick Hess (SP's 5-foot office boy): To grow to be 6 feet, 4 inches.

Eunice Fischer to Denver

In early 1947, Eunice Fischer, SP's Sunday School consultant, traveled to Denver to take part in her first statewide convention. "Denver, according to Miss Fischer, is SP's farthest west contact in convention work to date," *Press Proof* reported.

In February, Glenn Ingram, of Glenn Ingram and Company, certified public accountants who for years made the annual audit of the firm's books, was named accounting counsel for the board of directors of SP. Plans were announced for Ingram to make a study of company operation methods and to recommend a more simplified system and all-round improvement.

Mary and Lois LeBar, SP's writers for Beginner and Primary manuals, respectively, had a lesson in "liberalism at its height" when, in December 1946, "they made a study of methods at church school of Riverside Church, New York City, of which Dr. Harry Emerson Fosdick was pastor until recently," *Press Proof* reported in February 1947.

After an "all-girls meeting" early in 1947, the lunchroom committee took action to provide a 50-cup coffee pot to replace small pots. "Now, as a gesture of kindness and sympathy toward male employees, the girls are willing to share their coffee," according to a news item. "Men who like the idea have been requested to see Marie Friesen (Shipping), who will see that the proper portion of water is added to the pot."

In March, a 206X Multilith press arrived and was expected to enable SP to build up a sufficient inventory of Suede-graphs so there would be no more disappointments for customers.

"Also, the latest news out of the Printing Department concerns the rapid-fire sounds recently resounding through the halls," according to the same report. "They have been caused by the operation of the new four-way folding machine, busily folding letters and other advertising matter."

Employees whose duties included writing or transcribing letters got tips on writing better letters after nine employees returned from a course offered by the Dartnell Corporation. SPers who attended were Lois Gustafson, Mildred Vaters, Elvira Hardel, Mildred Haglund, Helen Spyker, Clara Sander, Jean Say, Muriel Erickson, and Elaine Springborn.

Lessons they learned included: "Relax. Be natural. Just talk when you write or dictate"; "Shave off the whiskers, those stilted, old-fashioned expressions"; "Think before you write."

In the session on shaving off the whiskers, a quartet sang "The Whiskers Song" to the melody of "Believe Me, if All Those Endearing Young Charms":

> We beg to advise
> And we wish to state
> That yours has arrived
> Of recent date . . . .

ABVS sales up

The June 1947 *Press Proof* published the good news that ABVS sales had increased over sales for the same period in 1946, far above expectations. "The books are going ahead of the usual 30 percent increase, having now reached between 720,000 and 740,000 books," the report stated. "The total will probably be 180,000 to 300,000 over last year. The Gospel-graph, 'Christian Birth and Growth,' used in connection with the Junior ABVS, will have to be put on the press at least a month early."

And more good news: "SP employees will drink Coke and water this summer [1947]. A spanking new drop-a-nickel-in-the-slot-and-get-a-Coke machine has been installed in the shipping room. Thus Coca-Cola will replace the orange, grape, and root beer drinks of past years." The Coca-Cola Company supplied the machine. It would have been necessary, otherwise, to charge seven cents on other drinks. Cost of ice was blamed as the cause.

But while shippers and others were enjoying "The pause that refreshes," management was still praying about and searching for a new location for the growing company.

A New Home in the Loop

1948–1956

THE YEARS IMMEDIATELY FOLLOWING WORLD WAR II saw great changes and progress in the world. Abroad, Emperor Hirohito, in an imperial decree, shocked Japanese citizens when on January 1, 1946 he declared his divinity a "false conception" founded on fiction. At home President Truman ended all wage, price, and salary controls except ceilings on rents, sugar, and rice, thus cutting the nation's economy loose from the shaky moorings of a four-year-old stabilization program. On October 14, 1947, former fighter pilot Chuck Yeager, flying a Bell X-1 rocket plane, reached 600 mph, breaking the sound barrier.

President Harry S. Truman

In Chicago the postwar period found Scripture Press becoming more and more a victim of growing pains and about to burst out of the walls of its North Clark Street facilities of 17,500 square feet. The fifth floor hallways were being used for working space, as well as storage. Several employees, needing privacy, struggled under the working conditions. The Printing Department needed additional space. *Press Proof* for April 1947 bemoaned the fact that expansion at that address was not feasible even if a new lease could be negotiated.

"We want to make this a matter of much prayer," President

Cory reminded employees. He went on to say that several buildings were being considered for relocation that would give the firm at least another 5,000 square feet of floor space.

A wish list

Division and department managers, along with other employees, made up a wish list, including:

Privacy for editors and writers
Better lighting conditions
A centralized library
More drinking fountains
Conference rooms
A prayer room
A chapel area
Time clocks on each floor
Private offices for all managers

By June the focus was on two buildings: the 111 North Canal Street building and the building at the northwest corner of Congress and Wabash, with the address of 434 South Wabash Avenue. Shippers favored the Canal Street building, whereas others favored the more prestigious Loop location.

The move to South Wabash

The South Wabash building got the official nod, especially because it would be a much more desirable location for the Supply Center, as the bookstore was then called.

VEC signed a five-year lease on June 13, and plans were quickly made to occupy the new home by early November 1947, after Rochelle Furniture Company vacated its space and renovations were completed. Controller R.A. Ginter announced that Quin Young would oversee the details of the move. *Sunday* magazine and Evangelical Teacher Training Association would also be housed in the newly leased space.

On the evening of January 12, 1948 some 250 people—employees, relatives, and friends—enjoyed a turkey meal served by Plunkett's (a Christian caterer SP used regularly in that era) at the firm's 14th anniversary banquet held in the brilliantly lighted third-floor general office area of the new quarters. Three evenings later nearly 600 persons crowded into the same area to help dedicate the new home to getting out "The Whole Word to the Whole World," which had been the theme of this annual banquet.

As key speaker at the dedication program, Dr. H.A. Ironside, famed pastor of Moody Church, touched on the history of publishing as it related to the Gospel. Paying tribute to Scripture Press for its accomplishments, he mentioned that he "once worked on the west coast in a Christian publishing house but never dreamed any Christian publishing firm would have such magnificent offices as these." Other speakers included Freelin Carlton, manager of Sears Roebuck's mammoth State Street store, who welcomed the organization to the neighborhood, and Harry G. Saulnier, superintendent of Pacific Garden Mission and secretary of the board of Scripture Press. George Beverly Shea, introduced as "radio's best-known Gospel singer," sang several numbers.

Following the dedication service, guests toured the new quarters and enjoyed refreshments served in the Supply Center. Charts reflecting the growth of SP's publications were on exhibit. (See Appendix for charts, and floor plans of the new quarters.)

Among the new employees at the grand opening was Russell T. Hitt, for nine years director of public relations at Moody Bible Institute and manager of SP's newly created Public Relations Department. He once remarked that his SP office had a great view of Lake Michigan—except for the fact it was blocked by Roosevelt University. Hitt was later to become editor of *Eternity* magazine and author of the best-selling missionary books *Jungle Pilot,* the story of Nate Saint who died with four others trying to evangelize the Auca Indians, and *Cannibal Valley,* the thrilling account of Christian missionaries who daily risked their lives to bring the Gospel to Stone Age Dani tribespeople in Dutch New Guinea.

Nine years on South Wabash

Scripture Press served churches for nine exciting years at 434 South Wabash Avenue. The company weekly, *Press Proof* (renamed *Spotlight* by Robert Tindle, a shipper, in a contest in October 1950) contains numerous highlights and other items of interest relating to this era. Much of the remainder of this chapter is based on accounts from *Press Proof/Spotlight.*

To get to work at SP's new location, 77 SP employees (72 percent) took CTA transportation—bus, subway, or elevated. Of that number, 16 took two different methods of transportation and six rode three. Twenty-six employees (24 percent) depended on suburban trains: Burlington, Chicago-Aurora-&-Elgin, Chicago & Northwestern, Illinois Central, Milwaukee Road, North Shore, and Rock Island. Several employees drove regularly, and one walked 11 blocks, besides riding the CTA twice.

Upon arrival at work each morning, the Scripture Press family gathered for the traditional chapel service, usually lasting 15 minutes, but sometimes 30 minutes if an outsider was scheduled to speak. Each Tuesday morning in February 1948, A.W. Tozer, editor of *The Alliance Weekly* and widely known pastor of South Side Christian and Missionary Alliance Church, highlighted chapel services with his studies on "the Holy Spirit and the Deeper Christian Life."

From the beginning, employees began each day looking to God. Chapel service at 434 South Wabash.

Dr. Walter L. Wilson, the beloved physician of Kansas City, Missouri, was another speaker, among many other outsiders, whom employees enjoyed from time to time in the '40s and into the '50s. Jim Adair especially recalls Dr. Wilson's kind demeanor. When in downtown Chicago, he would drop into Scripture Press to chat with VEC and would stop for a few minutes to encourage Adair. Dr. Wilson gave him a pair of surgical scissors early in his career that he used at his desk throughout his years with Scripture Press and still treasures.

Dr. Wilson deeply believed in the ministry of SP's take-home papers and once gave a watch as a prize for a contest run in *My Counsellor.* [The winner of the watch, Barbara Timm, a Canadian, wrote: "The four new scholars I got to go to Sunday School as a result of the contest are still attending, and one was saved this morning!"]

Especially known for his unique teaching, Dr. Wilson once held a series of soul-winning workshops up the street from Scripture Press at the Palmer House. Several SP employees attended those sessions. Emboldened by Dr. Wilson's teaching, one employee witnessed in the Palmer House lobby to Philip Morris' widely known Johnny. He was the midget bellhop, who with a hand to the side of his mouth, cried out on early TV and radio the cigarette maker's slogan, "Call for Philip Morris," clearly enunciating and emphasizing *Philllippp Morrrisss* until his call faded in the distance.

Exciting new VBS materials

Excitement ran high in the spring of 1948 as Scripture Press looked forward to the sale of its new VBS materials, especially in relation to the Junior curriculum. Editorial and salespeople believed the theme, "The Christian's Walk and Talk," with a new Gospel-graph by the same title, would pave the way for a red-letter summer for teachers in reaching Juniors, and their expectations paid off with excellent sales.

To produce the materials, writers did a lot of literal homework: Mornings in Wheaton found Ruth McNaughton, of the Editorial Department, and Marie Frost, an elementary school teacher, and BTC working separately in their homes on their individual assignments. Mrs. Cory used a SoundScriber, borrowed from the Adjustments Department, as she worked on the Gospel-graph and the manual lessons. It was a big help, since she usually worked in longhand, but arthritis had been inhibiting her work at that time. VEC looked forward to his wife's completing the project so he could lose no time in taking her on a vacation trip to start on that "complete rest" her doctor had ordered.

After taking the Northwestern in from Chicago one spring day in 1948, VEC and BTC drove to Aurora to promote DVBS materials at the First Presbyterian Church in Aurora. Mrs. Cory was sad, for she had left her white-bearded, ten-inch Pharisee puppet on the train. Telephone calls to the yardmaster in West Chicago brought no results. After being introduced at the meeting, Mr. Cory made some general remarks on the summer school curriculum when in walked Bob Walker with the little Pharisee. He had conducted a one-man search via the telephone which ended in a trip to West Chicago, a meeting with the "friendliest" of conductors, who came from his home to help, and a rescue of the little white-bearded puppet from a dark corner of a Northwestern coach in the rail yard. Mrs. Cory literally bubbled as she presented the merits of the DVBS materials.

In the offices of *Sunday* magazine in May 1949 there was pleasure over the fact Sunday was taking over *Christian Life*

Speakers table at 1949 banquet. Left to right: The Corys, the R.A. Ginters, the Lloyd Siegfrieds, the James DeForrest Murches, and Dr. Clarence E. Benson.

and Times, published by Clyde Dennis and his Good News firm. Combining the best of each magazine, the new monthly would be called *Christian Life.* It was to become the most popular general interest magazine in the Christian field.

And out in the field, Bob Bear, SP's first bookstore rep, was making news traveling the highways and byways of a large chunk of the U.S. The June 1948 issue of *Press Proof* invited readers to sit up front with Bob as he drove the highways:

> You're with Bob on his recent trip East. In Sturgis, Michigan you meet Mr. Griffith, who has a nice bookstore in connection with his jewelry store. He's a Plymouth Brethren and does this for a testimony in his community. "An evangelist held a meeting here recently and used flannelgraph for the youngsters," he tells you. "Fifteen were converted too!" Griffith is quite happy as Bob shows him Gospel-graph and Suede-graph products. Bob gets a conservative order, and Griffith hopes to sponsor a demonstration for that area.
>
> At Three Rivers, Mrs. Nellie Smallcomb has a Scripture Gift Shop in her living room. She isn't doing a booming business, so can't be counted on for an order.
>
> At Otsego you meet Mr. La Huis, who operates the Soul Winner's Service. Now this is about the most humble and simple little place you have ever seen to be called a store. The furniture is of the plainest sort, and the floors are bare and the curtains are of white gauze. Several children are running about. But you soon realize that Mr. La Huis has the respect, cooperation, and confidence of his neighbors for miles around. He's a real missionary at heart, and Bob leaves after Mr. La Huis orders a generous supply of SP lesson manuals.

After his Michigan calls, Bob Bear headed for Ohio, Pennsylvania, New York, and other points east. He was the pioneer of a ministry that paid big dividends in later years as more reps were added to make dealer and church calls.

ABGS sales booming

Sales of ABGS materials were booming, according to a memo Vic Cory issued to division and department heads:

> Inventory on ABGS manuals as of 4/25/49 shows the shipment of 519,457 books, which is a 5.56 percent increase over the same date a year ago. From our graphs, the projected total for the quarter will be 526,000, compared to 498,085 a year ago. Dollar sales comparisons will differ somewhat from the above.
>
> While the 5.56 percent increase in units isn't as big as we have had in some other years, it is much larger than we had expected in view of the Presbyterian defection. Furthermore, this quarter's total represents a gain of 20,000 over the January quarter, and this is the largest numerical gain made in any but the October quarter for a good many years. This would indicate that some of the Presbyterians have come back!
>
> For all of this, we praise our Lord and with increased faith, we can continue singing, "Great Is Thy Faithfulness," and, of course, "God Leads His Dear Children Along."

When Bob Bear resigned, Willis Grimm became SP's sales rep in August 1952. He lived in Williamsport, Pennsylvania before moving to Glen Ellyn, Illinois a few years later. In June 1953 Laurin Zorn, who had started *Power* and *My Counsellor* back in 1943, returned from Van Kampen Press, a division he headed at Bob Van Kampen's Hitchcock Publishing Company, and became SP's Wholesale Department manager in early 1955. He hired Leo Polman to become the company's rep to service stores west of the Mississippi. Zorn himself often went out with Grimm and Polman.

It was perhaps in the late 60s when Zorn ran into a problem with VEC. In Cory's opinion, Zorn was "giving away the store" by allowing too much discount to dealers, and the president had a notion to fire Zorn. He relented when Jim Lemon, relatively new on the job as head of the Marketing Division, persuaded him not to.

Dealer workshops boost business

Dealer workshops helped bookstores boost business in the field and at home. Frederick Armbruster of The Bible House, Pomona, Calif., wrote, "Your workshops last year increased our June business by $600 over the preceding year. Your workshop and conference program was largely responsible for an increase of $2,000 in our sales over 1949. Better than the financial side, we have been able to supply churches with material that reaches children with the Gospel and gives them a knowledge of far more of the Bible."

At Scripture Press the total number of pieces of mail received in 1950 reached 192,690. With 115,000 orders recorded in 1950, the company counted 4,000 more opportunities to serve customers than 1949 afforded.

Convention speakers were driving and flying to distant places in the late '40s and '50s. In the 12 months from July 1950 till the next July, the Convention Department sent its experts to 21 states and two cities in Canada for a total of 110 speaking engagements. Eunice Fischer was constantly on the road, along with Nels Andersen; other speakers included Alma Gilleo, Pearl Troxell, Stella Daleburn, BTC, and Mavis Anderson. In early spring of 1951, Mavis became stranded for two days and two nights with other train passengers between Regina, Saskatchewan and Medicine Hat, Alberta in the area's worst blizzard in 40 years. Passengers ran out of food, water, and almost out of heat. After two nights with little sleep, tired and bedraggled, Mavis arrived in Medicine Hat to find she had to speak in an evening service, then show camp pictures, and later conduct a Sunday School workers' meeting. She reported that the Lord got her through with renewed strength.

Bob Walker's Christian Writer's Institute conferences, featuring workshops on many phases of journalism, began to take on momentum in the late '40s and drew writers from afar. The conference in November 1948 held in the offices of Scripture Press and *Christian Life* featured, among others, Henry Sellinger, who wrote and produced such popular radio shows as "Ma Perkins," "Little Orphan Annie," "Clara, Lou, and Em," and "Terry and the Pirates." Wendell P. Loveless, who had been director of WMBI, shared honors with Sellinger in conducting a radio workshop.

Dale McCulley, associate producer of Cavalcade Productions, taught conferees how to write scripts for movies. Ken Anderson, editor of *Youth for Christ* magazine and who later headed Gospel Films, taught how to write novels, and Laurin Zorn, then with Van Kampen Press, told how to get books published.

BTC headed a workshop in Sunday School lesson preparation. Know-how in juvenile writing was given by Jim Adair and Florence Beabout. Alvera Johnson, managing editor of *Christian Life,* and Elise Fraser, CL's fiction editor, taught short story writing. And Bob Walker headed workshops in magazine writing, feature, and news writing. William F. McDermott, religion editor of the *Chicago Daily* News and famous Christian journalist, spoke at the closing dinner.

Convention Department begins workshops

With a strong emphasis on Daily Vacation Bible School in the early '50s, the Convention Department began workshops. In May 1952 three workshops were held in the SP chapel. On May 12 Bob Walker moderated a group discussion on "Departmentalized vs. Combined Worship Services." Panel members were the Rev. Robert Swanson, BTC, Nels Andersen, and Ruth Von Busch. The following handled departmental sessions: Marie Frost, Nursery; Stella Daleburn, Beginner; Lois LeBar, Primary; Mrs. Cory and Gladys Siegfried, Junior; and Swanson and Lloyd Cory, Intermediate.

Also in May 1952, Lois and Mary LeBar, both professors in the Christian Education Department at Wheaton College and long associated with SP, each received the Doctor of Philosophy degree from Biblical Seminary, New York. From that time on Vic Cory often humorously referred to the duo as SP's "pair-o'-docs."

In the early '50s, after President Truman ordered U.S. air and naval forces to help defend South Korea from the invasion of North Korean Communist troops, several SPers went off to war. An impressive chapel service was conducted on Friday, June 22, 1951 as employees pledged their prayer support to "our servicemen." Flo Shoemaker, who chaired the devotions committee for the month, suggested the program. Among those from SP who entered the armed forces in the early '50s: Dick Hess, Manuel Carrera, Art Modrzejewski, Dell Harris, Neil

Barringer, Bill Rowe, and Ken Nelson.

Later Hess returned to SP for a long stint. In May 1952 *Spotlight* apologized to Corporal Hess for marrying him to the wrong girl. His wife was *Marian Andersen* instead of *June Anderson.* The error occurred, according to the publication, because the name was given by a supposed "reliable informant." Hess was stationed at Ft. Lawton, Wash., awaiting shipping out to Japan.

SP shut down for General Douglas MacArthur.

SP shut down for a time on Thursday, April 26, 1951 to let employees go to a parade on Michigan Avenue to see World War II hero General Douglas MacArthur. Art Director Vic Erickson reported that he caught MacArthur's eye and that he waved at him as the procession passed the Stevens Hotel [now the Hilton].

A trophy for best film

A decision was made in May 1951 to name SP's new film on soul-winning in the Sunday School "Stars in Your Crown." It was one of a series of SP films produced by Dale McCulley's Cavalcade Productions. Harriet Salios, especially known for her singing, suggested the name and won $10. In the spring of 1952, SP got a trophy for the best Sunday School film produced in 1951, "Doorways to Decision." *Spotlight* failed to mention the name of the organization that presented the award.

In October 1951, SP welcomed Henry Jacobsen as editor of Adult lessons. He came from Suffern, N.Y. (Vic Cory called him "the wise man from the east") and had been general manager of the American Tract Society. In the first *Adult Teacher* (October 1952), Jacobsen urged readers not to neglect *Decision,* the weekly paper with study helps, written mostly by Henry's wife, Marion. Several years later, after sales for *Decision* stayed flat because not many adults were into really studying the Word, management decided to drop it. About this time Billy Graham had a radio program called "Hour of Decision." George Wilson, his business manager, phoned VEC and asked if the Billy Graham Evangelistic Association could name their upcoming magazine *Decision.* Cory gave an OK without hesitation, which likely surprised Wilson. "This got VEC and SP brownie points with the BGEA," Lloyd Cory quipped.

The same month SP had welcomed Jacobsen, BTC spoke

at the NSSA convention in Detroit, and afterward a woman came up and gushed, "Oh, Miss Mears, I just love your Junior High material!" A slight case of mistaken identity.

In April 1952 President Cory moved out of his office for a short time while Bob Walker conducted a photographic interview with Billy Graham.

At a meeting in May 1952, employees already in SP's pension plan or about to enter it were given details of the revised integration with Social Security. It was pointed out that there would be no increased cost to employees, and they would receive a larger pension at retirement. Forty-three were already in the plan, started in 1947. Those about to enter were: Mildred Stock, Betty Stock, Alma Gilleo, Marita Root, Lloyd Cory, Ben Kroeker, and Walter Hylen.

Pattibooks for ages 2 and 3 were popular in the early '50s and were published into the '80s. Wholesale Department workers chuckled over an order that came from a dealer in March 1952 for "3 copies of 'Who Loves the *Chicken*?' " He really wanted "Who Loves the Children?"

Joyful evidence of growing sales of SP products: the purchase in March 1952 of four "new, modern Burroughs billing machines." Nora Newman's billers were delighted in getting acquainted with the mechanics and looking forward to "greater heights" in output. First to use the machines were Marie Elliott, Ethel Johnson, and Florence Smith.

Conveyor belt installed

More efficient handling of orders resulted from the installation of a new conveyor belt, extending the length of the building. Henry Staalsen and his crew of workmen installed it in March 1952. This relieved congestion of skids stacked in front of offices on the second floor. To make room for the conveyor, the Printing Department moved to the seventh floor.

Another indication of growth came in June 1952 when Everette Schoenthal's warehousemen transferred stock to 14,000 square feet of much needed warehouse space at 521 South Wabash. The transfer was made from a smaller area at 66 East Randolph. The lease was for three years, to coincide with the lease of SP's office space at 434 South Wabash.

Great emphasis was put on reducing tardiness and absenteeism in the '50s. *Spotlight* told it as it was. For example, the

October 12, 1951 report for September revealed Wholesale Sales had no tardiness, whereas *Power* and *My Counsellor* and Editorial employees were guilty of the worst records. The March 21, 1952 absenteeism report for February showed "for the third consecutive month, Andy Jessen's Advertising Department had no absenteeism." Five other departments were perfect, whereas the Distribution and Convention Departments got the lowest rating.

There was also a companywide focus on sharing the Good News with vendors and others, not just through the output of Christian education materials. Pauline Seigfried, widow of Lloyd, passed on a notation written by Lloyd in his diary on May 3, 1950 that attests to this concern:

> "Now Is Our Hour"—this has been the theme of the past two SP Executive Committee meetings sparked by Robert Walker's report on revival and a statement that we felt a more constant witness to our vendors, salesmen, customers, etc. was necessary. The group spent much time in prayer. We could feel the moving of the Spirit and a decision was made to formulate a statement of SP's convictions regarding the nearness of THE HOUR and the way of salvation. R.A.W. wrote up an excellent word of testimony, and I am sure that the Lord will use it mightily in . . . whatever way He chooses. The plan of salvation is there and the challenge.

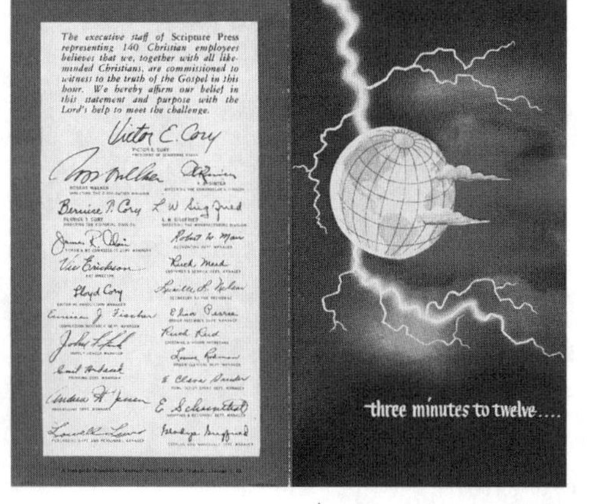

The "excellent word of testimony" referred to was a Gospel tract titled "Three Minutes to Twelve . . . This Is Our Hour" (Appendix). It was signed by 22 members of the executive staff. By October 1950, 50,000 copies of the tract had been distributed by SPers, and another 50,000 had just been printed to herald the Good News.

An item in *Spotlight* for June 1, 1951 further indicates the spiritual fervor of that day:

> It may have become commonplace to us—we see it every day, the sign, "Remember to Pray," in the back of the chapel. It struck home to the heart of a colored messenger

> as he left the *Power* and *My Counsellor* office recently. He asked for help—spiritual help. Tonight he will be given the Good News of salvation. Pray for Jim Adair and Harry Saulnier as they deal with him.

Morale was high when SP was housed in the Loop. *Spotlight* for February 20, 1953 reported:

> Cliff Richards of Public Relations, University of Chicago, said last week at the Industrial Editors' Institute that only about one-fourth of the companies they have surveyed have had good morale. This ties in with the report published in *Spotlight* about SP's morale survey made July 1, 1952: morale here was higher than in 77.7 percent of the companies surveyed.

Well into the '50s most employees reacted enthusiastically as management talked of relocating the growing firm. Several locations were considered. Sites at Des Plaines, Lincolnwood (Chicago), and Melrose Park were correctly zoned for commercial use, but applications for rezoning would have to be made for sites in Park Ridge and Wheaton. The Corys favored moving to Wheaton, where they lived, if a parcel of land on College Avenue could be rezoned. But Controller R.A. Ginter opposed the idea openly, favoring a site on the Des Plaines River, closer to his home. After the move to Wheaton, his preferred site in Des Plaines flooded several times.

Sadly, Ginter wasn't around to make the move. On Monday, November 22, 1954, the announcement that Ginter, 49, had died stunned and saddened SPers. After his collapse in a downtown Chicago store and an extended stay in Wesley Memorial Hospital, he had been presumably on the road to recovery. But his autopsy report showed that his death was caused by arteriosclerosis of the coronary arteries.

Only a short while earlier, on September 18, Dr. Benson, originator of SP's ABGS lesson materials, had died at the age of 75 in a hospital in Orlando, Florida. Both men were greatly missed as SP prayed and planned for its westward move.

More Memories of the Wabash Years

When a company is prospering, there are times of celebration and rewards for those responsible for growth. On Friday, November 14, 1952, 257 persons, including some 200 employees and guests, observed Scripture Press' 19th anniversary at a dinner in the Congress Hotel Gold Room. It was billed as SP's Safari, "Conquest for Christ." A month later, on December 19, management announced that for the fourth consecutive year employees would receive length of service bonus checks. The checks would be figured the same as the previous year, according to the announcement—half of one percent of an employee's present annual salary times the number of years employed by SP. Temporary employees would be given a cash remembrance. Employees serving in the armed forces would be treated as if they were still at work.

On Friday, February 27, 1953 employees lined up in the parking lot alongside the 434 building for X-rays at the TB mobile unit. In those days everyone 15 years or older was urged to have chest X-rays annually.

At the same time SPers were praying about SP's petition for rezoning of the property on College Avenue, Wheaton. It had been referred back to Vic Cory for more information. The city wanted more information regarding whether SP had made contact with five property owners or others living near the College Avenue site. None had been contacted, but contact was made and the petition had been returned to the city and was in the hands of the Zoning Board, awaiting a public hearing at a later date.

Employees regularly helped conduct services at Pacific Garden Mission, a few blocks from 434.

SPers serve other organizations

In the early '50s SPers were faithfully involved in conducting noonday Gospel services at nearby Pacific Garden Mission. Usually there were willing volunteers, but one spring week the Personnel Department had to "draft" people to help in the services. Those lined up for duty that week were: Jim Eshenaur, Ruth Reid, Lloyd Siegfried, Ian Walker, Art Modrzejewski, Elinor Rice, Ruth Mead, Vic Anderson, John Fish, Walter Hylen, Lee Temples, Iva Mae Johnson, Zenobia Hawkins, and Dick Hess.

SPers were also serving other organizations. In September 1952, VEC accepted the invitation of the Board of Trustees to serve on the Advisory Council of The King's College, then in Delaware. He was already on several other boards. In 1953 Bob Walker, among other outside connections, served as vice-president of Evangelical Press Association, and Jim Adair, as treasurer. Both were involved in the early meetings at Lawson YMCA that brought EPA into existence, particularly Walker, who was honored for his contribution by EPA in 1998.

Still hoping to move west, SP got word in April 1953 that the zoning board in Wheaton reported favorably to the City Council on SP's petition for rezoning of the site under consideration. However, the City Council, in turn, referred the matter back to the Zoning Board for more reasons as to why they recommended rezoning. Meanwhile, as SPers prayed, management was reaching out for more information on other sites still under consideration.

In July, convention and editorial people geared up for the first entirely SP-sponsored Sunday School conference, to be held at Mount Hermon in California. Those lined up to speak included President and Mrs. Cory, Robert Walker, Ruth

Streblow, Al Sedgwick, and Lois and Mary LeBar. Leo Polman was to be in charge of music. After the conference, the Corys, with son Phil, planned to leave for a vacation that would take them to Vancouver, B.C. to see Esther Van Fleet Post, their former housekeeper. En route back to Wheaton, they planned to visit Lake Louise and Banff.

In July of that year Lucille Nelson rescued an eight-year-old from drowning at her Sunday School picnic in Elgin. She noticed the little boy jump into deep water and realized he couldn't swim when he started going down for the third time. She jumped in and brought him out. Too modest to tell the story herself, someone else reported the rescue to *Spotlight.* Lucille was known throughout her 35 years at SP (1947–1982) for jumping in where needed. At first she served as secretary for President Cory but was best known as an important cog in Production and New Products.

SPers hear the sound of music

On Thursday, September 3, 1953, Warren Zorn, musical son of Laurin, auditioned voices for the SP Chorale, getting ready for the chorale's first program of the season. By March 1954, the following were singing in the chorale: Beverly Akens, Allan Anderson, Dan Blycker, Dorothy Bolman, Ruth Buelow, Rae Ann Christensen, Muriel Erickson, Vic Erickson, Ed and Mona Felske, Marjorie Ford, Lois Gustafson, John Hall, Virginia Horne, Tallie Kohler, Ben Kroeker, Miriam Levengood, Marion MacDonald, Marjorie Milhuff, Milton Miles, Ted Miller, Art Modrzejewski, Zoe Moore, Nora Newman, Louise Rodman, Gladys Siegfried, Pearl Troxell, Jerry Tunney, Betty White, and Bonnie Wright.

In November 1953, Billy Graham's book *Peace With God* was available in the Supply Center for $2.50 a copy, less the employee 20 percent discount.

General Memorandum No. 20B, released on May 28, 1954, announced the hiring of William O. Hall as Production Division Head. He came with 25 years' heavy production experience with R.R. Donnelley & Sons. He became known for his saying, "Work smarter, not harder." To the disppointment of Editorial, he soon switched some of the lesson manuals from Poole Bros. to his old firm, Donnelley.

The following week Emil Hudacek, longtime head of the

Printing Department, took a position with Zavodny Printing Company. A group of friends surprised him with a luncheon at Toffenettis'. It was the beginning of the end for printing on the premises of SP.

In July, announcement was made that "with a nickel and a dime, you can have yourself a sweet roll and a large candy bar or a third of a quart of Borden's milk."

In August, John Fish was elected president of the Christian Booksellers Association at the fifth annual convention at the Morrison Hotel, Chicago. He had been active in the Association since its beginning.

In February 1955, SP announced that Sherman Williams would come to head the Convention Department [later, CREDEX—Christian Education Extension, coined by Bob Cook]. He was closing out his pastorate at Beacon Chapel, Spokane, Washington and was expected in July. He served as CREDEX head till March 1960 when he left to pastor Redwood Chapel in Castro Valley, Calif. (See Appendix for "Five to Ten Year Plan for CREDEX.")

William Sundin arrived on March 1 to begin as controller, but he left a few months later, and Norman Finke became controller in July.

SP into filmstrips

In June, Bob Walker announced that SP was getting into an entirely new field of service, having signed a contract with Beacon Publishers of Toronto to produce filmstrips. SP was to have exclusive worldwide distribution rights. "The filmstrips," the announcement read, "will run in three different series. By August we expect to have ready for release six Bible stories, three Gospel stories, and three missionary stories. . . . All in color, the filmstrips will sell for $5 each. . . ."

SP introduced the forerunner of today's fax machine when in September employees were advised they could send and receive telegrams at a "Desk-Fax" machine at the switchboard.

Through the years, Bernice Cory entertained employees with detailed reports of her exciting trips. Perhaps the highlight trip of all her jaunts was her tour of the Holy Land with a party organized by Dr. Joseph Free, archaeology professor at Wheaton College. Before she left in March 1955, women department heads presented her with a gold and purple orchid to match her going-away outfit. She sailed on the SS *Constitution* and landed at Naples, Italy. The party went from there to Jerusalem. For years BTC had looked forward to visiting the Holy Land in order to enliven her lessons with first-hand material.

Following is an excerpt from a BTC letter to SPers:

> I have been deep in the earth in what is reputed to be the tomb of Lazarus, and in another deep pool supposed to be the pool of Bethesda. I've seen both traditional sites of Calvary, Gordon's Calvary, and that within the Church of the Holy Sepulcher. We had our last Sunday's service at the Garden of Gethsemane and shall have another on the Mount of Olives. Yesterday we saw the excavation of Jericho, and before that at Dothan.
>
> We expected to swim in the Dead Sea, but the King of Jordan was monopolizing the shower rooms, so we just waded. We all agreed we'd not want to swim in the muddy Jordan and wondered if it could possibly have been that bad when Christ was baptized in those waters. Dr. Free is a terrific guide. He knows the location of every significant spot. I'm taking lots of pictures—hope they turn out well. Am ever so grateful for your prayers. I can hardly wait to tell you all what I'm seeing. Everywhere people know of SP and use our materials. God bless you!

BTC had been back only a short while when VEC was off on a trip to attend the seventh World Congress on Evangelism at Sao Paulo, Brazil. His primary burden was for translation work, particularly of SP's visual aids. Many missionaries, he pointed out, had asked for them in the languages of their people.

In October President Cory, Bob Walker, and Norm Finke flew to Washington to talk with attorneys about SP's tax case that had been ongoing since the mid-'40s.

Orders roll in "like a flood"

December had Order Clerical people and shippers "working like beavers the past ten days," *Spotlight* for December 9, 1955 reported. "Orders have been rolling in like a flood!" The news item went on to tell that workers were "keeping their heads above water" but might need more help. "Order fillers and shippers have tried valiantly to give 24-hour service, but the volume has far exceeded anything imagined," the report continued. "To encourage shippers who are seeking to 'up' their output, Norman Finke has had a [large] board prepared to post daily the names of shippers placing first, second, and third in 'shipping points per hour.' Similar recognition would be given to those in other departments, but Shipping is the only group with a point system in operation. . . . Top man yesterday was Charles Walker with 43.6 shipping points per hour. Close behind was Robert Nickel with 42.6, and next Jesse Cotton [SP's first black employee], 40.6. The department average was 35.0"

The same issue of *Spotlight* announced the hiring of Robert H. (Bob) Hawkins of Spokane, Washington, a former West Coast rep for Van Kampen Press, as a field staff rep effective January 1, 1956. (Sometime earlier, Carl Frederickson, another former Van Kampen rep had joined the sales force.) "Hawkins will make two trips annually calling on dealers in Washington, Oregon, Idaho, western Montana, and parts of southern Canada," according to the news item. During the spring he was slated to help conduct workshops for dealers. (By April, the field staff had held 165 dealer DVBS workshops.) Hawkins worked for SP several years and later founded Harvest House Publishers, Eugene, Oregon.

SPers go abroad as missionaries

On January 8, 1956 Ed McCully, Jr., died at the hands of Auca Indians in the Ecuador jungles, along with Jim Elliott, Pete Flemming, Nate Saint, and Roger Youderian. Their deaths sent shock waves throughout the evangelical world. At Scripture Press, many employees remembered Marilou Hobolth, who had worked in Order-Filling and Inventory Control before she entered Moody Day School; she had later married Ed McCully. Now, in Ecuador, she was a widow of a martyr. SPers prayed fervently for comfort for Marilou and the other wives and that the valiant mission of the five men would pay spiritual dividends in future years—as it did.

Marilou was one of many SP employees who had gone to missionary service abroad. Others, over the years, include Mabel Lindsay and Florence Beabout, Japan; Leonard Messenger (what an appropriate name for a missionary!),

British West Indies; Betty Hagberg, Mary Kook, Lee and Irene Temples, Venezuela; Dorothy Svendsen, Peru; Marilyn Monson, India; Gloria Wallace, Zululand; Gloria Inniger, West Pakistan; Tom Cosmades, Turkey; Eleanor Timmerman, Mexico; Virginia Viets, Brazil; Beulah Clegg, Africa; Jerry Leonard, Brazil; Johannes and Loriene Vanderwal, Holland; Paul and Faith Schoming, Alaska; Burt and Ruth Long, Niger; and their daughter, Sue Hammack, Nigeria. More employees would go out to heed the Great Commission in subsequent years, though in the eyes of the Corys—and the Lord's, the Corys believed—those working for SP were already missionaries through literature.

In early 1956, Eunice Fischer wrote employees, saying, "If you're thinking of asking the boss for an afternoon off, Friday, January 27, would be as good a time as any, and you can come out to my graduation from Wheaton College. I'm not sending out announcements to kith or kin, but since I really consider you my kithin cousins, I do send you this word. Yes, I'm now on my last lap." She continued, in part:

> Today I've been thinking back over the Lord's wonderful provision. I landed in Wheaton a little over two years ago equipped with: a third less money than I needed, a determination to get through in half the regular time, and ambition to graduate as an honor student, a lonesomeness for my mother and family, a yearning to hang on to a little convention speaking [for SP] and magazine writing, and no regret at all at leaving Chicago's dirt and CTA system.
>
> The Lord in His goodness has prospered my way, checked me when I attempted the impossible, and supplied all my needs. What now? It seems best for my family responsibility and my own inclination to go on to Northwestern University for the M.A. in evening school. Perhaps I'll see some of you up there studying too. Nothing like a good old exam once in a while to keep one's spirits up.
>
> And to those of you planning to move to Wheaton—and without even the hardships of exams and term papers—I can assure you that you'll love this clean, folksy, tree-lined, safe-feeling little town. CTA, here I come!

Eunice returned to Chicago and enrolled for her M.A. at Northwestern and worked for several years on Beginner and

Primary lessons in SP Editorial.

SPers rejoiced when Olga Kononowa, a tiny woman from Ukraine who later changed her name to Anne Conway, became an American citizen on Tuesday, January 24, 1956. An employee in the Order Clerical Department, she was best known for her chapel appearances when she, with her charming accent, would recite long passages of Scripture from memory, pronouncing every word precisely and with no flubs.

The Dillon Brass Quartet at SP groundbreaking ceremonies in Wheaton in 1955. Lloyd Cory is second from left and player with hair flying is Bill Dillon.

Lloyd Cory was a bit scared in the early morning hours of Monday, February 13,1956 after arriving in Wheaton on the 1:35 a.m. "Roarin' Elgin" out of Chicago following a Dillon Brass Quartet engagement in Neenah, Wisconsin. As he walked across the Eddie Ruch property in downtown Wheaton on the way home, a flashlight, a revolver, and a shotgun suddenly appeared before his face. The Ruch service station had just been broken into and the robber had fled on foot. Two policemen thought they had their man until they searched Lloyd, finding only his trumpet, his Bible, an income tax book, and pajamas. They sent him on his way, relieved but his heart still aflutter. "It was the first time I had faced a gun since World War II," Lloyd said afterward.

A new bookstore on Wabash

In light of the fact a move out of the Loop was imminent, SP opened the Scripture Press Book Shop at 135 South Wabash in March 1956. "With the sound of the trumpet, hymns of praise, and a dedicatory prayer by Harry Saulnier," the new store opened to a large crowd, many of them curious passers-by, according to *Spotlight*. Billy Graham visited the store in the afternoon and was featured in a documentary film on the store and its ministry. In May, Art Saul joined bookstore manager John Fish in serving customers. Art had been pastor of Mansfield Gospel Center in Ohio for five years and prior to that Sunday School pastor of the Cicero (Illinois) Bible Church. In June 1956 SP also opened up a summer conference store at Winona Lake, Indiana.

Walker resigns, Frykman joins SP

It wasn't a big surprise in May 1956 when Bob Walker submitted his resignation from SP, for he had been on leave of absence since September 1955 because of heavy responsibilities in connection with *Christian Life* magazine. "A 13-year association is hard to break," the announcement read, "so the decision was made with reluctance on Mr. Walker's part and accepted with sincere regret by Mr. Cory. . . . The Lord sometimes leads in breaking of business ties as He has done in this case, but we can all sing unitedly 'Blest be the tie that binds our hearts in Christian love.'" Later, Walker announced that *Christian Life* would stay in Chicago rather than move with Scripture Press, to be able to catch newsworthy people when they were in town.

In June 1956, SP announced the forming of a fifth division, Personnel-Public Relations, to be managed by Wilfred C. Frykman. "Among the activities Mr. Frykman will direct are recruitment, interviewing, and screening of applicants; orientation of new employees; counseling; public relations; *Spotlight*; job evaluation and merit rating; training programs outside the firm; on- the-job-training; chapel services," the announcement stated. "Louise Rodman . . . will continue pretty much her present duties [as Personnel Department head]."

Frykman had been international extension director of Gideons International since July 1952. From 1945 to 1952 he was advertising manager of the Lincoln (Nebraska) Hatchery, doing editorial work on the firm's monthly newspaper and handling radio programs and personnel matters. Further preparation for his SP job, the announcement continued, was received in guidance and teacher relationships when he served as associate principal of a junior high school in Rochester, Minnesota. He received his B.A. degree from the University of Minnesota.

In July, John Fish was back in the news, having received a letter from President Dwight D. Eisenhower expressing his appreciation for the part SP and the Christian Booksellers Association (of which Fish was president) had in building up the White House Library. "The range of spiritual wealth covered by your selection is wide and deep," Ike wrote after he had inspected the collection personally. "I know the books will be a source of strength to me and others in the days and years ahead."

August saw a "coming and going" when Ben Wood arrived to head the Art Department and Lillian Swanson sailed from Montreal to minister to Scandinavian countries as a representative of SP. Wood left in December and Carl Lindgren came aboard as Art Department director. Wood continued to supply artwork for SP. Miss Swanson expected to be gone at least a year to promote the Gospel through the Sunday School and to determine what SP could do in translation work. A visit to Europe in 1955 had opened her eyes to the spiritual needs of people there.

Lillian Swanson

SPers were saddened upon learning of the drowning of Ed Pike, a former SP artist, on Saturday, September 11, 1956 in Lake Michigan while on a Moody Church young people's outing at the Crowell estate, Winnetka. SPers Zenobia Hawkins, Frances Crowder, and Bea Maxfield were with the group. Ed was one of five young men who experienced difficulty because of a sudden drop in the lake bottom, high waves, and a strong undertow. The other four made it to shore. Ed was a close friend of Jim Adair, who recalls: "It was Ed who invited me in 1954 to Moody Church Week at Canadian Keswick, where I met my wife, Ginnie, who was singing with two of her sisters on the program. Ed loved the Lord and volunteered his services as an artist for Pacific Garden Mission and the Best Seller Publicity ministry of Miss Jo Peterson who, in the '40s and '50s, placed Scripture posters created by talented artists in Chicago trains and buses."

BTC took a wrong turn in September when she entered the LeBars' home in Wheaton and plunged pellmell down a flight of stairs, landing on the cement basement floor. X-rays showed not even a cracked rib, and back at work she was praising the Lord for His deliverance. VEC, "feeling the need perhaps of a little sympathy directed to him," as *Spotlight* put it, lost a finger nail when he caught a finger in a collapsible chair.

On Saturday, October 8, 1956, SP took part in a big Sunday School parade up State Street. Velma Ammann and Emil Vosicky, both of Accounting, rode the SP float.

During the fall of 1956, final preparations were being made for the move to Wheaton, and some employees had already moved to the western suburbs and were taking the Northwestern train to work.

Westward Ho!

For several years the Corys and many Scripture Press employees looked to the day when the company would move to Wheaton and join a growing list of Christian organizations, headed by Wheaton College. Some humorously referred to the city as the "Protestant Vatican."

After SP made application to the Wheaton City Council in the early 1950s asking that the Bird property on College Avenue be rezoned from Class A residential to Class B commercial use, the council asked the city's zoning board for its decision. Later the zoning board came back to the council in favor of rezoning to permit Scripture Press to build on the property. But some council members wanted more information—particularly Commissioner Wallace M. Conley—and asked the zoning board to study the matter further and respond again with more detailed information.

The issue hit the front pages of Wheaton newspapers:

SPARKS FLY AS COUNCIL APPROVES
REZONING FOR SCRIPTURE PRESS

WOULD SCRIPTURE PRESS BE
AN OFFICE OR PUBLISHING FIRM?

Some residents strongly opposed rezoning to allow a noisy "printing" firm to erect a building on the swampy area, though builders had already determined that the land was unsuitable for houses. One reporter wrote that the site was "rat infested and covered with debris, and a mosquito breeding dumping ground" and after a heavy rain, water often flooded into College Avenue. Ignoring the fact that the area would be cleaned up and enhanced with a new building and attractive landscaping, these residents argued that, if allowed to build there, Scripture Press would not pay taxes, resulting in more children going to school and higher taxes for home owners. Another thing, they contended, College Avenue traffic would increase and become a problem.

Public hearings were conducted. Petitions began to be circulated. In July 1953, a man visited Stan Edgren, a Wheaton Free Church member, with a petition, and asked Edgren if he wanted to do something about the high taxes in Wheaton, and, if so, he should sign the petition barring Scripture Press from Wheaton. He questioned the man, who said some women from the Wheaton church were also getting signatures on the same matter. Edgren correctly explained that SP promised to pay taxes, but the petitioner said he didn't trust the company.

In city council meetings, Commissioner Conley, who seemed to oppose most progress in that day (see Van Kampen letter, Appendix), argued doggedly that allowing Scripture Press to build on the property would not be in the best interest of the city. For one thing, he said, it was his understanding the firm had a Multilith press and, furthermore, if the firm was only a publisher, it should be limited to 20 employees and not 200 or more as planned.

Finally, the city council voted to have citizens themselves decide the matter, and the October 30, 1953 *The Daily Journal* headlined:

REFERENDUM ON ZONING IS TOMORROW

The article read in part:

> The controversial Joseph Bird property zoning issue, which has been hanging fire nearly a year, will be decided at the polls, to be open from 7 a.m. to 6 p.m. tomorrow. The issue before the public is: Should the Joseph Bird property

> on College avenue, located between Kar-Lee greenhouses and the east city limits, be rezoned from Class A residential to B commercial?
>
> Scripture Press, a publisher of religious magazines, applied for the rezoning [last December] in order to build an office building and warehouse on the land. Two hearings were held and the zoning board, with a three to two vote, recommended that the land be rezoned. In April the board withdrew the recommendation because of the question of Scripture's ability to operate under the C-14 classification that prohibits a printing or publishing house from employing more than 20 persons.
>
> Another public hearing was held after which the zoning board recommended against rezoning. In July, the council, with Commissioner Wallace Conley casting the only negative vote, turned down the zoning board's recommendation and voted to rezone the property...A group of citizens then petitioned the city council to rescind their vote or hold a referendum. Technically the property is already rezoned [in favor of Scripture Press], but if the issue is defeated tomorrow the ordinance will then be rescinded. Again, over Conley's negative vote, the council voted to call the referendum.

Seeking to give residents the true picture, Scripture Press ran a full-page ad in the same issue of *The Daily Journal,* urging a yes vote and pointing out that the tax paid by SP would be one of the highest in the city and that its building and landscape would enhance the property on College Avenue. SP also placed other newspaper ads, distributed brochures, mailed out letters, and made numerous personal contacts to inform voters of the real facts, that a no vote would not be in the best interests of the community (Appendix).

The Daily Journal urged residents to vote, pointing out that the property in question had never been sought for residential purposes. "So ... keep it on the tax rolls as commercial property," the editorial continued. It also pointed out that the Glen Ellyn grade school district would reap the most benefits in taxation but that would be expected "since that part of Wheaton is in the Glen Ellyn school district and [some of] our children are attending the Glen Ellyn schools."

Carl A. Gundersen, a builder and a Christian, placed a half-page "political advertisement" in *The Daily Journal* that read in part:

> I am a home owner in Wheaton and . . . have no interest in Scripture Press Foundation, and no one asked me to place this ad. . . . I am not interested in seeing Wheaton become a commercialized community. . . . However, I believe there are some hard facts which we must face up to.
>
> One of these is the fact that we need more and better school facilities. . . . The only possible relief I see in sight is that provided by high type organizations like Scripture Press being located in the community. . . . Like some of you, I had heard that Scripture Press Foundation would not share the tax load . . . . In checking carefully, however, I discovered that this is not true . . . .The agreement . . . would be legally binding and therefore they would be carrying their share of the tax load. . . . Go to the polls [with me] and vote "Yes" in the referendum Saturday.

On Monday morning, November 2, 1953 *The Daily Journal* banner headline read:

> REZONING APPROVED BY 4-1 MARGIN
> 2,058 Favor Commercial
> Use of Land; 563 Against

The article (see Appendix) began:

> Wheaton voters Saturday upheld by nearly a 4 to 1 margin a July 6 decision by the city council to rezone some College Avenue property from Class A residential to Class B commercial in a special referendum requested by objecting citizens. The voting turnout smashed zoning referendum records as 2,733 persons took time out to cast 2,058 favorable and 563 unfavorable ballots. There were 112 spoiled ballots.
>
> The property in question is a 5.2 acre plot of ground owned by Joseph Bird on College Avenue, between the Kar-Lee greenhouse and the east Wheaton city limits. Scripture Press, which has an option on the land, applied for the

rezoning in order to erect a modern office building on the site to carry out their publishing work. The firm, which publishes religious magazines and Sunday School materials, estimated it would pay between $3,000 and $5,000 yearly taxes. This would be split between the Glen Ellyn school district, City of Wheaton, and the county.

SP purchases Wheaton property

On November 18, 1953 Scripture Press purchased the property for $17,500 (total for all Wheaton property purchased by SP from November 1953 to August 1967 was $143,500; see Appendix for breakdown). The company hoped to be in Wheaton by January 1955 after hiring the architectural firm of Friedman, Alschuler & Sincere to start plans for the new building. But by April 1954 management realized the move couldn't be made that soon. President Cory asked employees to pray fervently about the tax case that hadn't been decided. The decision, he thought, would determine when ground could be broken and the kind of building that the firm could afford to build. "The architects," he said, "have the first drawings finished and are going full steam ahead on the working drawings. They will then be ready to get bids for construction, but everything will have to wait until the tax matter is settled." He went on to assure employees that there was no danger of the firm being "put out in the street," since SP had the option of staying in Chicago after April 30, 1955, when the lease would expire. "All through SP's 20 years, the Lord has undertaken," he concluded. "Times without number the impossible has become the possible, because He has wrought it. He will not fail us now. Let us all pray that the Lord's will may be done, whatever that will is."

Despite the fact the long-going tax case continued to drag on, SP management decided in 1955 to go ahead with plans to build. Additional parcels were eventually purchased and added to the Bird parcel to give a total of 12 1/2 acres of property, extending from College Avenue back to Anthony Street in Glen Ellyn. In September 1955 Massachusetts Mutual Life Insurance Company approved a plan to finance the new building for the sum of $600,000; the actual cost was $1,019,730.[1]

Vic Cory (center, hatless) digs deeply in ground-breaking ceremony for the building at 1825 College Avenue, Wheaton. Among those participating: (third from left) Dr. V. Raymond Edman, president of Wheaton College, and (far right) Wheaton City Council Comissioner Wallace Conley.

Ground broken

With about 300 persons in attendance, a ground-breaking ceremony took place on Sunday afternoon, September 25, 1955 (Appendix). Initial clearance of the ground had been done the previous day, and the actual lines of the new building were staked out. Flowers were given by Kar-Lee, the florist. A printed program had a little shovel glued inside (Appendix). The Dillon brass quartet opened the ceremonies with "Onward Christian Soldiers," after which President Cory expressed his pleasure in God's bringing Scripture Press Foundation headquarters to Wheaton and summarized the 21-year history of the firm, "from log cabin to the White House," as he termed it (Appendix). He pointed out that SP was not a printing establishment, that the actual printing of its products would be done by printers in Ohio and Indiana. "Our happiness is of solid joy, for it stems from God's faithfulness," he asserted. "We repeat what was said by Samuel F.B. Morse on the occasion of the first telegraph message: 'What hath God wrought' (Numbers 23:23)."

Vic Cory addresses gathering at ground-breaking ceremony of the Wheaton building in September 1955.

Acting on behalf of vacationing Mayor Edward R. Farrar, Commissioner Conley, who had initially opposed the firm's coming to Wheaton, welcomed SP to the city. Emcee Robert Walker introduced Architect Raphael Friedman,, and C. William Kuhnen, representing Algot B. Larson, Inc., the firm under contract to build the structure. Wheaton College

President V. Raymond Edman spoke, pointing out that "Scripture Press is dedicated to the express purpose of publishing the best in Sunday School lessons." Immediately after the ceremony, SP employees and their families gathered at the Cory home at 412 North Washington for fellowship and a buffet supper.

Over the ensuing months, many articles appeared in *Spotlight* informing employees of matters relating to the new building and moving plans. Management offered help in finding housing and reimbursed employees who moved early and had to commute to Chicago. After the move, the company arranged for transportation for those still living far from Wheaton after the move. *Spotlight* told of construction workers driving 469 long piles, like telephone poles, into the swampy land to support the new structure. And there were articles on what to expect, such as:

> The Management Systems engineers have turned over to SP their layout for the merchandise handling areas in the new Wheaton building, says William O. Hall, Production Division manager. Designed for the simplest movement of goods from Receiving through Order Filling and Shipping, it will provide, among other things, plenty of room. New order-filling bins, especially designed for our stock, embody all the latest findings in fatigue-reducing operations and adequate visibility. Color selection should help to make them even glamorous. Lighting will be comparable to that of an office.
>
> Those who have been wrestling tonloads around by brute strength will be glad to know a power-operated truck has been ordered that will lift and transport a 4,000-pound load simply by pushing a few buttons. New shipping tables have been designed after the engineers' study of SP needs, with the thought of reducing effort and fatigue. A pilot model is now being made so that we can try it out.

Spotlight's "roving reporter" kept employees updated with such articles as:

> BRICKLAYERS ARE LAYING DOWN
> GOOD NEWS—STEEL ARRIVES!
> NEW BUILDING ALMOST FLOODED

LIFE ON THE WESTERN PLAIN
"LOOK FOR THE TOWER"

The article relating to the latter headline mentioned that "Look for the Tower" had for years referred to the Wheaton College tower, but now the words had new meaning—"the dazzling white tower at our Scripture Press plant." (Original plans called for a prayer room in the tower, but the idea did not prove feasible. The stairs to the tower were removed in 1972.)

The transformation of a swamp is under way.

By November many employees had relocated to the Wheaton area and had gladly said good-bye to the Northwestern and other methods of commuting as they began working in the new building. Norm Finke had filmed the erection of the building at various stages (see script, Appendix). Then came the move.

In an article in *Spotlight* for November 23, 1956, President Cory reminded, "Let's all sing the song of the Psalmist, 'I will praise Thee forever, because Thou hast done it' (52:9) "His remarks read in part:

> Orchids are deserved by just about everyone involved in the building itself and the entire Moving Operation Westward Ho. The first on the list would be the architects, Friedman, Alschuler & Sincere. Imagine seeing the whole building in their mind's eye "complete to the last detail" even before the first pile was driven! The contractors headed by Algot B. Larson and the 15 or 20 subcontractors are also deserving of orchids. . . . The Illinois Bell Telephone Company had men working Saturdays and overtime to give us phone service when needed. . . . Large orchids are due Engle & Son Cartage, who, besides doing our regular haul-

> ing, rose to the occasion with as many as 11 trucks and vans for night work in bringing out our office furniture and terrific inventory tonnage. . . . Haven't you admired the landscaping? And who was responsible for all of this—Mr. Lee Pfund, Sr.! [Trees that he added to the property included 30 bolleana poplars at $11 each and 15 pin oaks at $15 each.] . . . So many of our own people went the second or third or tenth mile in the moving operation. . . . Dick Hess and his crew just about did the impossible. . . .

VEC could have also included American Tractor Corporation in his remarks. Weeks of heavy rain threatened to stop work on the new building until the general contractors licked the problem by bringing in a 3,500-pound capacity TerraTrac M-3 forklift, with its 21-foot extension. Because of its positive crawler traction, plus ability to maintain power on both tracks while turning with a load, TerraTrac was able to "walk" through two feet of water and mud to keep 16 masons supplied with brick, block, and mortar. "We would easily have lost five weeks' work if we hadn't had the TerraTrac," according to Masonry Superintendent Morton Juhl. "In addition, we saved on labor and practically eliminated material breakage." The American Tractor Corporation featured the partially erected SP building in a full page ad on the TerraTrac in a number of construction trade journals (Appendix).

Escutcheon stone on front of SP building.

Also deserving of orchids was Wladyslaw Gawlinski, a Chicago sculptor who chiseled the SP logo into the escutcheon stone, a granite block weighing one and a quarter tons near the front entrance to the building. The logo, it was explained in a news article, "portrays an open Bible with the initials SP forming a great tree flourishing with 'the fruit of faith,' because its roots are deep in the Word of God. Below is the 'All Bible Teaching Material' banner."

Building dedicated

Dedication ceremonies were held on Friday night, December 7, 1956 in the chapel area of the new building, with several hundred persons in attendance. Longtime employee Bernice

Bosmann received $2 for inviting the most people; she wrote and sent out 60 invitations and 33 of her invitees came. Warren Zorn opened the dedication service with an organ prelude and the Rev. Kenneth E. Churchill, associate pastor of College Church of Christ, pronounced the invocation. Henry Jacobsen, editor of adult publications, served as emcee.

Presto! The transformation is completed.

Other SP employees taking part were: a male quartet composed of Ed Felske, Arnold Kruse, Ted Miller, and Emil Vosicky, with Madeline MacDonald, at the piano; Controller Norm Finke; vocalist Zenobia Hawkins; and President and Mrs. Cory.

Greetings were brought by Mayor Farrar, Architect Friedman, David L. Roberts, president of Wheaton Kiwanis Club; Wheaton College President Edman; and Dr. Robert A. Cook, president of Youth for Christ International. Dr. Carl Armerding of Wheaton College offered the prayer of dedication, and the Rev. Malcolm Cronk, pastor of Wheaton Bible Church, pronounced the benediction.

President Cory reviewed the steps that led SP to come to Wheaton. He mentioned in his address (Appendix) that "we laid the matter before the Lord and received definite leading and assurance to go ahead here on College Avenue." This occurred, he said, despite the fact engineers rated the site as the poorest of several that management was considering. He concluded: "This is a dedication service. The dictionary says that to dedicate is 'to set apart and consecrate to God and a sacred purpose; to devote formally to a particular use.' Dedication applies not only to the building, but dedication is a consecration of the heart, to be clean, holy and devoted. God guides only when He governs. We dedicate this building to Him and for His glory. We renew our consecration to Him for His service."

Open House followed the dedication and tours continued on Saturday and Sunday afternoons. Visitors received a four-page brochure containing Victor Cory's welcome and a detailed layout sketch of the 84,000-square-foot building (Appendix). Many were the compliments and interesting happenings, according to a compilation made by PR Chief Will Frykman.

For example, a local retired paint store owner was so impressed by all he saw that he got his son on the phone and insisted that he "get down here before closing time." (This was about 5:30 Sunday night, December 9.) The son tried to beg off, but Dad was so insistent that he loaded his family in the car and drove over to 1825. By the time he arrived, tours had ended, but he and his family were given a private tour of the building. Again and again his son said, "How glad I am that Dad insisted we get down here—I wouldn't miss this for anything!"

A police officer came in Sunday afternoon to confer about the traffic jams on Pennsylvania Avenue/College Avenue. He remarked, "I was told your work was worldwide, but I didn't think all these friends would be here!" For a while, those directing traffic could admit cars to the SP parking area only when they saw others leaving.

Mayor Farrar was given a quick tour before he spoke on Friday evening. His comment: "I never would have dreamt this building was so big on the inside, from the outside. Your architects have certainly done a magnificent job of camouflaging its size."

OMAC Bulletin features SP

The November 1957 *OMAC Bulletin,* the monthly magazine of Office Management Association of Chicago, featured SP as company of the month (Appendix). The article quoted Architect Raphael Friedman describing the plant as "not a commercial building in the usual sense of the word. Rather," he continued, "it is a structure that represents the deep, dedicated viewpoint of the people working there. As designers, we had to evaluate properly and accurately the tangible 'soul' of such a building. Scripture Press, with its ten-acre campuslike landscaping, was designed to fit properly into a setting which is largely residential. The desire was to add another touch of beauty to the Wheaton-Glen Ellyn community."

The article continued, in part, to describe the features of

the building and the functions of the various departments:

> As one enters the spacious lobby . . . , he is at once conscious that everything has been designed to carry on this unique publishing ministry as efficiently as possible. Artistically planned color schemes, not only in the executive offices but throughout the building, add to the pleasant surroundings and ideal working conditions. All offices are air-conditioned.
>
> The Editorial Wing of the plant houses 15 editors and writers, each a specialist in his or her own right. This area was designed with particular care. "The Editorial Division of Scripture Press," says Architect Friedman, "is not the same as the Editorial Department of the average publishing company. Rather, it is an area set apart and conducive to inspired writing—a research and study room for religious writers and teachers."
>
> In this section some 80 publications are created . . . each year. . . . More than 3 million . . . in 60 plus denominations . . . regularly use one or more of these publications.
>
> The Order-Clerical Department . . . is one of the largest departments. . . . In an average year, more than 225,000 pieces of mail arrive from practically all parts of the world. . . . A stencil file is maintained for more than 100,000 customers and 2,200 dealers.
>
> The Customer Service Department is made up of four sections—Adjustments and Returned Goods, Credit, Wholesale Collections, and Retail Collections. . . . With about 25,000 accounts, collection activity is a major project. . . .
>
> Publications Sales Department correspondents . . . advise Sunday School teachers in the United States and foreign countries regarding methods of teaching most effectively. . . .
>
> Expediting . . . workers are responsible for "riding hard" on all the details connected with from 200 to 250 printing jobs in various stages of production. . . . It should be pointed out that no printing of Sunday School materials is done at the Wheaton location. All printing is done in several . . . plants.
>
> Shipping and Receiving . . . [handles] more than 2,400 skids of merchandise . . . each year. . . . More than 1,000 skids of materials are on the floor in various stages of processing at all times. . . .

The Convention [CREDEX] Department operates as a service to the Sunday Schools of America and Canada. Five full-time staff members and more than a dozen other Sunday School specialists are on call to represent Scripture Press at Sunday School conferences and conventions, and their services are in great demand.... It is not unusual for a speaker to handle as many as eight speaking engagements at a two-day conference.

The Wholesale Department [has] a staff of four trade representatives who call on retail bookstores throughout the United States and parts of Canada and Mexico. Other departments include Accounting, Personnel and Public Relations, Office and Building Services, Catalog, and Advertising.

Cory envisions training institutes

In a meeting of members/directors of SPF on January 11, 1957, Chairman Cory stated that, "although the Foundation was presently and had been conducting and assisting in the conduct of various seminars, instructional classes, conventions, and Vacation Bible School institutes through the various Sates and even in Canada, these programs were not of sufficient duration to fully take advantage of the opportunities to promote the growth of the Sunday School." He went on to stress the need for three separate training institutes for pastors, Sunday School superintendents, and teachers, and even asserted that "if these training institutes are to be a success ..., it will be necessary to construct dormitories to house and feed the Christian workers attending these institutes." Training institutes came to pass, but the dream of constructing a dormitory did not materialize.

For the next 40 years the new building would be a flurry of activity in getting out "The Whole Word for the Whole World." And some people were bordering on sacrilege, singing:

"My hope is built on nothing less
than Gospel Light and Scripture Press."

---

[1] "In the United States Court of Claims," motion for relief from judgment and brief in support thereof, filed March 6, 1962, p. 6.

CHAPTER 10

SPF, Plaintiff vs. USA, Defendant

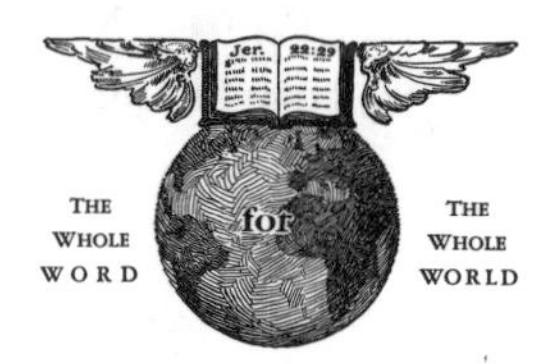

In April 1959, Bob Cook, Scripture Press Foundation's vice president of the Marketing Division, returned from Washington, D.C. to give a report on the progress—or lack of it—in regard to the tax case that the company had been fighting against the Internal Revenue Service since the company's exempt status had been revoked as of January 31, 1953. He gave a brief report to employees and urged "earnest, intercessory prayer in behalf of those who must weigh and balance all of the evidence in their hands." As a result, on May 5 SPers prayed throughout the day, with department groups going to Conference Room A at specified times to pray specifically for God's guidance in all things regarding the tax case. Few employees understood the complexities of the tax case, but they knew God did.

Dr. Robert A. Cook brought back a report from Washington.

On May 5, 1945, the Corys had organized the company as a nonprofit, nonstock corporation and filed with the IRS for exempt status (see "Scripture Press Foundation," Appendix). The stated purposes were set forth in its charter as follows:

> The dissemination of the Gospel, the distribution of the Scriptures, of extracts therefrom, of devotional and other lit-

> erature relating thereto, and of helps and supplies for use in Christian activities.
>
> The organization and support of organizations, institutions, and movements exclusively devoted to Christian missionary, educational and other evangelical efforts [through] the production, purchase, circulation, distribution, and sale of Christian literature, including books, periodicals, pamphlets, tracts, placards, mottos, and supplies; and the conduct of publication and printing establishments.

IRS advises SP to keep paying income tax

In a letter dated June 16, 1945, the commissioner of Internal Revenue acknowledged receipt of the application for exemption and advised that no ruling would be made until "you have operated for a period of time sufficient to disclose clearly the method of operation." SP was advised that the firm would have to continue paying income tax and that a new exemption affidavit would need to be submitted. This was done on August 28, 1946, and attached to the papers was the financial statement for the fiscal period ended May 31, 1946, reflecting one year's operation. Sample materials and a catalog also went to Washington. The financial statement showed SPF's total assets, $219,324.19; liabilities, $185,808.01; capital, $33,516.18; net sales, $640,794.60; excess of income over expenses, $2,806.07.

On September 11, 1946, SPF got good news: the IRS declared the corporation tax exempt "under the provisions of Section 101 (6) of the Internal Revenue Code of 1939." Contributions and bequests to SPF were declared "deductible by donors, inasmuch as Plaintiff was organized and operated exclusively for religious purposes."

Status reconsidered

Then in a letter dated September 30, 1953, the IRS advised SPF that "in view of recent changes in revenue legislation subsequent to the issuance of [SPF's exempt status], it is necessary to reconsider your status at this time." On November 5, 1953 SPF replied to the IRS, describing the type of materials and literature the corporation published, and stated that "the Foundation is not affiliated with any particular church group or denomination," that it "is truly interdenominational in that it serves presently churches in approximately 52 different denominations," and that there was no distribution of profits. Also SPF advised the IRS that it had started a reserve toward the acquisition of a suitable building for its headquarters outside Chicago and had increased its capital account to $400,000 for this purpose.

Then came bad news: On December 31, 1953, the IRS issued a ruling that SPF would not be exempt from federal taxes effective for the fiscal year ended January 31, 1953. A protest against this ruling was filed on April 28, 1954, but on December 31, 1954 the IRS reaffirmed its prior ruling denying an exemption status. "Our ruling," the letter stated, "was premised on the ground that your primary activity, which is the publication and sale of religious publications, periodicals and supplies, constitutes a business of a kind ordinarily carried on for profit, thereby precluding your exemption from tax." The directive ended, advising SPF that tax returns were to be filed retroactive to the fiscal year that ended January 31, 1953.

On March 18, 1955, SPF filed tax returns for the taxable years ended January 31, 1953 and January 31, 1954, reporting net taxable income for those years of $18,827 and $18,544, respectively, as representing profits from store sales, which SPF classified as "unrelated business income." Taxes for those years of $5,648.10 and $5,563.20, respectively, were paid; however, SPF immediately filed claims with the IRS for refund of those taxes, believing that store sales should not be considered taxable. When no action was taken in regard to the claims, SPF filed its original petition in the U.S. Court of Claims on March 6, 1954, to recover these tax payments with interest. This began the long court action.

In 1957, the company paid additional taxes amounting to $147,410.38 as demanded by the IRS and also filed for refund of the money plus interest in the Tax Court of the United States. No further taxes were paid while the case was pending. The case went back to the United States Court of Claims on June 24, 1960.

In a lengthy brief, the Washington law firm of Smith, Ristig & Smith went into a myriad of details, including:

A listing of officers giving their backgrounds; the fact that the company employed 240 persons, all of whom "are expected to abstain from tobacco, alcohol and the theater"; that 26,000 Sunday Schools use the company's materials; and that the building was used for institutes, seminars, workshops, and clinics; that the company planned to build dormitories and related facilities for free housing and care of persons attending "Plaintiff's year-around Sunday School Teacher Training Institute." It was also mentioned that SPF, beginning in 1946 and through 1957, had made cash donations and merchandise grants totaling $285,283. And from January 31, 1951 through January 31, 1957 it had expended $432,842 for providing free instructional service to pastors, Sunday School superintendents, teachers, and other Christian workers at religious conventions, institutes, and workshops.

A further plea for tax exemption

The brief went on to plead that SPF should be considered tax exempt inasmuch as the IRS did not collect taxes from denominational publishing houses, some of which had much larger volumes of sales than SPF and realized profits of more than $200,000 annually. The National Geographic Society, the brief pointed out, was tax exempt and "a completely independent organization, unaffiliated with any other exempt scientific association." The Society, the brief further stated, had a membership that was "no more than a built-in customer list eliminating any guesswork in the number of publications to be printed by the Society, and the membership dues are no more than the purchase price for the magazine." The Society in 1956 had receipts of nearly $18,000,000 and a profit in excess of $1,200,000. The brief contended, therefore, that SPF should also be tax exempt.

On January 18, 1961, Chief Judge Jones of the United States Court of Claims rendered the court's opinion in the case of Scripture Press Foundation vs. The United States, declaring after many pages of review "that Scripture Press Foundation's activities do not warrant tax exemption . . . [that] therefore, plaintiff's petition will be dismissed." Judges Durfee, Laramore, Madden, and Whitaker concurred.[1]

A motion for rehearing the case was turned down by the Court of Claims, and the Washington law firm took the case to the Supreme Court for the October term of 1961.

Meantime, at SP much prayer was going up in Executive Committee meetings and in special prayer sessions. Also management was looking at the effects of the tax case and steps that might need to be taken for the future. Lloyd Cory, in his succinct manner, jotted down the following notes, likely in an Executive Committee meeting held on February 6, 1961:

> Smiths surprised—results [Court of Claims decision] didn't agree with grapevine or points of law.
>
> 1945-54—SP made lots of $s, plowed back into work.
>
> Wash. attys. advised us to keep expanding, not to build up reserves.
>
> We built up co. on govt. money—had use of $100-200M/yr. working capital, available at 6%, from govt.
>
> Need: 1. drastic reduction in expenses 2. healthy increase in sales
>
> BA&H to start this a.m. on stencil section. "Business can carry corporate fat only at the risk of a corporate coronary" (Pres. of Ind. Standard Oil).
>
> Why is SP in this position? We've gotten fat in some areas. Should cut it down.
>
> SP must get its income from sale of products. Should become more profit-minded, dept. by dept.
>
> Need to be in a better net profit position.
>
> Dollar sales: Have leveled off, thanx to switch to dealers and lower increase rate.
>
> Increases in sales going downhill—only 2.2% this year.
>
> Need to get along longer w/fewer people/equipment for a while.
>
> "Everything we do from now on must pay off in net profit." (Bob Cook)
>
> "Production has been boiling off fat; will keep doing so. Take hard look at everything. Is this trip necessary? Have saved about $102,000 in Order Clerical in the past 3 yrs." (Bill Hall)
>
> "It's good to be afflicted. Cut down drastically on products, some on people. Satan likes to get Chrs. becalmed, w/lack of passion for souls." (Bernice Cory)
>
> "Re going on diet—always feel better when I'm down to where I should be. Pay—more for better people—no bonus." (Wilfred Frykman)

The following notes[2] are those of Victor Cory used either for an oral presentation at the same Executive Committee meeting on February 6, 1961 or for writing a memo to managers:

> Decision from Court of Claims adverse. Smiths surprised [since] verbal argument and rebuttals well received. Examination of decision: several errors and sidestepping important points of law.
>
> Friday tel. talk. Should go to U.S. Supreme Ct. If SC accepts case [there's] a good chance of overruling. But SC could refuse to take it on.Then CC binding. Pray that SC will accept jurisdiction.That may mean another year of prayer! But we tend to say that we have been praying, so long, so many times, days of prayer, etc. I believe the Lord at times wants us to ask why if honestly, in faith, in praying, in studying the Book. It will be a blessing and make us stronger! And we will praise Him!
>
> A little history! We started publishing in '34.After a few yrs., daylight and 3 meals a day. By 1945 God's blessing was upon us; the future looked limitless!
>
> We didn't want to be a Cory-owned business; it was the Lord's! We asked H. Fischer to set up SPFn. to which we surrendered our stock and became employees just like you all.
>
> From 1945 to 1954 the Fn. made money! There being no stockholders requiring dividends and no 52% Fed. income tax, [profits were] all plowed back. Plowed back? [Yes], during those 9 yrs. we probably had our biggest % of growth, doubling and redoubling. But every increase in vol. [meant] more development expense, more inventory, more A/R, more F & F. But thanks to these 2 breaks—no dividends and no taxes—we had green lights all the way.We were the fastest growing Christian bus.-Miss. orgn. I knew of!
>
> And SP has continued [to follow the] policy as to finance, expansion, and promotion on the direct counsel of our Wash. attys. and our Chicago accts.We've gone well toward doubling on our redoubling since 1954.
>
> Of course, that meant no reserve blt up for an adverse decision. Our legal counsel tells us that even if ultimately we must pay, the govt. will extend time.They don't want an empty mortgaged bldg.—they'd rather have a taxpayer.
>
> Maybe this has all been a blessing and part of God's program. If we ultimately lose, we've had the use of a lot of govt. money at 6% interest. Ever try to borrow money from

a bank? Just before our move to 434 [South Wabash], I tried Continental for $100,000. Nobody else would loan us money, yet SP had between $100,000 and $200,000 ea. yr. of additional working capital available at 6%!

W/O use of this money, turned over many times, SP [would not be] what it is today, not half the vol., no bldg, and [would still be] at 434.

Our acct. and our legal counsel believe that, with this adverse ct. decision, we should prepare to pay. This doesn't bar possibility of our yet winning and owing nothing, in which case we [will be] much stronger for having tightened up.

The new program we're embarking on has 2 parts: 1. A drastic reduction in expenses; 2. A healthy increase in sales.

The first outward move in both directions was for the Exec. Comm. to endorse the arrangement w/BA&H [Booz Allen & Hamilton Inc] to make a study in certain areas and an overall look at our entire organization. Most of you will recall their original visit on job evaluation, wage and salary admin. and organ. set up and their 2nd visit touching up these points.

Mr. Thornton Snead has been selected—will be here later this a.m. Where will BA&H begin? The spot chosen is manned by people who are smart & are hard & conscientious workers. But it is strategic & directly concerns 3 divisions. It is the Stencil Section. They're overloaded now & yet still more is required by Sales, Marketing, & others. Now costing $50,000. Whether we go into punch card equipment, we don't know. Automation & Unions not always answer. Eq. Kent State Normal College, O. Has over 7,000 students. 560 got dismissal notices. From Stencils, move into other areas. Bill Hall's slogan: work smarter not harder.

In a subsequent meeting held in auditor Glenn Ingram's office in Chicago on February 8, 1961 that included Robert V. Smith of the Washington law firm, Lloyd Cory took the following notes[2]:

All courts seem to be more collection agencies for the govt.

Think govt. will ask for $200,000/yr. + taxes.

SP's tangible assets—small.

Believe we can work out a deal (for time payments) w/govt.

Net worth of SP: $1,800,000.

Mortgage now $488,000 (was $600,000).

Govt. wants $s—wouldn't put us in position where we couldn't pay them.

SS development—not to exceed 5% of net income—cut from $109M to $35M.

The following comments by Attorney Smith:

The more publicity we give this case, the more chance we have of getting this to Supreme Ct.

Legally, the Natl. Geographic & denom. publishers are now as liable to taxes as we.

Don't have right to go to Supreme Ct.—can appeal only. [Supreme Ct.] turns down 90% of cases. Accepts only cases that affect the public—or people's lives.

Ct. of Claims acted hastily. They dismissed our petition entirely. They ignored 5 mistakes they made. Did not answer our legal arguments.

Move for rehearing before appealing to Sup. Ct. is usual procedure.

Have to file appeal to Sup. Ct. within 90 days after result of appeal to Ct. of Claims.

Possible to hook up w/org. that could pay part of taxes . . . [such as] Standard, Moody, D.C. Cook. Might need to in order to keep going.

Could reorganize as separate stock co., with foundation for [tax-exempt work].

Govt. may accept only 5% of net income for SS development deduction.

Think we might make a deal w/govt. to pay back taxes in 10 years.

Could sell bldg. to ins. co., lease it back. (Smith doesn't believe ins. cos. are allowed to do this.) Maybe a real estate co.

* * *

VEC thinks Bolton (Standard's owner) might be interested in taking over SP, or in loaning $s. VEC will contact Bolton.

Could have public bond issue—or have churches buy bonds.

WOH: Could raise income $125,000/yr. by raising price

on books 2¢.

Smith will visit Wash. wheels re. possibility of getting a 10-yr. repayment deal.

RAC believes we could raise $s from friendly millionaires.

Smith: When decision comes, Willi (govt. attorney) may get jeopardy assessment vs. us.

Will know in a year if Sup. Ct. will take on case. If they do, we'll know outcome in another yr.

CREDEX is the reason (Smith) for claiming exemption. Pare it down a bit, but don't eliminate it.

Smith's concerned a lot over switch from retail to wholesale. But SP has no choice. Dealing w/a dealer is commercialism.

Dealing directly w/churches, w/o middleman, isn't considered so commercial.

In May 1961 death took Robert P. Smith, senior member of the firm negotiating the tax case. Victor Cory attended the funeral in Washington, D.C.

Supreme Court refuses to hear case

Finally, in February 1962, SPers got the word from President Vincent Hogren and Board Chairman Victor Cory that the Supreme Court had declined to hear the case. A news release (see *Spotlight* for March 2, 1962) stated: "On February 19, 1962, the United States Supreme Court declined to review a judgment of the Court of Claims which denied Scripture Press Foundation of Wheaton, Illinois, a return of income taxes [$159,588] paid under protest in 1953. The United States Supreme Court made no comment when it announced that the issues involved would not be reviewed." The release went on to state that "legal authorities believe this decision of the Supreme Court could affect many other tax-exempt foundations, both religious and secular." No decision had been made, the release concluded, as to what further steps SPF might take to seek reversal or modification of the opinion. [No further steps were taken.]

In an article that appeared in the May 25, 1962 issue of *The* [Wheaton] *Daily Journal,* noted church writer Louis Cassels, of United Press, considered the implications of the lost tax case. He wrote, in part:

> Had Scripture Press happened to be owned by a church, it would be tax exempt even if it chose to publish comic books—or racing forms.... For example, if a church happens to own a profit-making business enterprise—such as a printing plant, a department store, a winery or an apartment house . . . under present law and policy, the Internal Revenue Service makes no attempt to assess income taxes . . . however remote [the] activities [of the church] may be from religious worship.
>
> There are church-owned hotels, bakeries, warehouses, radio stations, office buildings, parking lots, printing firms, and similar businesses in many parts of the country. The Roman Catholic Church and the Mormon Church are most often mentioned in this connection,but a number of Protestant churches are also engaged in tax-free business enterprises. Some Protestants are deeply troubled about what they regard as abuses of the tax exemption granted to churches. The Rev. Dr. Eugene Carson Blake, clerk of the United Presbyterian Church, has asserted publicly on several occasions that churches should pay regular corporate tax rates "on income from business unrelated to the religious purpose of the church."[3]

SP must pay more than $1 million

At the meeting of the Members of SPF on February 27, 1962, VEC reported that as a result of the Supreme Court decision, SPF faced payment of federal income taxes for the years ended January 31, 1953 through January 21, 1962. Estimated tax liability, he said, would be in excess of $1 million.

The court decision immediately set off organizational changes at SP, especially in the Production Division under Bill Hall. *Spotlight* for February 23, 1962 stated: "Print runs, paper stock, proper layout, and a multitude of other factors must be carefully watched from a cost standpoint. Then too, new typesetting and printing techniques in the marketplace must be investigated to determine their value to SP production needs." As a result, Bill Hall, it was pointed out, would need more time to work more closely with the president on production cost objectives. Therefore, Merchandise Handling would be under

Wendell Anderson, and Building and Grounds, handled by Will Frykman.

About the same time Booz Allen & Hamilton, consultants, completed a reorganization of the Distribution Division and the development of new distribution policies (see Members' minutes, February 27, 1962).

On June 26, 1962 VEC reported as follows to SP employees in the morning chapel session:

> The Tax Case, for which so many of you have prayed so faithfully for years, is now entering its closing phases. We in management are very much encouraged by the events of the last few days as we met with our attorneys and accountants. We came away from the meetings with a peace and a joy in our hearts as we saw and sensed the definite leading of the Lord as we now plan to expand the ministry of Scripture Press in what we believe to be the last days before our Lord's return. Details of our expanded ministry are now being worked out and will be revealed to you as soon as plans have been completed. We want you to know what is being done, and I am sure you will be as enthusiastic as we are about the future of SP. I expect to give you this report within the next two weeks or so, even though the new program will not become effective until August 1. You will also hear about our expanded promotional program to extend the use of SP products into new areas. In the meantime, you can thank the Lord for His guidance and answers to your prayers in the tax case and other aspects of Scripture Press.

VEC enjoyed showing his charts, especially when sales were good.

On July 30, 1962, directors of SPF adopted the "Plan of Reorganization, drafted by General Counsel, effective August 1, 1962, so that the Foundation could continue its existence as a tax-exempt organization with a view to carrying out the objective of the Foundation to promote the betterment of Sunday Schools through rendering free instruction to pastors, Sunday School superintendents, Sunday School teachers, and other religious workers with respect to Sunday School teaching and organization." As a result, the Foundation would transfer its publishing operations "to its wholly owned subsidiary, Scripture Press Publications, Inc., a profit corporation organized . . . under the former name of Christian Family Publications, Inc., with the Foundation to depend upon its rent, royalties, dividends, and donations and other types of passive income for funds with which to carry on its operations in the field of religious education." (See "The Relationship of Scripture Press Publications to Scripture Press Foundation," Appendix.) On June 20, 1962 the board of directors had approved changing the corporate name of Christian Family Publications, Inc. to Scripture Press Publications, Inc., and increased authorized capital stock from 250 shares of par value of $100 each to 2,000 shares of par value at $100 each.

At the September 18, 1962 directors' meeting, Board Chairman Cory reported that the Foundation would need to raise in excess of $1 million. As a result, directors approved a proposal from Washington National Insurance Company for purchase of SP's Wheaton building for $1,375,000, with a leaseback for 25 years and options for subsequent renewals of 5 consecutive 10-year periods. The money from the sale would be used for payment of back taxes. Taxes and interest for years 1955 through 1961 totaled $914,098 and were paid; taxes totaling $100,916 for 1953 and 1954 were paid in October 1963, closing the tax case.

The Corys difinitely saw the hand of the Lord in the entire matter. SP had used money for growth that otherwise would have been paid to the IRS, and at a lower rate of interest than if it had been borrowed from a bank. On the other hand, the tax case put a stop to plans for a dormitory and other facilities for students enrolled in classes at SP. But the newly organized Foundation could and would proceed without any further foreseeable problems with the IRS. Tax exemption was granted by the IRS effective August 1, 1962.

---

[1] Details relating to the tax case taken from the brief filed June 24, 1960 with the United States Court of Claims. See Tax Case box in SP Ministries Archives.

[2] Lloyd Cory and Victor Cory notes in Tax Case box.

[3] Clipping in Tax Case box.

The First Decade in Wheaton

1957–1966

It all happened in 1957: Dwight D. Eisenhower and Richard Nixon were sworn in as president and vice president on January 21. Billy Graham conducted a 3 1/2-month crusade in New York that drew more than 2 million people. And Charles Van Doren got $129,000 for answering questions on NBC's Show 21, but a congressional investigation revealed he had been supplied answers prior to the telecast.

At 1825 College Avenue, Wheaton, 1957 began with SP hosting the Trade and Convention representatives in a week-long conference. Sessions emphasized the tremendous opportunity and responsibility that SP had as a leader in supplying the materials to foster and promote Sunday Schools around the world. Speakers spoke of the importance of SP employees, remembering that working at SP was a No. 1 missionary endeavor. VEC emphasized the significant phrase: "When a nation is to perish in its sin, 'tis in the Sunday School the leprosy begins." The conference concluded with the company's 23rd anniversary banquet held in the new building in Wheaton. The theme: "Encouraging Workers Together."

President Dwight D. Eisenhower

Also in January 1957, the SP Bowling League was formed (it later became the Wheaton Christian Bowling League and still continues as of 1998). But more importantly, Dr. Robert A. Cook, president of YFC, International, accepted the position of vice president and distribution manager in charge of SP sales. He coined the name FIREPIN (Field Representatives Institute) for the conferences of field reps at the home office. It was Bob Cook who early in his tenure prayed: "Lord God, help us to remember that we here at SP are linked together and to eternity. Help us, O God, not to get lost in the ecclesiastical sawdust of our own carpenter shop, but rather genuinely appreciate each other's problems."

Gladys Siegfried Halleen confers with marketing director Bob Cook.

In February, SP became the exclusive distributor in the U.S. for the products of Ward Studios, Warsaw, Indiana, including the widely known Video-graph flannelgraph backgrounds and stories.

The February 21, 1957 issue of *Spotlight* contained a layout of the east wing of the new building and showed the following organizations as tenants: Great Commission Prayer League, Rural Bible Crusade, Evangelical Teacher Training Association, Evangelical Literature Overseas, and Winona Lake School of Theology. The east wing of the SP building is in Glen Ellyn, with the Glen Ellyn-Wheaton line running through the front door.

In March, BTC shared some of the gems she had culled from sermons, including:

> "God gives both the disposition and the dynamic to serve according to His good pleasure so that we want what He wants and that His plans for the ages may unfold through us."
>
> "Our conduct should bring less and less reproach on Christ while at the same time bringing more and more honor unto Him."
>
> "We live in a perverted, warped society, but because we are transformed we are sent as light into the community to shine. Lights don't have to try to shine—that is their nature.

Light is information for those ignorant of God. Wheaton needs your testimony: 21,000 people live in Wheaton, yet fewer than 10,000 go to church."

On March 19, Dr. C.B. Wyngarden came to administer polio injections to employees, at $2.50 per shot.

The directors of SPF on May 16 amended the Employees Pension Trust effective June 1, 1957 to change the basic plan from one providing for fixed benefits to one providing for fixed contributions by participants and the Foundation.

On June 3, SP welcomed Wendell G. Anderson of South Roseland, Ill., as controller. He had served as controller of the Zonolite Corporation for 15 years. His brother, Vernon, was the former business manager of *Christian Life* magazine. [Vernon's story was featured in the May 20, 1951 issue of *Power*, telling of God's delivering him on May 25, 1950 from the fiery crash of a "Green Hornet" streetcar on which he was a passenger and a gasoline truck at State and 63rd Streets in Chicago that killed 34 people.]

In early June, Lloyd Siegfried was chosen president of the Scripture Press Credit Union after it was organized to serve SP employees. Other first-time officers: Bill Custard, vice president; Velma Ammann, secretary; Emil Vosicky, treasurer. As of June 6, 43 employees had joined and 85 had indicated an interest. Five dollars bought the first share and there was a service charge of 25¢.

On June 26 BTC was crowned "Queen for a Day" to celebrate her birthday anniversary. It was a complete surprise, for VEC had been telling her that "some secretary around the place is going to be queen." Harold Eavey and Lloyd Cory trumpeted the fanfare, and Ruth Buelow and Ruth Von Busch attired the queen in her royal robe. Gladys Siegfried placed the crown on her head, Eunice Fischer vested her with an appropriate scepter, and Jim Adair read one of her favorite Scripture passages, 1 Thessalonians 4.

In August, VEC was off on another trip to Europe, and John Fish resigned as bookstore manager, to manage his own store in Kalamazoo.

The final filming of SP's 1958 production, "Exploring God's Wonders," took place in November at SP. And in December SP welcomed Peter DeGraff as Sunday School rep in the eastern U.S. Dr. Torrey Johnson, founder of YFC International, spoke in chapel on the last Friday of 1957.

On December 12, the directors of SPF approved acquisition of the remainder of adjacent land owned by Glen Ellyn Dairy Company (remainder of Lot 7 in Block 3 of Robertson's Seventh Addition to Glen Ellyn, approximately one acre) for $25,000.

On December 27, SP acquired Christian Family Publications, Inc., bringing in *My Chum* and *The Christian Parent* magazines from The Christian Education Company. With the magazines came Dr. Martin Simon, a Lutheran minister who originated the magazines and was their editor.

Also in 1957, the Corys donated a new Hamilton Baldwin piano for use in SP's chapel.

1958

On January 10, 1958, VEC reported to members and directors in relation to implementation of establishment of free Training Institutes on the premises of the Foundation for pastors, Sunday School superintendents, and Sunday School teachers. It would begin in February by the institution of a 12-week evening training course for Sunday School teachers, called Leadership Training Institute (LTI). Curriculum and announcements for similar institutes for pastors and superintendents were in the process of preparation.

Apparently SP was still paying off its lease at 434 South Wabash, for in February 1958 the fifth floor was rented. The second floor continued to be a liability—13,500 square feet of space, and management was requesting employees to keep praying.

In March the Convention Department was renamed Christian Education Extension (CREDEX, coined by Dr. Bob Cook).

In April, SP's Martin Simon was bustin' his buttons over the fact that his son Paul, one of America's youngest legislators who had served as state representative from Madison County for two terms, had just won again in the Primary. Paul Simon spoke in chapel on May 6. He, of course, was later to become a U.S. senator for several terms.

At Wheaton College's 99th annual commencement in June, VEC received an honorary Doctor of Laws degree. In July the Victor Corys, Gladys Siegfried, and Marjorie Ford left for a month abroad, including a tour of the Holy Land. BTC fell in London while visiting Lillian Swanson and required several stitches to close a wound to her head; the accident could have been fatal, the doctor said. VEC had returned home and met her in New York in late September.

In June, Bill Hall informed Vic Cory that the post office had refused to accept cartons that had the slogan, "Handle with Prayer," printed on them. The boss had thought it a great idea.

Also in 1958, SP purchased an old fire truck to pump water in case of flooding. It was sold a year later to Bob Van Kampen, Sr. after a new storm sewer system was installed. Coffee was selling at 5 cents a cup. Lorraine Ackley came as secretary to the president, Bill Bratkovich as Order Clerical manager, and Howard Unser as Advertising manager.

1959

In January 1959, Art Saul resigned as manager of SP's Chicago and Wheaton bookstores, effective February 1, to devote full time to his growing church. Bob Main took over management of the store. Jim Adair returned in late January from the annual convention of Evangelical Press Association with the news that *Power* had received the Award of Excellence in the Sunday School paper category. SP's *Christian Parent* magazine was accepted as a new member of EPA.

Corys at SP's 25th anniversary banquet, January 1959.

In February, Moody Bible Institute presented trophies to SP writers Drs. Lois and Mary LeBar, honoring them each with the Alumnus of the Year Award, the first time two people had received their annual tribute. "A jolly group of nearly 30 SPers" rode a chartered bus to Moody Church, where other SPers joined them for a buffet supper at which the presentation was made to the LeBar sisters, according to *Spotlight* for February 6, 1959.

The same issue of *Spotlight* greeted readers with a new design, featuring a blue-and- silver nameplate containing a line calling attention to the fact SP was marking its twenty-fifth anniversary in 1959. SPers celebrated at a banquet, and the company presented them and key friends with ballpoint pens with the inscription:

Scripture Press Foundation
Wheaton, Illinois
1934 OUR Silver Anniversary 1959
YOUR Golden Opportunity
All-Bible Graded Sunday School Lessons
"The Whole Word for the Whole World"

Lillian Swanson set up an office in April 1959 at 69 Upper Street, London, to officially begin Scripture Press Foundation (U.K.).

In June, BTC became Dr. Bernice T. Cory when Biola College gave her a Doctor of Literature degree. In September Roy Zuck joined SP as director of Training Hour publications, scheduled for release in October 1960.

SPers attended the Billy Graham Wheaton Crusade in October and rejoiced at the report there were 2,812 decisions, 64 percent being for acceptance of Christ as Savior. The same month Eunice Fischer said good-bye after two terms of employment and took up duties with David C. Cook Publishing Company, joining Gilbert Beers, who headed the Cook Curriculum Division at that time.

The speakers table at SP's twenty-fifth anniversary banquet. Left to right: Dr. Mary LeBar and Dr. Lois LeBar (Vic Cory called them "the pair-o-docs"), Mr. and Mrs. Casper Henning, the Robert Walkers, Dr. Howard Hendricks, the Robert Cooks, the Corys, Mr. and Mrs. Glenn Ingram, Gene and Harry Saulnier.

Also in October, the Billy Graham Evangelistic Association requested rights to the title *Decision* to use as the name of a new publication to tie in with Billy Graham's "Hour of Decision" radio program. For seven years, SP had used *Decision* as the title of the adult student paper correlated with the *Bible Knowledge* quarterly. Now SP was abandoning the title in favor of a new publication called *Adult Student*. Yet, according to a letter VEC wrote George Wilson at the Graham Association, SP was considering using the name *Decision* for a "paper similar to *Power*." But nevertheless, VEC wrote, "For the Gospel cause, you may consider this letter our promise to abandon the use of the word *Decision* as a publication title, and give our free and formal permission to the BGEA for its exclusive use."

In his letter, VEC added: "The Wheaton [Graham crusade] produced results that thrilled us all. Some of the city leaders have received the Lord, and in two churches that I know of with very modernistic programs and pastors, regular Bible study classes have been requested by the converts. Again, 'to God be the glory'" (see Appendix).

1960

SPers enjoyed steak on the evening of January 8 at the company's 26th annual banquet at Elmhurst Country Club. The theme: "Horizons Unlimited."

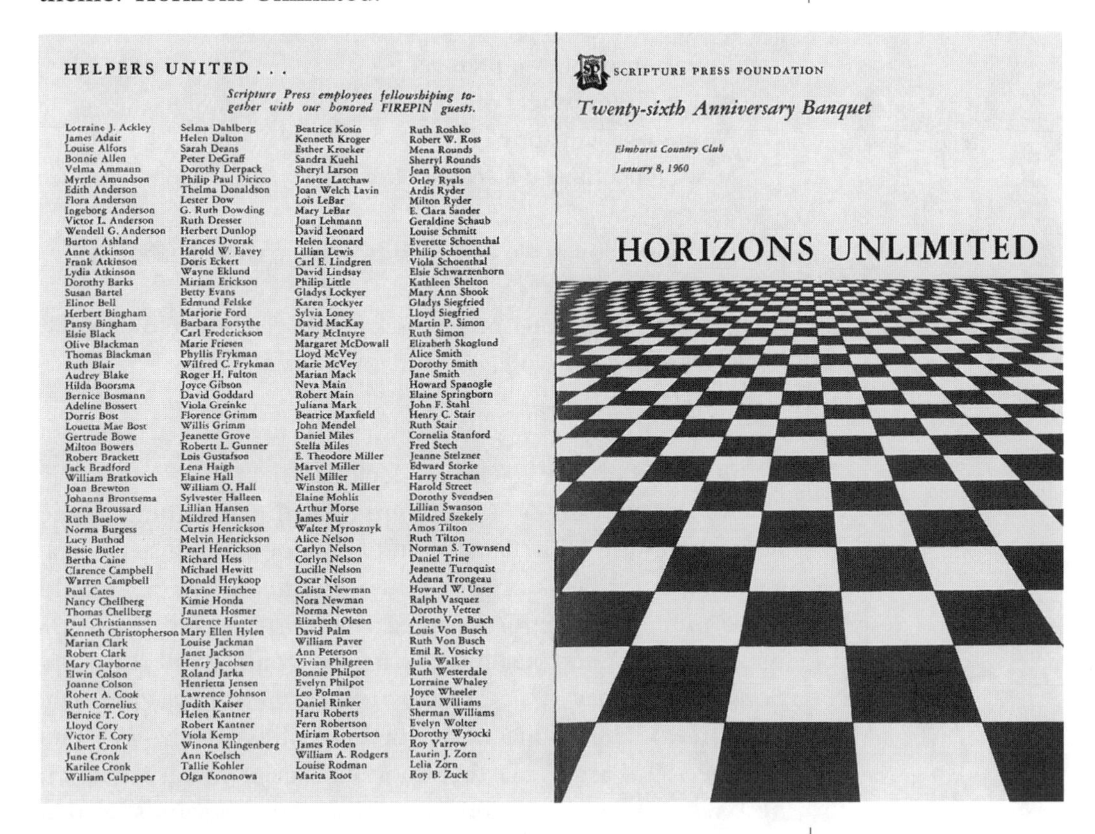

HELPERS UNITED . . .

Scripture Press employees fellowshiping together with our honored FIREPIN guests.

Lorraine J. Ackley
James Adair
Louise Alfors
Bonnie Allen
Velma Ammann
Myrtle Amundson
Edith Anderson
Flora Anderson
Ingeborg Anderson
Victor L. Anderson
Wendell G. Anderson
Burton Ashland
Anne Atkinson
Frank Atkinson
Lydia Atkinson
Dorothy Barks
Susan Bartel
Elinor Bell
Herbert Bingham
Pansy Bingham
Elsie Black
Olive Blackman
Thomas Blackman
Ruth Blair
Audrey Blake
Hilda Boorsma
Bernice Bosmann
Adeline Bossert
Dorris Bost
Louetta Mae Bost
Gertrude Bowe
Milton Bowers
Robert Brackett
Jack Bradford
William Bratkovich
Joan Brewton
Johanna Brontsema
Lorna Broussard
Ruth Buelow
Norma Burgess
Lucy Buthod
Bessie Butler
Bertha Caine
Clarence Campbell
Warren Campbell
Paul Cates
Nancy Chellberg
Thomas Chellberg
Paul Christiannssen
Kenneth Christopherson
Marian Clark
Robert Clark
Mary Clayborne
Elwin Colson
Joanne Colson
Robert A. Cook
Ruth Cornelius
Bernice T. Cory
Lloyd Cory
Victor E. Cory
Albert Cronk
June Cronk
Karilee Cronk
William Culpepper
Selma Dahlberg
Helen Dalton
Sarah Deans
Peter DeGraff
Dorothy Derpack
Philip Paul Dicicco
Thelma Donaldson
Lester Dow
G. Ruth Dowding
Ruth Dresser
Herbert Dunlop
Frances Dvorak
Harold W. Eavey
Doris Eckert
Wayne Eklund
Miriam Erickson
Betty Evans
Edmund Felske
Marjorie Ford
Barbara Forsythe
Carl Frederickson
Marie Friesen
Phyllis Frykman
Wilfred C. Frykman
Roger H. Fulton
Joyce Gibson
David Goddard
Viola Greinke
Florence Grimm
Willis Grimm
Jeanette Grove
Robertt L. Gunner
Lois Gustafson
Lena Haigh
Elaine Hall
William O. Hall
Sylvester Halleen
Lillian Hansen
Mildred Hansen
Curtis Henrickson
Melvin Henrickson
Pearl Henrickson
Richard Hess
Michael Hewitt
Donald Heykoop
Maxine Hinchee
Kimie Honda
Jauneta Hosmer
Clarence Hunter
Mary Ellen Hylen
Louise Jackman
Janet Jackson
Henry Jacobsen
Roland Jarka
Henrietta Jensen
Lawrence Johnson
Judith Kaiser
Helen Kantner
Robert Kantner
Viola Kemp
Winona Klingenberg
Ann Koelsch
Tallie Kohler
Olga Kononowa
Beatrice Kosin
Kenneth Kroger
Esther Kroeker
Sandra Kuehl
Sheryl Larson
Janette Latchaw
Joan Welch Lavin
Lois LeBar
Mary LeBar
Joan Lehmann
David Leonard
Helen Leonard
Lillian Lewis
Carl E. Lindgren
David Lindsay
Philip Little
Gladys Lockyer
Karen Lockyer
Sylvia Loney
David MacKay
Mary McIntyre
Margaret McDowall
Lloyd McVey
Marie McVey
Marian Mack
Neva Main
Robert Main
Juliana Mark
Beatrice Maxfield
John Mendel
Daniel Miles
Stella Miles
E. Theodore Miller
Marvel Miller
Nell Miller
Winston R. Miller
Elaine Mohlis
Arthur Morse
James Muir
Walter Myrosznyk
Alice Nelson
Carlyn Nelson
Corlyn Nelson
Lucille Nelson
Oscar Nelson
Calista Newman
Nora Newman
Norma Newton
Elizabeth Olesen
David Palm
William Paver
Ann Peterson
Vivian Philgreen
Bonnie Philpot
Evelyn Philpot
Leo Polman
Daniel Rinker
Haru Roberts
Fern Robertson
Miriam Robertson
James Roden
William A. Rodgers
Louise Rodman
Marita Root
Ruth Roshko
Robert W. Ross
Mena Rounds
Sherryl Rounds
Jean Routson
Orley Ryals
Ardis Ryder
Milton Ryder
E. Clara Sander
Geraldine Schaub
Louise Schmitt
Everette Schoenthal
Philip Schoenthal
Viola Schoenthal
Elsie Schwarzenhorn
Kathleen Shelton
Mary Ann Shook
Gladys Siegfried
Lloyd Siegfried
Martin P. Simon
Ruth Simon
Elizabeth Skoglund
Alice Smith
Dorothy Smith
Jane Smith
Howard Spanogle
Elaine Springborn
John F. Stahl
Henry C. Stair
Ruth Stair
Cornelia Stanford
Fred Stech
Jeanne Stelzner
Edward Storke
Harry Strachan
Harold Street
Dorothy Svendsen
Lillian Swanson
Mildred Szekely
Amos Tilton
Ruth Tilton
Norman S. Townsend
Daniel Trine
Jeanette Turnquist
Adeana Trongeau
Howard W. Unser
Ralph Vasquez
Dorothy Vetter
Arlene Von Busch
Louis Von Busch
Ruth Von Busch
Emil R. Vosicky
Julia Walker
Ruth Westerdale
Lorraine Whaley
Joyce Wheeler
Laura Williams
Sherman Williams
Evelyn Wolter
Dorothy Wysocki
Roy Yarrow
Laurin J. Zorn
Lelia Zorn
Roy B. Zuck

SCRIPTURE PRESS FOUNDATION

Twenty-sixth Anniversary Banquet

Elmhurst Country Club
January 8, 1960

HORIZONS UNLIMITED

Once again SP came away with first prize for the best commercial float in Wheaton's Fourth of July parade. The float displayed a large eagle and a banner proclaiming, "Trust ye in the Lord forever" (Isa. 26:4). Dan Miles served as chairman of the committee who built the float.

In August, Adeline Bossert became the first employee to retire under SP's pension plan. She had worked at SP ten days short of 19 years. VEC presented her with a walnut electric chime clock as a farewell gift.

It is generally agreed that Viola Greinke was SP's sharpest proofreader. In September 1960, SP editors took her to lunch at Four Seasons for her birthday. Henry Jacobsen wrote the following poem in her honor:

> Dear Viola, as a proofreader you have an unpleasant occupation:
> Your work seems predestinated to arouse considerable indignation,
> For you not only uncover the sins of the printer,
> But also find a lot of mistakes that we editors let enter
> The manuscripts we prepare,
> Which makes us tear out what's left of our hair.
> We are very unhappy
> As we reflect that we should have caught those booboos in our copy.
> But, Viola, though we may have an occasional inclination to shove you,
> We want to tell you, one day after your birthday, that in spite of all your good work,
> WE LOVE YOU!

In October, management decided to close the Sunday School Supply Center in the Loop after the beginning of the new year, citing limited space and a lack of parking as the reason. In November, decision was announced that SP would cease publishing *My Chum* magazine with the January 1961 issue and Back to the Bible Broadcast would fulfill subscriptions with issues of its *Young Ambassador* magazine. *The Christian Parent* magazine ceased publication with its October 1961 issue. Martin Simon had resigned earlier when he knew SP would no longer publish the magazines he had brought to the company.

Also in November, SP opened its distribution point at Long Beach, California and completed the purchase of the adjoining Frost property in Wheaton ($10,000 plus $1,000 for improvements).

Final frames for the 1961 VBS filmstrip, "Living by God's Time," were shot in early December.

Also in 1960, Beth McDaniel began at SP as Beginner and

Primary editor, and Helen Gorges as secretary in Training Hour programs.

1961

SP reps from the U.S., Canada, and England gathered on January 9 for the annual FIREPIN conference. Lillian Swanson spoke to employees in chapel. The week culminated with the 27th annual banquet, again at Elmhurst Country Club. Employees were especially happy after receiving another generous bonus at Christmastime.

In March, Sherm Williams, manager of CREDEX, accepted the pastorate of Redwood Chapel, Castro Valley, Calif. "The bright spot in the picture for SP is that we have never had a more loyal, dyed-in-the-wool booster than Sherm Williams," according to *Spotlight* for March 24, 1961. "For that reason he will speak for SP on the West Coast as often as his schedule will allow." Jack Bradford stepped in later in the year as acting director of CREDEX.

Also in March, *My Counsellor* became *Counselor* and announcement was made that it would be printed in four bright colors instead of the usual two. *Power* would be offered in two editions—one for teens, the other for adults.

In July, Art Saul became acting bookstore manager. He had formerly managed SP's Chicago bookstore.

Jesus said a "house divided against itself shall not stand" (Matt. 12:25), but the division that occurred in the Editorial Division in August was not "against itself"—it was for the good of the ministry. Lloyd Cory became editorial director, responsible for all materials for the junior age on up, Sunday School papers, and Training Hour. Dr. Bernice Cory's sphere of activity was narrowed to materials for the primary age on down.

Vince Hogren, who served as president of SP from January 1962 to March 1963, welcomes Russell Ingraham as marketing director.

Coffee—"the very best percolated kind"—was still five cents and Carney rolls, ten cents, according to the September 20, 1961 issue of *Spotlight*.

In November, VEC announced that he was stepping aside to become chairman of the board. Vincent C. Hogren would become SP's new president effective January 1, 1962. He had formerly served as executive vice president of Hitchcock Publishing Company. VEC said he himself would focus on the company's foreign publishing program and long-range planning. But Hogren resigned in March 1963. There was no announcement as to why he departed after such a brief tenure. VEC announced that "our Executive Committee will assume more of the load than heretofore, and I myself will take care of the remaining functions of the president's office until relieved by a new man." (VEC continued as president until his death in 1968.)

In December, management announced that Russell Ingraham, wholesale distribution manager of David C. Cook, would become distribution division director on January 1, 1962. And the same month Earl Swanson began a ministry in Canada that became Scripture Press Foundation of Canada and later Scripture Press Publications, Ltd.

Clarence McCall began handling distribution of curriculum to west coast customers out of Long Beach. Later in the year an SP office was set up, with Carl Gerbers as manager.

SP consultant Norman Townsend went to be with the Lord in 1961. Marilyn Schaer joined SP's Employment Department.

1962

In January, employees of the Long Beach plant planned to lay out the welcome carpet to their new resident manager, Carl Gerbers, but when they arrived he was already there. He was going by Wheaton time and arrived two hours ahead of the other employees. Gerbers wrote that his office was originally "Fibber McGee's closet," that it had been "cleaned out and has in it a nice (secondhand) desk, chair, and a file cabinet in which I store my lunch until needed."

In February, SPers learned through *Spotlight* that Dr. Bob Cook, whose presence and chapel messages had been such an inspiration, had been selected as the second president of The King's College, Briarcliff Manor, New York, effective March 17, 1962. He had left the company in November 1961. Many SPers believed, with his superb speaking ability and leadership style, he would have made a great president to lead the ministry of SP.

The Corys "had the surprise of their lives this morning" when they arrived in chapel and saw a banner wishing

"Happy 40th Anniversary, Drs. Cory," according to the June 15, 1962 *Spotlight*. The Corys' four sons hosted an anniversary party for their parents at SP on Saturday evening, June 16.

August 1 marked the beginning of Scripture Press Publications, Inc. Both Scripture Press Foundation and SPPI had new letterheads, invoices, etc. This division was a result of the close of the tax case (see chapter 10). Monday, August 13, Sam Postlewaite became the new SP art manager, replacing Carl Lindgren, who was transferred to advertising art director.

Also in 1962 SP became the first Christian publisher from the USA to have a Canadian catalog with a Canadian price list incorporated. SP produced a series of Royal Commission filmstrips.

1963

On January 21, 1963, SP directors approved the selling of the SP building and property to Washington National Insurance Company and leasing it back for 25 years (see chapter 10).

In June David E. Hall, formerly assistant to the director of accounting at Moody Bible Institute, became SP's new chief accountant.

August brought about promotions: Bill Hall to vice president of Production; Will Frykman to vice president of Personnel and Public Relations; and Wendell Anderson to vice president of Finance. They had formerly been division directors.

Characteristically, Bill Hall was continuing to show how to save money, for in October he dramatized for employees how saving "every single dollar on a job is just as though you had made this many more sales." He pointed to a 30-inch stack of *Power* papers. "A saving of $20 is equivalent to selling a stack of *Power* papers 49 feet high—almost to the top of the SP tower," he said. "One hundred dollars saved would extend the pile 246 feet high or 16 times the height of our building."

Also in 1963, secretaries with shorthand notebooks became obsolete with the introduction of a typing pool called Telecord in the Office Services area. Letters could be dictated over the phone and would be typed and brought to the dictator. Ruth Reid became secretary to BTC and Winona Walworth came as CREDEX manager.

1964

On February 1, 1964, the Christian Education and Extension (CREDEX) work of the Foundation was transferred to Scripture Press Publications.

Convention speakers: Sherm Williams, Dr. Ed Simpson, Dr. Frances Simpson, the Corys, and Norman Townsend.

In April, SPF directors got word that "counsel deems it impractical to apply for tax exempt status for the Canadian SP Foundation but [he would] investigate further." In July the directors authorized expenditure not to exceed $100,000 [for the next fiscal year] for proper uses in the field of CE—aids, grants, gifts, scholarships, literature, Sunday School development, etc.

Also in July, announcement was made that Bill Bratkovich would head a new division called Operations, to include Order Clerical, Merchandise Handling, and the Long Beach distribution point.

In August, Liebhart (Lee) Pfund, who was responsible for the landscaping of the SP grounds in 1956, died. And Kenneth J. Brouwer, director of Marketing and executive vice president of SP, retired. He had joined the company in early 1964 from Armour & Company, where he had been responsible for developing and marketing Dial soap. In the minds of some, he functioned a short time as interim president of SP, but he never signed correspondence as president, a longtime employee recalls. Don Baker became SP marketing director on September 28.

Sales conference, 1964: (front, l to r) Willis Grimm, Winston Miller, Dan Miles, and Lou Peckstein. (back) Mel Banks, Robert Spreckels, Harold Eavey, and John Stahl.

Dr. Roy Zuck began as executive director of SPF in November but planned to continue his work on Training Hour publications.

Also in 1964 the boards of SPF and SPPI formally adopted the Statement of Faith expressing the conviction of all officers, board members, editorial staff, and other key people to be signed annually (Appendix). Its 11 principles covered the great doctrines of the evangelical Christian faith, from trust in the verbally inspired Scriptures on to belief that "all Christians are called and commissioned by the Lord to live to the glory of God and to win others to Christ," with supporting Scripture references for each.

1965

In April 1965 employees learned that SP would go into an IBM computer system on or about July 1. Plans called for the equipment to be installed in the area occupied by Telecord and Mailing.

Floyd Robinson became SP's eastern field rep in June. Announcement came in October that the past fiscal year was SP's best sales year, though gross hours spent on work decreased by 13,500 hours from a comparable period the previous year. The total number of workers decreased from 216 to 210, including full-time, part-time, and seasonal employees. It was a matter of working "smarter, not harder," as Bill Hall often said.

In July, Dale McCulley, of Cavalcade Productions, declined to do any further work for SP "until you are able to clearly formulate and consistently implement a biblically based policy for racial equality." Cavalcade had produced more than two dozen motion pictures and filmstrips for the company, but reached an impasse in the association with SP, being "in complete disagreement with your decision to eliminate all non-whites from the 1965 VBS filmstrip." In time this policy was changed, as the company realized the wrongness of this practice that had been in effect for the sake of a biased segment of its market.

Also in 1965, Larry Morrison joined SP as a staff assistant to the president.

1966

In January 1966, VEC still had hopes of constructing a CE classroom center, long proposed by the Foundation for the Wheaton area, but advised directors that SPF's application to IRS was still pending.

In February, David Hall moved from Accounting Department manager to the post of controller, replacing Wendell Anderson.

In June, Raymond S. Bradshaw, Jr., joined SP as chief accountant. He had served Michigan Consolidated Gas Company as accountant for three years. Herb Sterling came aboard to head a new division known as Data Processing. He had been a key man in the Data Processing Division for a chain of California grocery stores. (For details relating to the introduction of computers in SP's Data Processing area, see Martha Lincoln's contribution to chapter 24.)

Also in June, Warren Wiersbe was critically injured in a head-on highway collision, and the word was that he was scheduled for plastic surgery "and may get a complete overhaul." At that time he was pastor of Calvary Baptist Church, Covington, Kentucky; years later he would become Victor Books' most prolific author.

In July, SP welcomed James E. Lemon as director of the Marketing Division, with Don Baker moving to Dealer and Denominational Sales. Lemon had previously worked for David C. Cook. Ed Kitch joined the Marketing staff as marketing research manager. He had worked for such firms as Aldens and J.C. Penney.

In October, VEC reported that the IRS had granted the Foundation exemption from payment of federal income taxes effective August 1, 1962 (see chapter 10). The Foundation's working capital, he said, would increase substantially as a result of the tax case settlement. Claims had been filed with the IRS for refunds of $63,000. The Foundation could not accumulate earned income but could accumulate unearned income, he continued.

Later in October, BTC and VEC were both in Europe, VEC attending the World Congress on Evangelism in Berlin and BTC continuing with the "Ladies' Tour of Europe." November saw 248 people out of a record 387 enrolled receiving certificates at graduation ceremonies as the fall LTI sessions concluded.

CHAPTER 12

Putting Power into Take-Home Papers

Prior to 1943, Sunday School take-home papers for children and adults alike generally failed to come to grips with life and therefore packed no punch. Children left them behind. They were colorless, with a 19th-century look, typically with black-and-white silhouettes of children and lambs playing in a meadow and fashionable ladies with umbrellas. These Pollyannaish papers featured "prayer meeting talks" and nice little stories that gave readers precious little that would make a real difference in their Christian lives.

Even Scripture Press, with its exciting new approach to teaching materials, wasn't helping the situation. Its *Upward,* an imprint for teens published by Faithful Words Publishing Company, St. Louis, simply wasn't in tune with readers and their needs. Recognizing this, in early summer of 1942, Vic Cory asked Laurin Zorn, fresh from the trade publications field, to pray about and create an electrifying take-home paper that would grab teen-age readers and give them a meaningful spiritual challenge. (See Appendix for issue of *Power for Living* relating to "25 Years of Power.")

Laurin Zorn: He put power into take-home papers. But what is he doing here???

Zorn gathered samples of as many Sunday School papers as he could to study. He began to look for a staff. The first young woman who came into the office looking for an editorial job was Betty Leslie, a Wheaton College graduate and daughter of the man who at that time was superintendent of men at Moody Bible Institute. Zorn hired her at once. The second was Esther Lou Young, who had just graduated from Wheaton College. Both were English and journalism majors, but inexperienced.

In the fall of 1942, Zorn reported that he had hit on a formula and format that he believed would impact teens. He showed VEC a pocket-size prototype and it had the name *Power*. Artist Joe Barcanic had given the new paper two-color eye appeal. It would have a modern journalistic touch and tell stories of people and what God had done in their lives. The lead article in the prototype was the human-interest story of First Mate Bob and his popular "Haven of Rest" radio program. SP mailed 45,000 sample copies to churches, and back came orders for 9,400 copies of the new paper, an appreciable gain over the 5,700 circulation of SP's *Upward.*

The first issue of Power, 1943.

Power *goes to Sunday School*

In January 1943, *Power* became SP's Sunday School take-home paper for teens, and a paper for Juniors with a similar approach, *My Counsellor* (a complete revision of a Faithful Words paper by the same name that SP got the rights to) was introduced the following October. Chris Egemeier, managing editor of the *Church School Promoter,* had suggested the name *Power* in a contest to go with *My Counsellor* based on a line from the second stanza of "Day by Day": "All my cares He fain would bear and cheer me, He whose name is Counsellor and Power." (Some years later the name *My Counsellor* was shortened to *Counselor.*)

"In creating the first issue of *Power*, we used up all our editorial copy and had to begin scrounging for some more," Zorn recalled in a report he wrote in 1967. "For the first month we did single issues. I think we may have done four for February and for a few months following. It may even have been that we did only four Sundays at a time for most of 1943, but VEC was breathing down our necks to get a larger number of issues ready to be printed at one time. We finally got up to eight, and it stayed at eight for a long time. The second quarter, circulation jumped to 13,500, then to 18,000, then 23,500, and then to 28,000, and for a long time afterward every quarter showed an increase. People were using the paper to send to members of the family away in the armed services. At the same time, the war effort offered us some very choice opportunities for real-life stories. We can well understand that VEC felt we had a comer."

In *Power* there was no attempt to use teen terminology or otherwise jazz up the content. The thrust was to answer the question that Zorn believed was in every teen's mind: "Does Christianity work today, and if so, who is making it work?" He coined the slogan, "Christianity in Shoe Leather," and patterned articles after grabbers like those found in *Reader's Digest.*

When Esther Lou Young and Betty Leslie left, Esther Lou to go to nursing school, and Betty to marry, Florence Beabout and Jim Adair replaced them. Beabout had graduated from Wheaton College, and Adair came in July 1945 from Asheville, N.C., where he had been a reporter on both the morning and evening newspapers, *The Asheville Citizen* and *The Asheville Times.* He had written numerous human interest articles and had been intrigued with R.G. LeTourneau, the "mountain mover" (with his big earth-moving machines) known for his faith and generous giving to Christian causes, the kind of person who made a good *Power* article.

A new-hire

After waiting to come to Chicago following a visit with Zorn in November 1944, Adair finally got word in late spring of 1945 that he was hired with the title associate editor. A month before he was to leave for Chicago, he was invited to play a round of golf with Billy Graham, who, learning he was a newspaper reporter and a Christian, urged him to apply for a job as an editor on a new magazine that Youth for Christ was developing, but Adair opted to accept the job he had been offered at SP. When Zorn left in 1947 to begin Van Kampen Press and publish Christian books, Adair became editor of *Power*, and after Beabout later left to become a missionary to Japan, he became editor of SP's Sunday School papers, from the *Primary Days* on up.

Zorn, and then Adair, reached out to some of the best

Christian authors of the day who specialized in either real-life articles or fiction or both. *Power* for January 2, 1944 featured John Witmer's article on Hudson T. Armerding, a "tall, lanky junior officer aboard a United States heavy cruiser," much later to become president of Wheaton College. A week later Bob Cook's article on Wendell P. Loveless was the lead story. Other top Christian writers included Bernard Palmer, Ken Anderson, Harry Albus, Don Hoke, Larry Ward, Phillip R. Newell, Ruth Hollander, and Dorothy C. Haskin. They wrote inspiring stories of athletes, war heroes, ex-gangsters, successful business and professional people.

When Adair was first hired, he was expected to write many of the articles. He used several pseudonyms: J. Robin Simkins, Jimmy Radford, and James Riden. Simkins was his mother's maiden name, and his father was Radford Riden Adair. Jim's first article was "Circuit Rider," the story of Peter Cartwright, the rugged, colorful Methodist circuit rider of the early 1800s. The new editor also came on board expecting to travel widely to interview subjects, but it wasn't until several years later that SP sent him out to search for hard-hitting stories. In the middle '60s VEC encouraged him to fly to Europe for stories, especially coverage of the Janz Brothers evangelistic Team in Germany. This trip resulted in articles not only from Germany but also from France and England. Trips with his family to Saskatchewan and New England paid off with articles for *Counselor* featuring his twin daughters, Mary Sue and Martha Lou, in visits with interesting people, such as a Canadian mountie, an Indian trapper, and a lobsterman. En route to Philadelphia on a train, to their surprise, the twins were recognized by a *Counselor* reader.

A Canadian Mountie fingerprints a couple of culprits—Mary and Martha Adair.

In the early years, Adair used a wire recorder, and at times bemoaned the fact the wire became hopelessly tangled, causing him to lose valuable portions of some interviews. Later he used a tape recorder, which could also get snarled. Following are some memorable subjects he wrote about in the '40s and '50s: Bob Lazear, manager of famous Wyoming Hereford Ranch; Louis Zamperini, Olympic track star; Kenneth Keyes, prominent Miami relator; Maxey Jarman, chairman of General Shoe Corporation; and Mitsuo Fuchida, the pilot who led the

Pearl Harbor raid and later became a Christian evangelist. After their appearance in *Power*, all of these subjects' stories appeared in Adair's first book, *Saints Alive,* published in 1951 by Van Kampen Press. Another memorable subject Adair interviewed in the early years of *Power* was future surgeon general Dr. C. Everett Koop, then chief surgeon at Children's Hospital, Philadelphia. His article later appeared in a second *Power* anthology, *God's Power Within,* published by Prentice-Hall in 1962.

A.W. Tozer wrote the foreword for Adair's *Saints Alive,* and his comments clearly communicated Zorn's original purpose, to show "Christianity on the hoof," as he put it, a variation of the original slogan. Tozer wrote:

> The author . . . quietly sets himself to show that there is such a thing as contemporary godliness and that a true saint does not need the protective covering of the centuries to prove himself one. He shows that the real saint is one who has turned to God from idols to serve the true and living God and to wait for His Son from heaven. Sober habiliments do not make a saint, nor self-torture, nor poverty, nor isolation from society. Not any of these, nor all of these can turn a sinner into a saint; much less can a saint be created by ecclesiastical decree. It is faith that puts a man through the fires of repentance and brings him broken and defenseless to the shelter of Christ's redeeming blood. . . . Far from being stories of persons who lived long ago and far away, these are stories of present-day men and women from different races, they have all the same message to proclaim. It may take any of several forms in telling, but the sum of each testimony will be: I have found the Messiah and my heart is satisfied.

Billy Graham had this to say about the collection of *Power* stories in Adair's later book, *God's Power Within:*

> I believe that these stories, so interestingly and vividly told, will go far to arouse slumbering souls and cause every reader to realize that the real and lasting effects of the Gospel are not hidden. God is still in the business of redeeming lost men through Jesus Christ.

Adults take to Power

Power went through various changes as the years passed. In 1948 designer Warren Wetherell gave the paper an up-to-date look, drawing on his own design talent and the talent of several young artists. His studio supplied art for many years. From the outset, adults took to *Power*, though it was intended for teen-agers. In 1961 SP began publishing separate editions, *Teen Power* and *Adult Power*, and sales increased. In time *Teen Power* became *Power Life*, and *Adult Power* became *Power for Living*. At its peak in the '60s and '70s, *Power for Living* had quarterly sales of well over 600,000. It was recognized as SP's No. 1-selling publication. In 1968 someone estimated that a year's issue of *Power*, if laid end to end, would stretch from New York City to Los Angeles and back and 600 miles out into the Atlantic.

A new look for these take-home papers, 1949-50.

In the early years, *Power* was produced in monthly sets and shipped to churches. This proved costly and inefficient. Later production chief Bill Hall worked with Standard Publishing to print and collate sets by the quarter. This helped keep costs down. But the system made it necessary to plan and publish so far in advance that the paper lost any possibility of being timely—everything had to be timeless. (Today *Power for Living* is planned 12-18 months in advance.)

***Power for Living* (formerly *Power*) turned 25 in 1968. Pictured with skids of this take-home paper: (seated examining proofs) Viola Grienke and Bruce Bucklew; (standing, left) Jack Houston, Anne Harrington DeWolf, Bill Krutza, and Henry Jacobsen (white shirt); VEC and Laurin Zorn (center); Jim Adair, Grace Fox Anderson, and Nancy Haupt.**

Power editors whose names are widely known include Ted Miller, who originated *The Christian Reader* magazine; Jerry Jenkins, who joined the staff in November 1971 from the sports desk at the *Tri-City Herald* in Kennewick, Washington, wrote his first book as an associate editor and since has written more than 100 others and assisted Billy Graham in writing his autobiography, *Just As I Am;* Stan Baldwin, who coauthored with Jenkins a biography of football star Walter Payton and since has written many books; and Don Crawford, himself a book author. Crawford took over as editor of *Power for Living* in the mid-'70s when Adair was asked to give full-time direction to Victor Books.

PFL *and* Counselor *take honors*

Power for Living and *Counselor* took "best paper" honors from time to time at conventions held by Evangelical Press Association. In 1962 *Counselor* was judged the top take-home paper among member publications, and *Power*, second best. Honors came also in 1954 for "best article,"Ted Miller's profile of General William K. Harrison, Jr. It was an "as told to" article from the viewpoint of Dr. Howard H. Hamlin, a friend of General Harrison, who described the general as a force on the battlefield and at the conference table and as having "the touch of God in everything he does."

SP take-home papers received several awards through the years. Here Ted Miller receives first place award for *Counselor* from Joe Bayly at EPA convention in 1962.

Though *Power for Living* and *Counselor* were regarded as SP's best known take-home papers, others were well received, among them, besides those previously mentioned, ***Bible-time** for 4s and 5s, Primary Days, Young Teen Power, FreeWay* (formerly *Power Life*), and *Connect*. *FreeWay*, with its newspaper format and somewhat wild contemporary artwork, was a sharp departure from the the look of other Sunday School take-home papers and instantly appealed to high schoolers and college students. Jerry Jenkins had charge of the content.

Over time, sales of all papers declined as production costs rose and prices for the papers increased steadily to well over a dollar per pupil for 13 issues.

"Red flag" matters

Editors took special care not to offend leaders of some of the more conservative churches, especially those belonging to Independent Fundamental Churches of America and the General Association of Regular Baptists. As a result, the company had a "Red Flag" manual that spelled out matters to watch. Also editors worked as if SPM Trustee Dr. John Walvoord of Dallas Seminary were looking over their shoulders. An episode in the '60s relating to the GARB proved most upsetting. A cartoon story appeared in *Counselor* about a Chinese Christian who "turned the other cheek" when a town official took over some of his property and it resulted in the Christian being spared when enemy forces took over the area. The item had appeared earlier in *Power* and got no flak, but the cartoon was regarded as Communist propaganda by some.

A woman belonging to a GARB church in the Cleveland, Ohio area phoned and awakened Adair at 6 a.m. on the Sunday that the issue of *Counselor* containing the cartoon was to be distributed. She demanded that all churches be called and alerted to the danger of the cartoon. It unnerved Adair to the extent that a doctor had to be called in later that day. To try to calm the waters, SP sent out a letter to all General Association of Regular Baptist (GARB) churches explaining that the editors had innocently erred and assuring that in the future they would be watchful of anything that smacked of Communist propaganda.

Many testimonials

That God has blessed the ministry of *Power for Living* and other SP take-home papers is evident from the many testimonials that have come by mail and word of mouth. For example, Carl Fredrickson, SP's trade rep for the eastern portion of the U.S., in 1960 gave a small boy named Steve copies of *Power* to take to his mother. The boy had come to Sunday School at Fredrickson's invitation after he gave the boy a Christian book to read. Steve's mother became deeply interested in the message of the Gospel through reading *Power*. Eventually, both she and Steve came to the Lord.

A Michigan pastor noticed a teen-ager reading his take-home paper during the church service. The first thought was to ask him to refrain, but his wife reminded him that he was at least getting a message that he needed. Sure enough, some time later the youth came to the pastor and told him he wanted to be saved, like the people he read about in his Sunday School paper.

A girl in Arizona, inspired by the weekly stream of testimonies, enrolled in a Bible school to prepare for full-time Christian service. A young man in an Illinois prison heard a reading of a *Power* story of a condemned murderer who received Christ and lingered afterward to get "what the fellow in the story had."

An inmate in Michigan State Prison wrote in 1965 to say that he came to Christ through reading *Power* issues that his wife sent him. "Yes, I was saved and reborn again in our Father through one of your *Powers*," he asserted. "It has been a real relief for me to get them even here in prison where there is a big need for God."

A royal marine came to Christ during a stay in Hong Kong. He became concerned about his fiancee in England. He witnessed to her in letters but said that a real help in her coming to know the way of salvation was the copies of *Power* he passed on to her.

Robert O. Ferm of the Billy Graham Evangelistic Association told of a Chinese in U.S. government service coming to the Lord during Graham's Washington, D.C. Crusade, then later reading an article in *Power* about Dr. Robert A. Cameron, a professor of math at the University of Minnesota. He immediately felt that here was a kindred soul. He told his wife, "This man is my friend. . . . I'm going to teach with him at the University of Minnesota." The university checked his qualifications, then welcomed him as a professor of aerodynamics. He continued to be a *Power* fan.

A reader of *Counselor* had this to say: "I want to tell you how much I enjoy reading your paper *Counselor*. I was not saved through reading your paper because I was saved when I was five years old. They are very plain and simple to read for kids of my age especially the ones that are not saved. Some materials I read are not explaining the way of salvation the way you explain it. You explain it plain and very understandable for me and many other kids to read."

Tommy was one of the children who received *Counselor* when he attended released time classes in California in the early '60s. He had been to three classes. Then, just before Easter vacation, he received Christ as his Savior. Five days later Tommy was grappling with a friend over a fishing rod when the fishhook pierced his eye and brain. Tommy never regained consciousness and went to be with Christ a short time later. The released-time teacher wrote SP a letter to say how thankful she was that she had been able to give copies of *Counselor* to Tommy and others.

"Bill" had tried everything

One of the more memorable testimonials came out of Waukegan, Illinois. "Bill" had tried almost everything and surprised himself by showing up one Sunday morning at a church in time for Sunday School. Greeted warmly, he was taken to a class. Though the lesson was good, he was unmoved until he read an article in *Power* about an ex-booze runner and dope addict who had been transformed by Christ. Later he went to the pastor's home and asked how to be saved like the story subject. That evening Bill told the church congregation that, despite the old khaki pants and patched sweater, he was "another kid whom the Lord had rescued." In time Bill joined the Army. His letter back to the church told of his progress to top sergeant, but the words that gladdened the hearts of church people most were: "I'm still telling people how I got saved by a story in that Sunday School paper. Several already have been won to Him by my testimony."

***

As this is written, Cook Communications Ministries continues to publish *Bible-time, Counselor*, *Teen Power* (in 1998 *Teen Power* was renamed *Real Time*), and *Power for Living*. The latter is now in four colors and is especially attractive. Cook also publishes *Zelos*, a product begun in Wheaton that is something of a combination of the old *FreeWay* and the student book for older teens.

The Second Decade in Wheaton

1967–1976

IN 1967 LYNDON JOHNSON occupied the White House, and in Vietnam 464,000 Americans were fighting a no-win war. The first heart transplant was made by a five-man team headed by Dr. Christian N. Barnard, but the patient, Louis Washkansky, died 18 days later of lung complications. British super model Twiggy arrived in New York, and thinness was confirmed as the new fashion standard.

President Lyndon Johnson

Also in 1967, Billy Graham spoke for the first time inside a Communist country, Marshal Tito's Yugoslavia. About the same time the World Council of Churches was again giving strong indication that liberalism wasn't about to go away. The WCC redefined the good news of the Gospel in terms of restructuring society instead of calling individuals to repentance and faith in Christ, according to Graham's autobiography, *Just as I Am* (page 568). "The WCC's Commission of World Mission and Evangelism carried the process further," wrote Graham (Ibid.), "focusing even more strongly on social and political justice to the exclusion of the redemptive heart of the Gospel to a lost world. . . . Implicit [in the statement of the commission] was the assumption that Christ had already given salvation to every human being (a belief known as universalism), so that there was no need for humans to repent or believe in Christ in order to be saved."

In light of this, SP's Bible-based teaching materials were needed in the '60s as much as in the '30s.

On Friday, January 27, 1967, work on SP's products slowed down briefly as only 15 brave and hardy people made it to SP because of "the snowstorm of the century," according to a memo in the 1967 *Spotlight* archives folder that took the place of the *Spotlight* issue that wasn't for that day. Snow piled up in drifts shoulder high when more than 20 inches fell, making roads almost impassable.

At a January board meeting, directors instructed the president to appoint a special committee to study granting financial assistance for, and possible consolidation of, marketing and/or financial interests with Gospel Light Publications. However, Gospel Light responded that the firm had no interest in pooling any of certain operational activities or a complete merger.

An indication of the scope of ministry of CREDEX came in March when it was reported that in 1966 experts held 988 workshops attended by 33,433 people. There were 163 individual church conventions with 7,112 in attendance at the 212 workshop sessions. LTI attendance was 666, representing 212 churches in 88 cities.

On Monday, June 5, 1966, SPers honored the Corys on the occasion of their 45th wedding anniversary at the company's annual banquet at St. Andrews Country Club. The theme of the banquet proclaimed "Mountains, Milestones, Miracles," and Dr. John Walvoord, president of Dallas Theological Seminary and an SP board member, paid tribute to the Corys, using their name to touch on factors in their lives: *C*hrist, *O*thers, *R*omance, and *Y*outh.

On June 19 BTC's Aunt Jennie, who some months earlier had gone into a retirement home, went to be with the Lord. She would have been 94. Till the last she was interested in the Lord's work and diligent in prayer.

Search for a new president

With VEC's health declining, in July 1967 directors appointed a special committee to select and appoint suitable individuals to comprise a presidential search committee to seek out, interview, and find a satisfactory candidate to become president. Many employees had, as previously mentioned, considered Bob Cook as a strong candidate, because of his leadership qualities, his charisma and platform presence; but VEC had decided that his background did not fit him for the job.

In April directors agreed that Stephen Slocum, head of American Tract Society, should be interviewed, but he advised that he was not interested in being a candidate. The search was eventually called off, with VEC continuing to preside over SP.

In August, Curt Henrickson transferred from manager at Long Beach to order processing manager in Wheaton, replacing Bill Bratkovich, who had relinquished his SP duties after he developed a severe case of rheumatoid arthritis. It was triggered by an auto accident in August 1966 while he was driving on the Eisenhower Expressway to a CBA convention in Chicago.

In October, directors directed the president to adjust the selling prices of curriculum and other products and at the same time effect adequate controls over cost of sales and operating expenses for the fiscal year ending January 31, 1969 so that the corporation should realize a pretax profit of 6 percent of net dollar sales.

Also in 1967, Personnel began giving service pins on an employee's fifth anniversary and at subsequent five-year segments, monetary awards.

1968

In early 1968, VEC was rushed to the hospital with a bleeding ulcer. This made Dr. John Walvoord, in particular, even more anxious that VEC turn over the leadership of the company to a qualified person. And at this time VEC began to have second thoughts about Bob Cook, who by this time was well along in his presidency of The King's College, Briarcliff Manor, New York. VEC consulted his division heads and other company leaders about approaching Cook. In a letter dated February 23, 1968, he wrote Cook that "the opinion and choice was unanimous!" that he be invited to be the next president of Scripture Press Publications (Appendix). "And what was my reaction? Enthusiastic!" he added. "So here I am, tendering you our unanimous and prayed-through invitation to be the President of Scripture Press Publications, Inc."

VEC's lengthy letter went on to detail that various phases of the business were in good hands, that SP continued to show an increase each year in sales. The salary would be generous, and "a new car and its running expenses [would be] thrown in!"

Cory continued: "Where would VEC be? I am Chairman of the Board and in a few months will be 75, and the Lord has definitely shown me that the reins need to be handed over to someone else."

To VEC and others in Wheaton, Bob Cook's negative reply came as a disappointment. He believed the Lord would have him stay at King's.

VEC called home

On June 2, 1968, SPers and the Cory family were saddened at the loss of Victor Cory a few weeks before his 75th birthday. The day before, a store door slammed on his left index finger, causing the loss of a little blood and necessitating eight stitches. His doctor gave him a tetnus shot, and it is likely this triggered his fatal heart attack that claimed his life the next day. He had had a heart condition for about two years.

Man of The Book.

Since his homegoing occurred on Sunday, he hadn't miss a day of work. He always said he wanted to die with his work boots on, and go from doing the Lord's work right into the Lord's presence. God granted him his wish.

The memorial service for SP's founder was held the following Thursday, June 6, at Wheaton Bible Church. Officiating clergymen and those paying tribute to him were Dr. Malcolm Cronk, Harry Saulnier, Dr. Lance Latham, Lt. Col. Lyell Rader, and Dr. Richard Seume. Ministering in music were Mrs. James Draper, Mrs. Geri Schaub, and Vernon Van Hovel. Dr. John Walvoord spoke briefly at the graveside.

Ushers, all from Scripture Press, were Victor Anderson, Ray Bradshaw, Paul Dibble, Phil DiCicco, Curt Henrickson, Art Saul, Lou Von Busch, and Laurin Zorn.

Pallbearers were Jim Adair, Will Frykman, Dave Hall, Bill Hall, Henry Jacobsen, Jim Lemon, Lloyd Siegfried, and Roy Zuck.

Honorary pallbearers were Carl Bergman, Wayne Buchanan, Robert Cook, Harold Halleen, Norman Lewis,

William McCarrell, Wesley Mills, Clate Risley, Herbert Taylor, William R. Thomas, William Volkman, Robert Walker, John Walvoord, and Waldo Yaeger.

Interment was in the Wheaton Cemetery.

Spotlight for June 7 was devoted largely to the founder of the company, eulogizing him with details from his life and comments from executives and other employees. The main article ended: "Dr. Victor Edwin Cory has always been quick to ascribe all greatness to God and not to take any credit for his remarkable achievements. One of his characteristic remarks was, 'The Lord had a job to be done, and I just happened to be standing around where He could use me.'"

Bill Hall wrote: "[Vic Cory's] abiding, intense, almost compulsive concern always seemed to be that more souls must be told the story of Christ and led to a saving knowledge of Him. . . . His efforts . . . enabled him to see that this message was carried to literally millions during his lifetime."

Jim Lemon: "Dr. Cory impressed us by his unusual combination of gentleness and firmness, rarely found in such wonderful balance—and here was his true strength."

Will Frykman: "At one time a management expert suggested to Dr. Cory that the daily devotional time was 'costing' the company $500 a day. He replied without hesitation, 'Since the beginning, we promised God the first part of each day. . . . We must not break this promise. Furthermore, our mathematics are not necessarily God's mathematics. It would cost the company dearly if we did not have these times of fellowship with Him.'"

Bernice Cory: "Victor, more than anyone I have ever known, literally *lived* in his Bible, which he called 'My B-I-B-L-E.' He steeped his mind and heart in God's mind and heart as this was reflected to him on the pages of Holy Scripture."

Lloyd Cory: "The main thing VEC taught me, besides digging daily in the Word, was to *work*. He never was one who loafed, and had little sympathy for those who live for themselves. He went along with Willard Wirtz, who said, 'People who want by the yard and try by the inch need to be kicked by the foot. . . . We haven't earned our rest yet. Most of us can—and should— work harder for our Lord, both on and off the job. The catch is that doing so means we have less time to spend on our own pursuits. But do we dare live to please ourselves in these perilous times?"

Frykman chosen president

On July 15, 1968 at a meeting of the SP Publications Board of Directors, Will Frykman was unanimously chosen president of SP, after having served as acting president following Vic Cory's death. VEC's widow had earlier stated that Frykman was the unanimous choice of the executive committee. Harold Halleen was elected chairman of the board. Frykman had joined Scripture Press, as previously mentioned, in 1956 as director of Personnel-Public Relations, just in time to work with Harold Eavey in coordinating the move to the new facilities in Wheaton. Frykman was named a vice president in 1963. A graduate of the University of Minnesota, he became active in public school administration, broadcasting, and served as director of foreign relations for Gideons International.

Wilfred C. Frykman, president from 1968—1976.

The reaction to the appointment of Frykman as president surprised some, including Frykman himself. Dave Hall noted: "Will knew nothing about publishing; he knew nothing about printing; he knew nothing about editorial, but he knew people." (Actually, Frykman had early in his career worked as an editor. See section at the end of this chapter relating to the Frykman presidency.)

New home for SP's west coast facilities

In August, announcement was made that Missionary Aviation Fellowship would soon build a two-story building in Fullerton, Calif. and that SP's new west coast facilities, called the SP ServiCenter, would be housed on the first floor, including the Long Beach operation, a bookstore, CREDEX and sales offices, and conference facilities. (Dedication was in June 1969.) Also in August, Floyd Robinson was appointed dealer sales manager, effective January 1, 1969. Robinson left the company in January 1974 to join Anchor Diversified.

October saw the appointment of three new vice presidents in addition to senior vp BTC and vp Bill Hall. The new appointees: Dave Hall, Finance; Jim Lemon, Marketing; and Lloyd Cory, Editorial. BTC would head the Children's Division.

Long-range planning team as it began in early 1970s, probably at Elburn, Ill. Front row: Lloyd Cory, Jim Lemon, Roy Irving; then, Ed Liden, Dave Hall, Bernice Cory, Jim Adair, Lorraine Ackley, Ray Bradshaw, Bill Hall, Phil DiCicco, Will Frykman, and Curt Henrickson.

In November, area directors were appointed: Jim Adair, papers and books; Roy Irving, research and development; Curt Henrickson, order processing; Ed Liden, advertising and sales promotion; and Phil DiCicco, office management. Later, in May 1969, Ray Bradshaw became an area director, with the title of controller. Veteran Willis Grimm joined the AD team in 1973. Editor Elsiebeth McDaniel became an area director in early 1974, and editor Joyce Gibson joined the group in 1975.

Also in 1968, the installation of flow racks in Merchandise Handling was completed.

1969

Laurin Zorn retired in January 1969 after 20 years with SP, and Larry Morrison, who had served since 1965 as assistant to the president, resigned to join Dr. Henry Brandt as chief developer of a new Farrell's Ice Cream franchise in Michigan. (Morrison died suddenly as a result of a heart attack a few years later.)

In August, SP held its annual picnic on the lawn west of the building.

In September, BTC left for her third trip to the Holy Land, taking with her cousins Lt. Colonel and Mrs. Lyell Rader. Punching time clocks became a thing of the past, as SP began using time distribution sheets.

Merchandise Handling welcomed its new shrink-wrap equipment in October, to improve the quality of packing and aid in a more efficient processing of orders. The first management planning session involving both the Executive Committee and the area directors was held at Elburn, Illinois. The area directors joined the conference on the third day and were assigned a number of projects for study and to make recommendations to the Executive Committee. In ensuing years this group met annually at various locations, from Wisconsin to Georgia. (For more details, see section near the end of this chapter.)

In November, BTC was off for Hawaii, where she was to bring seven messages at a Sunday School convention.

In December, Roy Zuck assumed the new position of executive vice president of the Foundation. Will Frykman was elected president of the Foundation. Everette Schoenthal, SP's much-loved theologian/shipper with 29 years of service, died. He often spoke in chapel services. And SPers packed 1,425 Lightbearer Christmas boxes that were delivered to the Manteno State Hospital. This was an annual affair for many years.

1970

SP welcomed Wayne Eklund in January 1970 as the new Purchasing Division director (he had formerly been employed at SP). His division included the Production, Purchasing, and Art Departments. Bill Hall assumed a new post as corporate planning vice president.

Valentine's Day 1970 marked the 50th anniversary of Aunt Jennie's valentine party which triggered both BTC and VEC's conversion to Christ. They always regarded themselves as "spiritual twins." And also in February, Mel Banks and the other incorporators of Urban Ministries, Inc. met, though actual incorporation did not take place until March 27.

In April, BTC and Helen Gorges attended the Asian Literature Strategy Conference in Singapore. In May, Helen was appointed by the Foundation's Roy Zuck to the position of administrative assistant.

In July, SPF directors authorized the purchase of 95 shares of Urban Ministries, Inc. stock at $210 per share or $19,950, after UMI raised $80,000 in capital funds. The purchase was completed in May 1972. (See chapter 17.)

August saw the return of BTC from another world tour. In October SPF became Scripture Press Ministries, and Irving A. Philgreen, formerly of Short Terms Abroad and an ex-YFC director, became director of stewardship for SPM in November. And it was in November that Roy Irving, who inherited Henry Jacobsen's desk when he moved to Arizona to continue his work there, found this memo in one of the drawers:

> In this room and at this desk I have spent some of the happiest, most rewarding moments of my life, aware of the pres-

ence of God's Spirit and enjoying the privilege of cooperating in His work. I don't know who will use this office or this desk, but I pray that yours too will be an enriching and fulfilling experience!

An aside about Henry Jacobsen: He was much loved by his colleagues and was a favorite chapel speaker. Once he blundered into an embarrassing situation addressing a Saturday morning seminar session at SP. As he taught, he let slip the phrase "a nigger in the wood pile." He suddenly realized what he said and turned his back to his class, facing the wall for at least a minute. Then he turned red-faced and apologized to blacks in the audience, who graciously forgave him for the unfortunate faux pas.

1971

In January 1971, Lillian Swanson, vp of SPF in London (SPUK), went to India to conduct CE workshops for six weeks. In February and March she was in the Philippines conducting workshops. Both trips were under the sponsorship of SPM.

Also in January, Barbara Cummiskey was welcomed back to SP after a long bout with pneumonia. She worked as a steno in the Sunday School Papers Department and later was diagnosed as having multiple sclerosis. In time she was often hospitalized and then bedridden for a lengthy time. On June 7, 1981 a well-documented miracle occurred. God spoke to her as she lay in bed at home: "My child, get up and walk!" She removed the oxygen tube from her throat, took off the brace from her arm, and jumped out of bed. Her legs had not held the weight of her body in over five years, yet she danced as she headed into the hallway. Her mother stopped short when she saw her, and, lifting the hem of her gown, exclaimed, "Barbara, you have calves again." Her legs had been atrophied. That evening she astonished the congregation and pastor of her church, Wheaton Wesleyan, as she walked down the aisle. The MS never returned. Her story was on the TV program "That's Incredible" and in the April 1985 issue of *Guideposts*. Over the years, she has spoken in many gatherings to testify of what God did for her. In 1998, Barbara (Mrs. Brad Snyder) was a pastor's wife in Vinton, Virginia.

On Thursday night, February 4, 1971, Charlene Maniaci of

Sunday School Papers was killed in an auto accident en route from work to her home in Rockford. She was driving on a two-lane highway and her car collided with a truck. Also in February, Art Saul became regional manager of the 11 western states, and ace proofreader Viola Greinke retired after almost 15 years of service. Phil DiCicco's VW became stuck on the icy crossing at College Avenue, and an instant after he jumped out, a commuter train rammed his car and pushed it 50 feet east of the crossing.

President Frykman announced in April an "Employee Participation Plan" designed to give all employees more opportunities to contribute to the success of the SP ministry and to share more in its benefits. The plan, which lasted several years, was a variation of the Rucker-Scanlon Plan and called for 40 percent of savings to be shared on a quarterly basis with employees, on a calculated percentage of individual wages, and 60 percent to be retained by the company. (In November 1983, a new profit-sharing formula was adopted, subject to annual review: share 50 percent of profits over net profit budget goal and a maximum of 10 percent of annual salaries, "sharing to be based on total compensation.")

The plan was built around a teamwork concept, and kicked off a program that brought employees together to participate in many discussions of how to improve production and make for a sharper ministry. A work team was organized to administer the plan. Some of the duties of the work team: receive copies of work team minutes, analyze surveys, review suggestions for changes in the plan, review quarterly income statements and the amount shared with employees, communicate progress of the plan and report to the executive work team on problems and suggestions concerning the plan. Someone mentioned that the plan related to 1 Thessalonians 5:12-13: "We beseech you, brethren, to know them which labor among you, and are over you in the Lord, and admonish you, and to esteem them very highly in love for their work's sake. And be at peace among yourselves."

Also in April 1971, SP began shipping freight shipments to customers from a warehouse in Bloomington, Indiana. This venture lasted only about a year.

Thirty-four new products were introduced by SP at the CBA convention in Denver in July. These included a new high school leader's resource book, six Little Glad Books for preschoolers, four new Discovery Books for Juniors, two Bible Story Books for Primaries, two Pop-up Books, and a new line of Youth Today Books (seven titles). There was good and bad news about July quarter orders. Sales were far better than anticipated but many items were sold out before the quarter began.

In September, SP began a new quarter system, the new quarters being September, December, March, and June, to parallel the public school year and the promotion of children to new grades. BTC was off again on a world tour in late September, with 16 others led by Dr. J. Palmer Muntz.

Longtime employees at a special event in the 1970s. Front row: Bernice Bosmann, E. Clara Sander, Gladys Siegfried (Halleen), Stella Miles. Second row: Lucille Nelson, Louise Rodman, Audrey Blake, Bessie Butler, Elaine Springborn Grimm. Back row: Jim Adair, Victor Anderson, Willis Grimm, Lloyd Cory, and Lloyd Siegfried.

In October, a dress code was announced: except for those working in the warehouse, women were to avoid sports clothing and hemlines should be modest in good taste; men in the office area were to wear dress shirts with ties.

In November, Bill Hall took semi-retirement after 17 years at SP and moved to Florida. He continued to serve in several capacities, including doing corporate-type projects for the president and board.

Also in 1971, Wayne Eklund was promoted to vice president. A policy specifying retirement at age 65 was approved. And the SP Pension Plan was changed to a complete company contribution, with benefits based on years of service and a final five-year average monthly salary.

1972

In January 1972, Dr. Mary Barbour, an associate professor at Slippery Rock State College in Pennsylvania, joined the Editorial Division as the new associate editor of Nursery materials. Her husband, Carl, was hired to work with B & G.

At the May meeting of the SPPI board, directors approved a reorganization plan to set up a corporation in Delaware and merge SPPI into that Delaware corporation, effective July 31, 1972. The purpose was to permit the issue of preferred stock, allowed by Delaware but not by Illinois. At a later meeting, the board amended the certificate of incorporation to allow issue of 2,500 shares: 500 shares of Series A Preferred Stock at the par value of $100 each and 2,000 Common Stock shares at par value of $100. Series A stock would be privately sold; holders would have no voting power nor right to attend stockholder meetings. According to the certificate book, stock was purchased by Tyndale House and later bought by Moody Bible Institute.

In June, Ward Studio Press of Warsaw, Indiana was purchased by SP when the owner retired because of a health problem. The small firm, renamed Screen Printers, produced Video-graph backgrounds for SP's Suede-graphs and also flannel backgrounds for Child Evangelism Fellowship.

In June, more than 175 attended SP's annual picnic at Pottawatomie Park, St. Charles. In July, announcement was made that both Sunday School and Vacation Bible School curriculum would carry the label "All-Bible Curriculum."

Fern Robertson and her Sunday School class. BTC expected all her editors to teach pupils for whom they prepared lessons.

In August, SP Editorial lost a faithful worker when Fern Robertson, manager of Youth Programs, died after being pulled from the water while vacationing at Laguna Beach, Florida. She had been with SP nearly 16 years. At her funeral, Joyce Gibson said: "Fern was what the rest of us talk about."

"The rainfall of the century" on Friday night, August 25, sent B & G workers scurrying. The first leaks appeared in the Employment Department, where rain began coming in "like a waterfall." Then the Bookstore stockroom was in trouble. Then about two inches of water was just everywhere. Furniture was quickly moved and everything humanly possible was done to save material of special value. Employees came in on Saturday to join in "Operation Mop Up." Eventually carpeting had to be ripped up and replaced. Victor Books employees were caught in the downpour en route back to Wheaton from Chicago, where they had a pizza party for Lynette Lewis, who was leaving SP. They had to find alternate routes to avoid flooded areas. Grace Fox found her Volkswagen Bug half submerged in the west parking lot. Employee Jim Sabinske tried to restore many antique books damaged at his home by putting them in a frost-free freezer. Margaret Armstrong had to move out of her flooded basement apartment, and Mary Roop had seven feet of water in her basement. The sewer system was improved by the city some years later to take care of the water problem on the SP property.

In September, SP hosted 53 guests from 26 denominations and publishing houses who came for the sixth annual Denominational Day. SP personnel presented new curriculum and other products.

On October 3, BTC was honored in chapel, the day marking her 40th anniversary with SP. On October 12, William R. Thomas, who had helped VEC start SP, died at the age of 90. On November 6, Martyn White became assistant to Lillian Swanson at SPUK. In November, many SPers attended the Basic Youth Conflicts Seminar conducted by Bill Gothard at McCormick Place in Chicago. His first public seminar was held in the east wing of the SP building in Wheaton.

On December 29, Marie McVey, of Merchandise Handling, retired after 21 years of service.

1973

In February, registration of SPPI as a Delaware corporation was completed. In March, Roy Zuck announced that he was resigning as executive director of SPM to take a position with Dallas Theological Seminary as assistant academic dean and assistant professor of Bible Exposition, effective July 1. In November, Helen Gorges was elected executive director of SPM, replacing Irving Philgreen, who had served in a supervisory role in the interim. Also, SP vice presidents Dave Hall and Jim Lemon were elected to the SPPI board, as was V. Gilbert Beers.

In chapel on Monday, March 26, Warren Wiersbe kicked off a two-week study of his first "Be" book, *Be Real.* Employees were assigned to ten discussion groups.

Lady of The Book

Bernice Cory with the Lord

SPers were saddened when Bernice T. Cory died on Saturday night, April 21, after suffering several strokes. She was 73. On Monday morning, a memorial service was held in her honor in SP chapel. David Hall led in singing "My Savior First of All" and read the following Scripture portions: Romans 14:7, 2 Corinthians 5:1-8, Philippians 1:20-24, 1 Thessalonians 4:13-14, 2 Timothy 4:6-8, 2 Peter 1:11-14, and Revelation 14:13. Alan Addy sang "Until Then." President Frykman commented on her life's work and testimony.

The funeral service on the following Wednesday was conducted at Wheaton Bible Church. Speakers were her pastor, the Rev. Christopher A. Lyons, President Frykman, Board Chairman Wesley Mills, Harry Saulnier, and Col. Lyell Rader.

Pallbearers were Wayne Eklund, David Hall, James Lemon, Dr. Roy Zuck, and grandsons Steven Cory and Tucker Cory.

Burial was in Wheaton cemetery alongside her late husband, Dr. Victor E. Cory.

At its meeting on May 14, 1973, the Scripture Press Ministries Board of Trustees adopted the following resolution as an expressing of appreciation for the service of BTC:

> WHEREAS, Dr. Bernice T. Cory, who went to be with the Lord on April 21, 1973, was co-founder with her late husband, Dr. Victor E. Cory, and has been editor in chief and successively treasurer, vice president, senior vice president, and director of the several Scripture Press organizations over the past 41 years, and has given fully of her time in complete devotion to the growth, outreach, and development of the Sunday School, and
>
> WHEREAS, this Board of Trustees recognizes the devoted service which Dr. Bernice T. Cory has rendered to the worldwide ministry of Scripture Press, and her guiding hand which has enabled Scripture Press to develop a teaching ministry devoted wholeheartedly
>
> —to the dissemination of the Word of God to millions of people
> —to the teaching of improved methods of Christian Education in Sunday Schools and churches
> —to the translation of these scripturally sound lessons into many foreign languages
> —to the distribution of countless thousands of pieces of Christian Education literature to missions, schools, and libraries
> —to a corporate policy of telling the story of salvation in Jesus Christ to as many persons as possible by means of the published Word

THEREFORE, this Board of Trustees, collectively and individually, in the person of each member, namely, Daniel L. Cory, Wilfred C. Frykman, Kenneth O. Gangel, Harold P. Halleen, Norman Lewis, Edward L. Simpson, Robert A. Walker, John F. Walvoord, and Roy B. Zuck, desires to express its appreciation for the 41 years of service of Dr. Bernice T. Cory to the Scripture Press ministries, for her single-purposed, enthusiastic devotion to the cause of Christian Education and the lifelong example of Christian walk that she set, and to emphasize a recommitment of each member of this Board to continue and, through His leading, to expand the work which was so faithfully carried on by Dr. Bernice T. Cory.

Three SPers in plane crash

On Tuesday, April 24, three SPers—Dave Hall, Ed Liden, and Phil DiCicco—were shaken up in a plane crash in Ottawa, Ill., with Hall at the controls. The small plane did not get airborne and ended up in a small lake. Liden saved DiCicco from drowning. (A detailed account by DiCicco is included in the final chapter of memories of former employees.)

In May the SPPI directors authorized a 7 percent dividend on the par value of the preferred stock for the first time. This was the stock that had been purchased by Tyndale House Foundation. Also in May, David and Helen Leonard were given retirement recognition for their service in Merchandise Handling and Order Clerical. Dave had served nearly 17 years and Helen, nearly 16 years.

In June, Lloyd Siegfried, who at that time had served SP for 35 years and 7 months, retired; he had worked longer than anyone else besides BTC. He had started as a seasonal shipper and worked several jobs, the final one as inventory control supervisor.

What apparently was SP bookstore's first annual pre-inventory sale began on Monday, August 20. The sale became a big event into 1997, with crowds coming early and employees parking their cars on the rear lot for the entire week.

In September, three former SPers died: Laurin Zorn in Texas at the age of 73; Bertha Caine, 65, formerly of Telecord; and Carl Gerbers, 73, ex-credit manager.

Will Frykman was elected president of National Sunday School Association.

On October 15, seven SP retirees returned for SP's first annual Alumni Day: Edith Anderson, Flora Anderson, Ethel Gantz, Miriam Given, Marvel Miller, David Palm, and Lloyd Siegfried.

In late October, VEC and BTC were honored at an impressive memorial service at the Mid-America Sunday School convention in Detroit's Cobo Hall, with 10,000 CE leaders in attendance. Lloyd Cory received a bronze-molded plaque in replica of the oil painting of his parents that hangs in SPM's Heritage Room.

In November, Jerry Jenkins, managing editor of *FreeWay*, left to become executive editor of *Inspirational Radio/TV Program Guide.* He later became editor of *Moody Monthly* and director of publications at Moody Bible Institute and still later, a writer in residence, continuing his prolific output of books.

Also in 1973, the cost of coffee went from 5 cents to 10 cents. The Editorial wing was carpeted. And news came that the 800 North Clark building, former home of SP, had been demolished to make space for a new structure.

1974

On January 2, 1974, David Hall began his new duties as executive vice president, responsible for the administration, coordination, and control of operations of SPPI. Ray Bradshaw became director of the Finance Division, and Curt Henrickson, director of the Order Processing Division. In making the announcement, President Frykman stated that he would still be "responsible for the conduct of all SP activities to achieve our established objectives in keeping with policies, long-range programs, and budgets approved by the Board of Directors."

In early 1974, Barbara Zuck, 17-year-old daughter of the Roy Zucks, was critically injured in an automobile accident on President Street, Wheaton, and was in a coma for weeks. But in May, she was able to cut her own meat and walk alone; she wrote a letter to SPers to thank them for their prayers and cards. In August, she had her 13th operation, major surgery to remove the softened cartilage in her trachea. After her recovery, Roy wrote a book, *Barb, Please Wake Up,* about the experience and Victor Books published it.

In March, Art Blakely, who had been with SP for nine years, became sales manager. Paul Mathews became assistant to David Hurst, accounting manager. In a few years Mathews left for a position with Tyndale House, where he later became corporate vice president.

In April, Gladys Siegfried Halleen was honored for 35 years' service at SP. She came to the firm as a part-time secretary to VEC and at the 35th milestone was advertising production manager. At one time she filled in as acting head of the Distribution Division.

In May, Clara Sander was honored for 30 years of service. The same month Henry Jacobsen retired and Jim Eckhardt became editor of SP's adult materials.

In July, Bernice Bosmann marked 30 years of service in Order Clerical. Personnel's Dale Chaddock congratulated her on her "record of achievement, faithfulness, dependability, and job knowledge."

In July, *Spotlight* revealed how SP's 80,048 square feet of floor space was used:

47% for warehousing and shipping
5% for writing and editing
9% for sales and marketing
3% for accounting and finance
7% for purchasing, production, and office management
4% for order and data processing
3% for building services
6% for employee conveniences
6% for chapel and conference rooms
4% for aisles and lobby
2% for SPM
4% rest rooms, lobby

In August, Marie Friesen was honored for 30 years of service (she retired in September 1976). She came as a stock girl and order filler and was later promoted to the Bookkeeping Department, then to Order Clerical.

In September, Dale Chaddock resigned as personnel director to devote more time to his counseling business. September also saw 12 employees retiring (years of service in parentheses): Syl Halleen (16), Melvin Henrickson 20), Viola Kemp (22), Tallie Kohler (29), Lola McClintock (12), Alice Nelson (14), Calista Newman (18), Laura Penney (13), Orlo Peter (7), Ann

Peterson (16), Emery Pugh (8), and E. Clara Sander (30).

In November, Lorraine Ackley was chosen to serve as corporate secretary for both SPM and SPPI, replacing Bill Hall, who had resigned.

1975

In February 1975, Marilyn Schaer, administrative secretary to David Hall, became personnel manager, working with Ruth Walker and Louise Rodman. Joyce Gibson became area director over Junior and Young Teen Editorial Departments and a member of the Corporate Planning Workteam.

SP trustees and Executive Work Team in 1975: Seated: Curt Henrickson, Lorraine Ackley (secretary), Wes Mills, Will Frykman, Lloyd Cory, Roy Zuck, and David Hall. Standing: Gil Beers, Dr. John Walvoord, Wayne Eklund, Ray Bradshaw, Harold Halleen, Jim Lemon, and Dan Cory.

In May, *You Can Be the Wife of a Happy Husband* was No. 5 on the *Christian Bookseller* magazine's best-seller list for the second month in a row, and *Fragrance of Beauty,* No. 10. Also in May, *Youth Illustrated* took first place in its category in Evangelical Press Association competition, Urban Ministries' *Inteen* got second place, and *FreeWay*, third place (tie).

In July, the SP family was stunned to learn that Victor Books author Paul Little had been killed instantly in a car collision near Barrie, Ontario, en route to a Toronto meeting. Earl Swanson phoned in the message. Also in July, Jim Adair, Sunday School papers and Victor Books director, marked 30 years with SP.

In August, Herald Christian Bookstore in Fullerton became a department under Marketing, with Marion Smith as manager.

In September, to help launch their book, *'Atsa Louie—I'ma Phil,* Phil and Louie Palermo served a five-course spaghetti dinner to 300 persons in SP's fellowship hall.

Also during 1975, SPPI became a charter member of the Evangelical Christian Publishers Association.

1976

Albertine Louise Rodman retired on January 30, 1976 after 37 years of employment, leaving as the employee with the company's then longest record of service. She began working at SP on November 30, 1938, the day after Seabiscuit beat War Admiral at Pimlico race track in Baltimore. She began posting accounts receivable and climbed to Employment Department manager and editor of 1,266 issues of *Spotlight*.

Good Friday became an official SP holiday.

In May, Anne Harrington brought back the first-place award plaque for *FreeWay* (Sunday School papers category) from the awards dinner at the EPA convention in Philadelphia. Since SP's pension plan was established in 1947, 30 retirees were receiving checks in June at an annual cost of $110,000. Lois Gustafson Buelow joined retirees after 33 years in Customer Service. Bessie Butler bowed out after 30 years in Merchandise Handling.

In July, SP took first place for the best booth at the CBA convention in Atlantic City. The SP building lease with Washington National was transferred from SPM to SPPI.

In October, full shipping operations began in Buchanan, Georgia for Baptist Literature Board imprint of SP curriculum for Southern Baptists.

In November, Millie Saul, who had started with her husband, Art, working in the SP bookstore, died after a long bout with amyotrophic lateral sclerosis (Lou Gehrig's Disease). And also in November, the SPM board authorized $15,000 to refurbish the Anthony Street house on SP property, to make it presentable for higher rental income. The Village of Glen Ellyn had refused to rezone it from Commercial.

Gross sales for the fiscal year exceeded $10 million for the first time.

Dave Hall named new president

Wesley K. Mills, chairman of the SPPI board, announced that Will Frykman had been named the new chairman of the board, and that David Hall would succeed him as president and chief operating officer, effective January 1, 1977. Mills became vice chairman. Frykman continued as president of SPM and chairman of the boards of SPF (U.K.) Ltd., SPF of Canada, Evangelical Publishers, and Beacon Distributing.

A graduate of Wheaton College, Hall later received his Master of Business Administration degree from DePaul University. He came to Scripture Press in 1963 as accounting manager after four years in the Finance Branch of Moody Bible Institute. As previously mentioned, he became controller in 1966, vice president of finance in 1968, and executive vice president in 1974. While serving nine years in active and reserve duty with the U.S. Army, he earned the rank of captain. He was also a licensed pilot and ham radio operator. He grew up in Michigan, where his father was a Baptist pastor.

David E. Hall, president, January 1977-May 1990, and SPM's Helen Gorges, probably at her retirement.

Will Frykman (WCF often hereinafter) announced that he would continue his active role in the overall direction of Scripture Press Publications and place greater emphasis on his leadership of SPM as president and as chairman of the boards of SP's Canadian and British operations.

Frykman discusses highlights of his presidency

In July 1997, WCF discussed some of the highlights of his presidency with the author of this book. When he was asked to become president following VEC's death, WCF said he felt inadequate. He talked earnestly with the Lord about the matter. *What do I know about being a president? Am I really the right person for the job? What does a president really do?* John 15:16 came to his mind: "Ye have not chosen Me, but I have chosen you, and ordained you, that ye should go and bring forth fruit. . . ." He took this as an indication that it was God's will for him to take the job and depend on the Lord to lead him and support him. God, he said, gave him the good sense to form teams to carry out the work.

His first move was to delegate authority similar to the way Moses had operated on the advice of his father-in-law, Jethro, to appoint "able men . . . [to be] rulers" (Ex. 18:25). Whereas VEC had had nine people reporting to him, and felt he had to approve many details, WCF arranged for only four division vice presidents to report to him: Lloyd Cory, Editorial; Jim

Lemon, Marketing; Bill Hall, Production; and Dave Hall, Finance. He began to meet with each on a weekly basis and charged them with the responsibility for meeting objectives that had been hammered out and approved.

One of WCF's first moves was to call a goals conference that was held in October 1968 at the Fellowship Deaconry in Elburn, Illinois. The four division heads, plus BTC, met with him. Bill Gothard spoke at the opening session.

Perhaps the most important decision made at the initial goals conference was to enter seriously into the book field, triggering the start of Victor Books. Jim Adair was elevated to a "new-level editor in charge of Papers/Books," according to a minutes summary. But children's books were to remain under Editorial. Editorial Research became a new department under Editorial. "Office Services and Control Services were elevated to a new level, Office Management," per the minutes, with Phil DiCicco heading the area.

The Strategy and Outreach teams, with President Will Frykman's Planning Commission at Corporate Planning Conference in 1975 at the Wagon Wheel, Rockton, Ill. Pictured (front row, l. to r.) Jim Lemon, Phil DiCicco, and Lloyd Cory; then (l. to r.) Elsiebeth McDaniel, Curt Henrickson, Frykman, Joyce Gibson, Earl Swanson, Wayne Eklund, Lorraine Ackley, Dave Hall, Jim Adair, Willis Grimm, and Ray Bradshaw.

Among other important decisions made at the conference, an area director level was established. The original directors appointed to lead areas were Adair, Ray Bradshaw, DiCicco, Curt Henrickson, Roy Irving, and Ed Liden.

At a management planning conference in September 1971, a long-range task force (later to be called the President's Planning Commission) was discussed, and in January 1972 decision was made to involve area directors and start setting down long-range plans. In 1973, two subteams, Strategy and Outreach, involving all members of the President's Planning Commission, were established.

The long-range planners met 38 times in ten years at various places, including the Fellowship Deaconry, Elburn, Illinois; Brown's Lake Resort, Burlington, Wisconsin; Camp Willabay, Lake Geneva, Wisconsin; Lake Lawn Lodge Delavan, Wisconsin; Clock Tower Inn, Rockford, Illinois; Barren River Lake Resort, Lucas, Kentucky; and Callaway Gardens, Pine Mountain, Georgia.

Adding area directors and creating the Employee Participation Program began to involve employees at other levels as members of work teams. Later WCF began the Scripture Press Employee Participation Plan (SPEPP), with its incentives that encouraged workers to strive to meet goals and share in profits. Teams were well organized. Everyone knew what had to be done. Costs were kept down, work was done more efficiently, and sales improved. As a result of SPEPP, the company enjoyed its best-ever financial year in 1974. (Records unavailable but likely the margin was close to 6 percent, the highest goal that had been set.)

A former editor himself before coming to SP, WCF began *tranSPirer*, a management information bulletin, in November 1968. About the same time, he asked BTC to write what she believed the SP purpose to be, leading in time to the formulation of SP's mission statement. The original mission statement was adopted by the Executive Committee in September 1971:

> "Called by God and committed to reach, teach, win, and train people for Him through proved and improved Christian Education products and ministries that are Bible-based, Christ-centered, and life-related."

It was later revised and approved in May 1989:

> "Called by God and commmitted to produce excellent Bible-based, life-related curriculum, books, and Christian Education products that will be used to reach and teach people for Christ."

"The Whole Word for the Whole World!" A sampling of SP products in foreign languages.

WCF took a strong hand in developing SP's translation program, extending the ministry to many foreign countries. His first trip abroad as president took him to such places as London, Brussels, Frankfurt, Basle, Milano, and Paris. Later he visited Holland to encourage the translation work of an organization called Timotheus headed by Meta Knecht, who made SP materials available in Dutch. He worked with other translators to make SP lessons available to Sunday Schools in Norway, Finland, Belgium, Germany, Poland, Greece and

Egypt. His knowledge of Spanish stood him in good stead in a visit with translators in Mexico, except for one time. Addressing a congregation of Mexican Christians, he intended to say that SP was glad for the dollars used to help them with translation work but used the wrong word, which translated to "pain in the neck," causing much laughter.

Other highlights of WCF's term as president included beginning Urban Ministries and overseeing the switch of SPM from a private operating foundation to a public charity.

In addition, WCF had a part in launching the Evangelical Christian Publishers Association. He recalls that in 1968 at a CBA convention in Minneapolis he and Gospel Light's Bill Greig concluded that publishers needed to get together to discuss their own problems at CBA conventions. This resulted in the establishment of ECPA, and the first meeting was held the next year in Denver. CBA people were apprehensive and felt threatened, but later John Bass, director of CBA, admitted that the formation of ECPA helped CBA.

WCF says he had his share of headaches and hard-to-tackle problems. For example, the Canadian operation gave him many challenges. Having to inform Lillian Swanson that time had come for her to give up the leadership at SPUK and let Martyn White take over was a tough one for him. She accepted it well. She became a Christian education consultant for SPF of Canada.

WCF forthrightly gives God credit for enabling SP to grow under his leadership.

SP in Great Britain

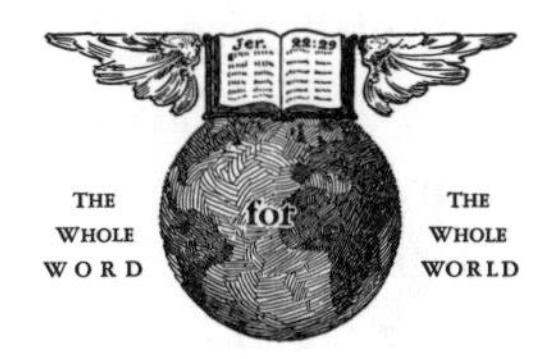

A THREE-MONTH VACATION, or "holiday," as the British call it, that Lillian Swanson spent in the British Isles in 1954 sparked a fire of real concern for the Sunday Schools of Great Britain. For wherever she visited in England, Sweden, Norway, and Ireland, the story was the same: "Sunday Schools are dying." Despite the fact Billy Graham had held his highly successful crusade at Harringay Arena in London in the spring of 1954, estimates indicated that perhaps only 1 to 4 percent of the population attended church regularly. Sunday School leaders were fighting a losing battle because of lack of funds, shortage of space and teachers, and indifference on the part of parents and even pastors regarding the Christian education needs of children.

Lillian Swanson goes to the Isles

The burden for Great Britain lay heavily on Miss Swanson's heart, causing her to obtain permission in 1956 from Scripture Press to spend a year in the Isles to conduct Sunday School conferences and teacher training sessions. She also had in mind working with key churchmen concerning the possibilities of translating SP materials into Swedish. She visited Norway again to get leaders in that country excited about Sunday School ministry. But she had the distinct feeling that she was intruding, for in July 1957 she wrote back to SP in Wheaton, "It is not uncommon for [my key contacts] to sit and look at me, scarcely saying a word, but with the expression,

'What does a woman from America think she has to offer *us?*'"

However, she was especially fitted for work there because of her Canadian citizenship and "a keen feeling to honor the Lord and represent SP to Europeans in the best possible light," according to Bernice Cory (see Appendix).

Miss Swanson set up 16 Sunday School conferences in Norway and others in England, Ireland, and Wales. As materials were used in demonstrations and conferences, the cry went up, "Where can we obtain such materials?"

The Rev. Stephen Olford, then pastor of Duke Street Baptist Church in Richmond, Surrey, England, encouraged Miss Swanson to ask the Board of Trade for permission to import sample lesson materials to England. She got a negative nod but persisted and, after further consideration, the board approved her request.

Miss Swanson then started a vigorous campaign of Sunday School conferences, pastor interviews, and teacher training sessions. Her efforts engendered interest in many to conduct an all-age Sunday School, for the entire family; to stress the Sunday School as the Bible study arm of the church; and to urge churches to supply teaching materials, instead of expecting teachers to purchase them.

First office on Upper Street

As demand for the lesson materials grew, Miss Swanson set up an office in April 1959 at 69 Upper Street, London. John Turnham joined her to serve as accountant, order filler, packer, and shipper. In 1958 the home office in Wheaton had agreed to a relationship with Norman Rich to distribute SP materials in Great Britain, but he was unable to get orders out quickly enough, and in August 1959 the London office was set up as a USA distributorship, receiving a 40 percent discount on lesson materials. But there were repeated problems getting shipments through Customs.

Lillian Swanson pictured with her brother, Earl, and David Hall.

In September 1961, Dorothy Braun, a CE teacher at The King's College, went to England to help in Sunday School conferences. She wrote from Filey, a Christian holiday conference:

"I think sales here are far surpassing those at Keswick. It is encouraging to hear the enthusiastic comments about SP products. Lillian is doing a marvelous job over here in selling people on the importance of the Sunday School and in acquainting them with SP materials."

In early 1962, the organization moved from Upper Street to larger quarters with the purchase of the building at 372 Caledonian Road, London. According to the SPF directors minutes for June 20, 1961, SPF approved $15,000 plus $300 for repairs/alterations, and VEC stated that eventually the building should be owned by a separate British foundation but until then SPF would own the building.

By January 1964, the staff had grown to include, in addition to Miss Swanson, D. Orton-Gibson, general administrator; John Turnham, accountant; Jennifer Godfree, receptionist-secretary; John Wilson, shipping and receiving manager; Victoria Lampert, church and office customer contacts; and Mrs. John Turnham, Mrs. Betty Cook, Mrs. Brenda Connah, and Michael Miller, order processors.

SPUK—a new foundation

In September 1962, SP management took steps to incorporate a foundation in Great Britain to be called Scripture Press Foundation, Ltd. (SPUK). (See Appendix.) Officially, on March 13, 1963, the British company was set up as a completely independent entity with no legal connection except as to name, management, and the purchase of materials from SP in Wheaton. The following October Lucille Nelson from the home office spent three weeks with the London staff, working on procedures and job descriptions.

About this time Victor Cory was telling SP employees in Wheaton about the booming business experienced by the London office. He reported that he had told the London office that "Wheaton is scared. Several years ago we were 200 times larger than you. Last year we were only 90 times larger. And if the present volume continues this year, we're only 65 times bigger!"

In the early '60s, Miss Swanson welcomed CE specialists from the USA, such as Dr. Bob Cook, Norman Townsend, Sherman Williams, Winona Walworth, Drs. Ed and Frances Simpson, Alf Orthner, and Marjorie Ford. In 1963 Vic and Bernice Cory, along with Stanley Mooneyham, spoke in conferences in England and Scotland, highlighted by a week at Filey, a holiday center in northern England.A. Lindsay Glegg of Kingston, Surrey, also endorsed SP in conferences. By then some 2,000 schools of many denominations were enthusiastically using SP lesson materials.

On September 13, 1963, VEC wrote back to SP as follows:

> There's a great market here in Britain for SP but "many adversaries" in the form of the prevalent practices of 1. afternoon Sunday Schools, 2. inadequate rooms and facilities, and 3. the quaint custom of teachers having to buy their own materials! But these walls are beginning to tumble, so our opportunity is great.
>
> Lillian has done a great job. We're IN here at Filey. From one to three SS conferences a day. Today is the closing day followed by two weeks of meetings in England and Scotland.

In September and October 1965, SP's Al Sedgwick joined five other guest speakers, plus Miss Swanson and three staffers in "Round Britain Conferences," to " bring skill into Sunday School." They conducted sessions in such cities as Birmingham, Bristol, and Derby in England; Glasgow, Edinburgh, and Dundee in Scotland; and Belfast and Dublin in Ireland.

Sedgwick reported that the next-to-the-last session in Belfast was something of a fizzle. "We had expected a much better turnout [than 150-175] and a more enthusiastic group in this city which is the stronghold of Protestantism in the British Isles. Some . . . felt attendance was down largely because the local organizer was a young man, a member of the Elim [Pentecostal] Church. . . . We were advised that any future conference in Belfast should be headed by a Presbyterian inasmuch as they have the greatest strength in this area." The last session held in Dublin was "by far more enthusiastic and responsive," he stated. "This was one of the best conferences of the tour, and I was grateful to wind up on such a high note."

Sedgwick's report went on to mention that "we have many very enthusiastic Christians who are completely sold on the job that Scripture Press materials are doing in their Sunday

Schools. Over and over again," his report continued, "people would get up in conferences and tell how their dying Sunday Schools have been revived and attendance increased after using SP materials. Some told of attendance doubling and some even tripling after the introduction of our materials." In one town of 3,000, 150 enrolled for a VBS and they publicized the event so well that "everybody was talking about VBS, even though many did not know what the letters stood for." Some 250 persons attended the closing program.

Criticisms were few. Some complained that the materials contained too many "Americanisms." The Rev. J.D. Pawson, an English minister who addresed a conference, estimated that only three percent of the total curriculum contained terms some British students would not understand. Staffer Graham Frost, who had studied in the U.S., had this to say to those who complained: "If you still have difficulty understanding the American expressions, ask your pupils, for they will probably know, inasmuch as they watch American TV programs." A Dutch girl at Filey pointed out that some of the artwork in SP Gospel-graphs was rather antiquated. She referred in particular to some of the women pictured with long, old-fashioned looking dresses and outdated hairdos, as well as shoes.

Beginning in December 1989, SPUK sent changes for pupil books, take-home papers through Junior age, and resource packets to Wheaton, and these products were Anglicized. However, costs became prohibitive, so in September 1994 SPUK began selling the U.S. version of the materials to keep the selling prices down.

The youth committee of the Elim Pentecostal movement asked for a confirmation in writing that nothing anti-Pentecostal would be included in SP lesson materials. But for some reason a confirmation was not given; instead an attempt was made to justify the inclusion of a paragraph by Dr. James Gray in the high school manual. This resulted in the committee refraining from recommending the acceptance of SP materials at the annual Elim conference. BTC wrote a lengthy letter of apology to J. Hywell Davies, national youth director of the movement, and painstakingly outlined "things about the Holy Spirit and His ministry that all Evangelicals agree on, no matter what our denomination" (see Appendix). Whether this reopened the door is not recorded.

In February 1972, the trustees of SPM established the Victor Cory Memorial Fund for the benefit of the ministry in Great Britain. Already, SPPI in Wheaton was subsidizing SPUK at about $10,000 annually.

Martyn White joins staff full-time

In November 1972, Martyn J. White, a man with a delightful, glowing personality who had worked part time for several years in the London office and had participated in many SP conferences, joined the staff full-time. In June 1973, SP employees pitched in to help him purchase a car, contributing a total of $1,000. By December 1973 he had put 30,000 miles on it, mostly to Sunday School conferences. In 1967, he had met Dr. Roy Zuck in Britain when Zuck was on a speaking tour, and Zuck had urged him to come to the States for study. This resulted in his coming in early 1968 to Wheaton to study at Wheaton College and Moody Bible Institute. He had married SPUK staffer Jennifer Godfree, and he and his wife lived with the Corys during the months Martyn was in school and spending time at SP. In September 1979, he became managing director of SPUK when Lillian Swanson left to become an SP consultant in western Canada.

Dedication Day, Amersham-on-the-Hill, England, November 4, 1978. Front row: Edith Ramsay, Mardelle Ayres, Martyn White. Back row: David Groom, Brian Roberts, Philip Brown, Ralph St. John, John Turnham, and John Hollington.

Earlier, in September 1978, the firm moved to a building purchased earlier in Amersham-on-the-Hill, Bucks, a suburb of London. Two months later, on November 4, the building was dedicated, with Lucille Nelson representing the home office. That December the board elected White as SPUK vice president, with David Hall as president and Wilfred Frykman as chairman.

In the early '80s, SPUK became a distributor of books published by Moody Press and NavPress. (For a chronological history summary, see Appendix.)

In discussion in July 1992, it was agreed that continued participation by council members from SP Publications created undesirable liability on the part of SPPI, as well as limits on

SPUK to move further in the direction of being an independent public charity. Therefore, the USA members resigned and SPUK added three British trustees. Martyn White became CEO and Ian Waterfield, general manager.

Effective February 14, 1996, SPUK became SP Trust, Ltd., with a new location at Triangle Business Park, Wendover Road, Stoke Mandeville, Nr. Aylesbury, Buckinghamshire, England. After White's retirement in the mid-'90s, Ian Waterfield became the chief executive.

"While all these moves have been taking place, however, some things haven't changed one bit," according to the March 1996 *European Bookstore Journal.* "The sense of ministry in the company remains the same. This is typified by the mid-morning break for Bible reading and prayer. The team believes in what they are doing. Each knows they have a part to play in the company and feel that this is what the Lord wants them to do. Prayer is vital and it is clear to any visitor that it is a happy organization. It is also easy to see why all who could have moved to the new premises. After all, it is where God wants them to be."

SP Trust merges with Valley Books

In April 1997, SP Trust merged with Valley Books to form the new company of SP/Valley. Waterfield stated soon afterward that the firm was both a "curriculum house" and distributor of books and videos. SP/Valley's association with International Films has established the firm as the leading Christian video distributor in the U.K. SP/Valley represented about a dozen American Christian publishers and Angus Hudson's Candle Books in England. The firm was an independent British limited company and a registered charity with its own board of trustees—all British.

With a different board and different management, staff changes took place in early 1997, as three senior long-term employees were laid off with two lower ranking workers. Actually, sales were sagging, and by September what had seemed serious was quickly becoming critical, according to Waterfield. By December 1997 Scripture Press had "disappeared from the British scene," as Martyn White termed it in a Christmas card to Lorraine Ackley of SP Ministries in Wheaton. On the verge of bankruptcy, SP/Valley had merged with an organization known as Send the Light.

"We did this rescue package because we believed SP/Valley was worth saving," stated Keith Danby of STL. "It added benefit to the trade; it was actually a 'dream ticket' for all concerned: for SP/Valley, SP/Valley creditors, U.S. and U.K. suppliers, and ultimately, we believed, for the U.K. trade."

Service from Aylesbury ceased in late December. The office staff, customer service, and administrative personnel were "made redundant" and offered reemployment by STL on new contracts from January 1, 1998. Ian Waterfield joined STL's executive board.

Questioned about reaction from publishers, Waterfield said everything was "overwhelmingly positive. All the SP/Valley publishers [such as Moody and Tyndale] have given wholehearted support."

Waterfield was quoted as saying, "I passionately believe the product[s] that we handle can have a life-changing impact on people, whether it's books, music or videos, or greeting cards."

SP Curriculum is now distributed through Kingsway, a Cook subsidiary.

***

If Lillian Swanson were living, her heart would be broken over what has happened to the work she started. God spared her the pain. On September 13, 1991, Lillian Swanson went to her heavenly home after a bout with cancer. In a tribute read at her funeral, Martyn White called her "a real, genuine pioneer." Following, in part, is his tribute:

> Dr. Victor Cory . . . sponsored Lillian to come to Great Britain. [In 1959] she draped a few flannelgraphs over a length of string at the Keswick Convention, she knocked on doors, made telephone calls, traveled thousands of miles by bus and train throughout the U.K. to introduce Scripture Press. Doors were closed in her face, some pastors were rude to her, others in no uncertain terms told her to go back to Canada. Lillian lived in a small rented room, she had no car, very little income. Sometimes a bowl of soup sufficed for her meal. But this splendid lady was undeterred in her calling. In fact, rejections made her more determined to champion Sunday Schools and teacher training in the U.K.

In fashioning and designing this unique woman, the Lord built in features exactly right for a pioneer. That strong jaw line—Lillian would never accept that something couldn't be done. She even removed the "im" from the impossible. God pumped into her two or three times the energy level of a normal human being. No one followed Lillian. We trailed her. He included the gifts of creativity and innovation.

Britain had never heard of Sunday School conventions and workshops and huge banners and American Sunday School materials until Lillian stepped onto our island! Lillian was a pioneer.

She wasn't easy to work with. Pioneers are often like that. Not that she was ever unchristian. It's just that we couldn't keep up with her. . . . Jennifer Godfree became her first secretary and it was through one of Lillian's training days that we met. Lillian never forgave me for taking Jennifer [away from her] to be my wife. I had to pay for it by leading conferences almost every Saturday! But Lillian encouraged me, mentored me, taught me, corrected me, motivated me.

Great Britain owes a huge debt to Lillian Swanson. Many, many thousands of churches, Sunday Schools, teachers, and children are being served today with Scripture Press Bible-based materials because of her. She laid a solid foundation for SPUK.

---

[1] See "Serving You Better . . . ," *European Christian Bookstore Journal,* December 1997, Appendix.

Scripture Press in Canada

Early in the history of Scripture Press, curriculum materials were shipped from Chicago to churches in Canada. Later, about 1956 when SP moved to Wheaton, an arrangement was made for a forwarding company in Toronto to receive materials and ship them to Canadian churches and stores. Billing and promotion were handled from the home office in Wheaton.

In 1961 a consultant's study recommended that someone, preferably a Canadian, be hired to promote SP in Canada, and on December 15 of that year Earl Swanson, brother of Lillian, became SP's man north of the border. Prior to his assuming this responsibility, he had served as a pastor and as director of Christian Education in the Christian and Missionary Alliance in both the Western District in Canada and the Central District in the U.S.

Gloria Akin, who later became Swanson's executive assistant, when Swanson became president and chief executive officer, described him as energetic, tireless, and a person with "great foresight and determination, one who accepted the challenge" of his work with a real dedication.

Besides Mrs. Akin, those initially joining the new venture were full-time employees Joyce Clarke, Olive Selby, and Betty Gabona; and part-timers Edna Swanson, Dorothy Lunney, and Verna Reimer. Gloria Akin remembers the small combination reception/office and work complex of three rooms in which sample packets were made, books sold, visitors and customers received, orders processed; also "the dark room" for photocopies, lunches eaten between phone calls, the small upstairs room acquired later for making up of displays, and the Volkswagen into and upon which display materials were heaped, and finally, as she recalled, "into which would crawl our 'fair-haired' boss."

In regard to Swanson's field work, Mrs. Akin put it in these terms: "How could we forget the many hours he traveled, the many dealer visits he made, the numerous conferences he manned? B-u-s-y! B-u-s-y days! The work," she recounted, "increased rapidly, and soon Joan Ferguson and Chesley House, our first field representative, joined the staff."

It should be mentioned that while Swanson promoted SP products for the first year, billing was still done from Wheaton, and the order fulfillment process was transferred to General Printers, Oshawa, Ontario. Soon it became obvious that the home office eventually should establish a substation in Canada, to handle all phases of the business, supplying literature for churches.

Office opened in Oshawa

In November 1962, an office was opened at 65 Simcoe Street, Oshawa, where order-clerical work was done. General Printers continued to warehouse and ship materials. Finally, on February 1, 1963, the substation became incorporated as a not-for-profit Ontario corporation called Scripture Press Foundation of Canada. In April 1965, the firm qualified as a charitable organization with the approval of the Department of National Revenue. It became active in providing tax deductible receipts for donations by Canadians to Power for Others and performed a receipting service for an array of organizations, the proceeds from this service being utilized to support a much-appreciated biennial National Christian Education Study Seminar.

The link between the Canadian foundation and SPPI, Wheaton, was in the interlocking board that included both Canadians and several senior executives of SPPI.

"It soon became evident," Gloria Akin recalls, "that a more spacious facility was needed and the first of two moves was made—first to Ajax, where we were located from 1965 to

1972, and then to our beautiful headquarters in Whitby, the fall of 1972. How unexpected was that severe snowstorm which so thoroughly wiped out most effectively our grand opening and open house in Ajax—but how delightful and successful our grand opening for our Whitby headquarters! Our dear Mrs. Cory was present, along with Mr. and Mrs. Frykman, and a host of well-wishers. A banquet, and a most successful consultants seminar (our first) were a part of this memorable occasion."

In March 1966, Floyd Neuen became the Canadian operation's first full-time salesman, and Wes Klassen was added to the sales staff in January 1967.

In February 1967, the firm received a certificate of exemption from the Department of National Revenue, Ottawa, exempting the Foundation from withholding tax on interest payable on bonds, debentures, or similar obligations issued after June 13, 1963. It also received an exemption from withholding tax on all income received in Canada.

In 1971, Beacon, a dormant subsidiary of Evangelical Publishers, with no assets, was transferred from the control of EP to the Canadian SP Foundation and renamed Beacon Distributing Ltd. In 1982, BD property and assets were sold to SPPL and became a division of SPPL. BD found a number of Christian Publishers and suppliers of other church-related products desiring its services and began to grow rapidly.

A new home in Whitby

In 1972, the firm moved to 104 Consumers Drive, Whitby, Ontario. To begin the warehousing and shipping of curriculum and related products, Joan Ferguson's husband, Gordon (Gord), came on board as warehouse manager. A number of very dedicated workers were added. Growth was enhanced greatly by the efficiency of this facet of the operation. Churches and bookstores appreciated being able to deal with one entity in Canada for all their SP needs. Gord maintained his supervision of the warehouse until Karl Gauweiler replaced him. Ferguson became inventory control officer.

At the peak of SPPL's activity in Canada, the organization had almost 100 employees who distributed SP products, along with products for 20 U.S. publishers, and operated five Christian bookstores in Toronto, Pickering, and Oshawa. For several years, Murray Tindale managed the EP bookstores and was instrumental in their becoming a major source for Christian literature in Canada's largest English speaking metropolis.

In May 1978, SPPI, Wheaton, acquired the business assets of SPF of Canada and EP, which became known as Scripture Press Publications, Ltd. As of October 1982 Beacon Distributing also became part of this organization. The move by SPPI, Wheaton, to acquire the Canadian operation came about because the IRS did not accept the nonprofit status of the work in Canada as being compatible with US laws; also heavy financial commitment to the Canadian operation by SPPI played a big part in the acquisition.

When SPPL celebrated its 25th anniversary at the Canadian CBA convention in 1988, Beacon Distributing was the largest distributor in Canada. But SPPI had serious concern about the financial status of Evangelical Publishers. Eventually, EP was sold, but the purchaser in time declared bankruptcy, and Evangelical Publishers, a Canadian institution since 1912, ceased to exist.

New facilities in Paris, near Toronto

In February 1990, SPPL moved from Whitby into new facilities in Paris, a city of about 8,000 southwest of Toronto. In November 1990 Miss Lana M. Bills was appointed to the office of president of SPPL, effective December 10, 1990. Earl Swanson, who had recommended her as his successor, received early retirement when Miss Bills took over leadership of the business. She came to the office with 15 years of experience in Christian publishing—with the Canadian Bible Society, CBA Service Corporation, and national sales manager of Word Communications, Ltd. Earl Swanson continued to work with the new president until January 1991. His retirement dinner was held on January 31, 1991.

In 1992 SPPI, Wheaton, began to pull back from its distribution interests in Canada, to focus on curriculum sales. Miss Bills resigned in August 1992. Large debts had piled up, and as a cost-saving move in 1994, SPPI sold the assets of Beacon Distributing, Ltd. to David C. Cook Publishing Company. In 1994, Cook bought the SPPL building in Paris, and SPPL leased a new office and warehouse space in Paris. Rod Toews took over the marketing of SP curriculum, with finance and operations managed from Wheaton by Curtis Henrickson. As a subsidiary of SPPI, SPPL was included in the sale of SPPI to Cook in February 1996.

Today, Cook aggressively markets SP curriculum from its Paris plant, and Beacon Distributing is recognized as a significant and growing distribution agency for Christian literature in Canada.

CHAPTER 16

The Third Decade in Wheaton

1977–1986

IT ALL HAPPENED IN 1977: Jimmy Carter became the 39th president, and Walter F. Mondale took the oath as vice president. Elvis Presley died on August 16 in Memphis at the age of 42 of "cardiac arrhythmia," according to the official announcement. And on September 19, Jackie Onassis received $20 million in a settlement with her late husband's daughter in return for abandoning all further claims to his estate.

President Jimmy Carter

At SP in January 1977, Bernice Bosmann retired after 32 years of service in several departments. She was especially known for her faithfulness. A small woman, she arose each morning at 3:30 and left at 4:30 from her home in Evergreen Park. She was always one of the first to arrive at SP, having used three transportation systems. To her, a 6 p.m. arrival time back home was a "good" trip.

Also admired for her faithfulness and travel distance in getting to work is Lorraine Ackley, who began at SP in January 1958. Till her retirement in late 1998, this Joliet resident drove daily to work and back home, a 51-mile round trip. She drove some 12,500 miles annually, sometimes in rain and snow, as many as 500,000 miles in 40 years—or about 20 times around the world!—in the nearly 40 years that she worked. Lorraine drove a dozen different cars and had only three accidents with property damage but, thankfully, suffered no injuries.

On February 18, SP entered into a contract with the Association for Bible Curriculum Development to revise and produce their Bible curriculum for Christian schools, the beginning of SP's LifeWay series. (In 1988 ABCD was dissolved.)

A new step.

Continuing a tradition they started, Mary and Carl Barbour in February again prepared a valentine box and placed it in the lunchroom so employees could give valentines to special friends.

Also in February, Will Frykman left for Europe. On his first stop, he contacted publishers in The Netherlands about translating SP materials into Dutch. He later attended the Christian Booksellers convention in London and conferred with leaders at SPUK. On Sunday, February 27, some 300 persons visited SP to greet the company's new president, David Hall, and Board Chairman Frykman. Hall was presented a specially designed and inscribed Bible, and Frykman received a portrait of himself that today is displayed in SPM's Heritage Room.

In March, Peggy Grow joined the sales staff. She was to later work in other departments, ending her employment in 1997 as secretary in the Victor Books Division.

In May, 524 readers of *Counselor* indicated they wanted to receive Christ, after reading a story entitled "Run-in with the Law" that ended with an invitation to come to the Savior.

In September, Lucille Nelson was honored for her 30 years of service. She began work on September 23, 1947 as secretary to founding president, Vic Cory, and later moved to other key positions.

October brought together 15 charter members of SP's Quarter Century Club: Louise Rodman, Clara Sander, Bernice Bosmann, Lloyd Siegfried, Gladys Halleen, Vic Anderson, Jim Adair, Bessie Butler, Elaine Springborn Grimm, Lucille Nelson, Audrey Blake, Lloyd Cory, Gertrude Bowe, Stella Miles, and Willis Grimm. Two additional members, Tallie Kohler and Marie Friesen, could not attend. A total of 526 years were represented by the 17 employees. They were guests at the Alumni Day luncheon at Indian Lakes Country Club.

In November, Ray Bradshaw and Curt Henrickson became vice presidents. Bill Hall, 69, former vp of Production, passed away on November 18 at the Boca Raton (Florida) Community Hospital. The funeral was in Wheaton.

New LifeWay materials for sixth-graders in Christian schools were available for the fall of 1977.

Also in 1977, Victor Books moved to the east wing (formerly Rooms 3 and 4) furnished with Westinghouse modular furniture. The Victor Books area became part of the president's team. Coffee went up to 15 cents. And Christmas Eve became a no-work holiday.

1978

On February 8, 1978, SPM trustees authorized purchase of The Christian Centre in Amersham-on-the-Hill, Bucks, England, for $48,500 (U.S.) and a lease agreement with SPF (U.K.) Ltd. In May, trustees authorized purchase of a building at 646 East Roosevelt Road, Glen Ellyn for relocating the SP bookstore but the purchase never materialized.

In June, Dr. Welsey R. Willis became executive vice president of SPM. He came from Fort Wayne Bible College, where he served as academic dean.

Gladys Siegfried Halleen retired in late August after 39 years and five months. She had held many jobs and at the time of her retirement was advertising manager. In September Lloyd Cory marked 30 years with SP.

In November, SPM trustees elected Dave Hall to succeed Will Frykman as president. John Walvoord became chairman of the SPPI board. In Canada, Dave Hall became chairman of the Canadian board; Murray Tindale, vp; and Lucille Nelson, secretary.

Also in 1978, Bill McVey began a graphics review of curriculum. The product planning function was restructured from Product Management Workteams to Product Planning Workteam (PPW) for policy decisions, Product Approval Workteam (PAW) for cost/pricing recommendations, and Product Scheduling. The No-Name Workteam was given responsibility for products 0-5 and 7; Victor Books for product line 6; and Marketing for product line 8. Jim Markle became advertising manager.

1979

Lorraine Ackley began January 1979 with new responsibilities as CE consultant in the Market Planning area, replacing Winona Walworth, who had retired and later became a home missionary in Arkansas. Lorraine continued as corporate secretary. Ralph Wetherbee became acting national sales manager (in May he became official sales manager). Vic Anderson, Production Department manager, was honored for 35 years of service.

In March, Mavis Sanders came aboard as public relations administrator in the Advertising and Sales Promotion Department. Formerly, she had served on the staffs of *Decision* and CBA and most recently had been assistant to astronaut Jim Irwin, president of High Flight, Colorado Springs.

In May, Bob Messner and LeRoy Scudder became field sales managers. Mary Roof retired after 11 plus years from the Credit Department. Former Personnel director Dale Chaddock died after a lengthy illness.

In early August, SPers said good-bye to Bob and Geri Schaub. Bob had come to SP in 1960 a year after Geri had begun working at SP, but left to work at Sears in Glen Ellyn, then rejoined SP in 1968. He managed B & G. Geri had served as Lloyd Cory's secretary.

October saw David Hall elected president of the Evangelical Christian Publishers Association. And in November Will Frykman was named chairman of the board of SPPI, effective January 1, 1980. He served as chairman for nine and a half years.

1980

Joyce Gibson became January 1980 employee of the month, and her name joined that of Stella Miles on a plaque that went on display in the main lobby a month earlier. In February, Rodney McClelland was honored; Stan Michalski, April; Harriet Salios, May; Lorraine Ackley, June. The honors were passed on from month to month. Each honoree got a special parking spot for the month, dinner for two at the Hamlet, one paid day off, a personal portrait, and a special plaque.

Also, Wes Mills, a former Spiegle executive, resigned from the SPM and SPPI boards in January because of ill health. He died in November 1981.

In May, Wes Willis was named vice president of the

Editorial Division, and Jim Kovalik replaced him as executive director of SPM. Lloyd Cory moved to a new role as an editor-at-large, assisting with editorial projects for both the curriculum and books areas.

In June, Audrey Blake retired after 32 years in Merchandise Handling and the Order Department.

In August, SPPI acquired the assets of the Baptist Literature Board in lieu of foreclosure, plus liabilities, and formed a wholly owned for-profit Delaware subsidiary with the same corporate name. (See chapter 19.) Also in August Al and June Cronk said good-bye after serving 23 years each. Al served in Merchandise Handling, Production, and the bookstore, while June worked in the Order Clerical Department, finishing as manager.

Talking with the manager of the New Wine Bookstore in Dundalk, Maryland in October, Myrtle Bina heard, ". . .we're being robbed!" and the phone went dead. Quick-thinking Ruth Shrigley called the police in Dundalk and learned later that the police arrested the robber just down the road.

In December, Ed Kitch became head of SP's new research Department, aided by Mary Barbour and Donna Hatfield.

1981

January 22, 1981 was Evelyn Christenson Day in Wheaton, proclaimed so by Wheaton Mayor Barger. The author of SP's first book to reach one million copies was presented with a leather-bound copy of *What Happens When Women Pray* by Dave Hall, who announced the establishment of a scholarship by SP in Evelyn's honor at Bethel College.

In February, *The Success Fantasy,* a Victor book by Tony Campolo, was named "Best of the Year" for 1980 by Group in Loveland, Colorado. Ginnie Adair had known Tony when she lived in Philadelphia and introduced Jim to him while on vacation in Ocean City, New Jersey, at which time Tony agreed to write a book for Victor. Also in February, Ruth Blair, assistant graphic arts buyer, joined the Quarter Century Club.

On May 18, SPPI directors adopted an Employee Stock Ownership Plan (ESOP) and Trust Agreement qualifying as a stock bonus plan, effective October 1, 1980. In addition to SPPI employees, SPM and Baptist Literature Board employees were also designated as participants in the program.

On May 26, employees began "flextime," permitting them to come early and leave early. This arrangement lasted until early fall and remained in effect during summer months until SP closed in 1996.

June marked 35 years for both Vic Anderson and Bessie Butler.

July brought about the completion of the installation of the newly purchased computerized Rolm phone system, replacing the 23-year-old Bell system. Announcement was made that a new workteam would be formed to coordinate and administer the ten-year-old SP Employee Participation Plan, replacing the SPEPP Central and Advisory Workteams. Marilyn Schaer would head up the committee consisting of eight other members. In October the following were chosen: Ray Bradshaw, Rosalie Bromann, Gene Geoffrion, Mike Kiss, John Litz, Fran Martin, Betty Riley, and Dan Tillman.

Jim Lemon, vp of Marketing, announced that he had submitted his resignation and would leave SP on August 14. He had worked for the firm for 15 years. He began a successful franchise bookstore business known as Lemstone, Inc. and in 1998 counted some 80 stores under the Lemstone umbrella. Gerald Wit replaced him on December 1, 1981. He had been a toy buyer for Marshall Field's.

On Tuesday morning, September 8, Gil Beers spoke in chapel and afterward autographed copies of his new *Victor Handbook of Bible Knowledge,* the largest project in terms of cost that Victor had published to date. Later in the month the Beers family and SPers were saddened at the death of Douglas Beers, the son of Gil and Arlie, following an auto accident.

On November 7, Margaret Frykman, wife of Will, went to be with the Lord. On November 9, Victor Books author Warren Wiersbe, with his wife, Betty, joined SPers in chapel as he was honored for the publication of more than a million copies of his "Be" books. The tenth, *Be Confident,* was about to go to press. There were smiles for Stella Miles as she was honored in chapel for 30 years of service. She had served at the switchboard since 1965. Elaine Grimm, assistant to Ray Bradshaw, was honored for 35 years of service.

Curt Henrickson and Wesley Willis were elected senior vice presidents at a meeting of the board of SPPI in November. President Hall stated that as a result of these changes, responsibility for operational decisions would be in the appropriate divisions, with the Executive Workteam dealing primarily with policy and planning. Hall said he would be giving greater attention to SP's long-range plans and to SP's subsidiaries. These new responsibilities were to become effective on January 1, 1982 and would result in much traveling. In December, Art Saul, who began with SP in 1956, announced he would leave in early 1982 to teach at Sacramento Bible Institute.

Also in 1981, an all-new five-day VBS course was introduced.

1982

In March, President Hall returned from a trip that took him to Canada for a long-range planning conference, England to visit SPUK, and The Netherlands to discuss translation matters. SPers were saddened to learn of the death of Don and Rita Crawford's 19-year-old daughter, Peg, found in 20 feet of water in the Loch Ness River in Scotland. She had finished an exchange program at Trinity University in Wales and was about to return home.

On June 1, Stella Miles retired from the switchboard after 30 years as an SPer, and Mary and Carl Barbour (Editorial and B & G, respectively) said good-bye after ten years and headed back to Pennsylvania. Vic Anderson, Production Department head, was honored in late June as he retired after 38 years.

Victor Books received recognition in the ECPA-sponsored Gold Medallion Book Awards competition in July. *Gaining through Losing* by Evelyn Christenson was the winner in the Inspirational/Devotional category, and *How to Really Love Your Child* by Dr. Ross Campbell in the Outreach category. Also in July, the Data Processing Department hosted a potluck luncheon honoring Bessie Butler, who was retiring after 36 years of service.

President Hall launched a series of informational luncheon meetings with employees in September, meeting first with Editorial and Victor Books Divisions.

One of SP's original writers, Mary LeBar, died on Sunday morning, October 3, in Mesa Verde, Colorado. She and Dr. Lois LeBar, her sister, had conducted workshops in Missouri and were en route to California. Mary wrote Beginner (Pre-primary) lessons that started in October 1938. She also wrote

Patty Goes to the Nursery Class (for 2s and 3s), that went on sale in 1948. This project was adapted from her thesis for her master's degree. She then wrote eight Pattibooks to accompany the course. She also wrote a number of other SP books. She and Lois were Wheaton College CE professors for many years. After retiring, they taught CE around the U.S., in Africa, and elsewhere. Lloyd Cory represented SP at a memorial service at Shell Point Village, Florida, the LeBars' home.

(Dr. Lois LeBar died on August 30, 1997, following a long illness.)

Also in 1982, SP discontinued publishing VBS materials, and text-editing equipment was leased to reduce typesetting and alteration costs and provide greater efficiency.

"The Lord gave the Word: great was the company of those that published it" (Psalm 68:11). SPers in 1983. (Photo by Dick Olson)

1983

On January 6, 1983, Lorraine Ackley joined SP's Quarter Century Club. Friends in Marketing, the Executive Workteam, and members of the Club honored her at a luncheon. The first of SP's take-home papers, *Power (Power for Living* and *Teen Power)* crossed the 40-year mark in January. Grace Fox Anderson, managing editor of *Counselor,* became the first employee to receive the new Outstanding Service Award. She not only maintained the schedule and quality of *Counselor* but took on the additional responsibilities necessary to meet *Teen Power* schedules, resulting in both cost and time savings.

She received a framed certificate, photo, a special parking spot, gift certificate for dinner at The Hamlet, and a day off with pay. The award replaced the Employee of the Month award. Jan Arroyo was the second employee to be honored.

February saw the departure of Elaine and Willis Grimm, who combined almost 68 years of service at SP. Elaine (a.k.a. Sally) came in 1946 from La Salle, Illinois and made her mark in the Finance Division. Willis joined the Marketing Division in 1952 and became a mainstay. They were married in November 1963. He was a favorite chapel speaker. They were honored at a breakfast at Indian Lakes Resort by the Marketing and Finance Divisions.

In March, Dave Hall, along with Wes Willis, was off again for Europe, to touch base with SPUK and visit translators in Belgium and The Netherlands.

May brought more honors to SP's Sunday School papers. Both *FreeWay* and *Counselor* received awards of Excellence at the EPA convention in Minneapolis.

In September, announcement came stating that SP's ESOP would become a "PAYSOP," according to a change in tax laws. SP would receive an additional tax credit for contributions made to the ESOP over the next five years. ESOP participants would receive a new benefit from PAYSOP contributions.

Doris Eckert, supervisor in the Office Services area, retired to Hot Springs Village, Arkansas after nearly 26 years on the job.

President Hall announced in November that Mark Sweeney had been promoted to vice president of the Victor Books Division and that Gerald Wit had been named vice president of the Marketing Division. "They will continue to fill a vital role as we move ahead into our 50th year of publishing," Hall said.

Longtime employee Ruth Camp Reid, managing editor the Nursery Department, retired in December after 31 years of service that began in 1945. Part of the time she worked as a free-lancer out of Wichita, Kansas, returning to SP as executive secretary to BTC, and then Nursery editor.

Also in 1983, Sunday School Papers editors began reporting to curriculum editors, to correlate papers more closely with lessons.

1984

Joyce Gibson received a certificate of membership in the Quarter Century Club on June 22, 1984. She began her work at SP on June 29, 1959 as secretary to BTC and later was promoted several times and had become Junior/LifeWay director.

During the summer the SP building received a new roof, after 28 years, suggesting that if the new one lasts as long, the second re-roofing would come in 2012.

In November, Helen Gorges was appointed administrative director of SPM, replacing Jim Kovalik. SPPI President Hall, it was announced, would take an active role in program development, policy decisions, and long-range planning for SPM.

Fiftieth anniversary banquet program listing names of employees working for the company in 1984.

Serving Together

35 or over
James Adair
Lloyd Cory

30 or over
Olga Kononowa

25 or over
Lorraine Ackley
Olive Blackman
Ruth Blair
Ruth Cornelius

20 or over
Margaret Berg
Phil DiCicco
Joyce Gibson
Helen Gorges
David Hall
Curt Henrickson
Crystal Knosp
Martha Lincoln
Beth McDaniel
Sam Postlewaite
Marilyn Schaer

15 or over
Grace Anderson
Ray Bradshaw
Marilyn Dunn
David Hurst
Darrell Johnson
Rod McClelland
Stan Michalski
Floyd Neuen
Sharon Noble
Ruby Nordtomme
Ruth Shrigley
Corinne Strating

10 or Over
Alan Addy
Cherilyn Addy
Chris Balsano
Scott Barngrover
Joyce Benson
Don Bovey
Marian Clark
Don Crawford
Wayne Eklund
Norma Felske
David Frykholm
Eleanor Hance
Myrna Hasse
Ardith Hooten
Anne Johnson
Leroy Kloese
Judy Kovalik
Louis Mackaben
Evelyn Mackaben
Beth McCulla
Dorothy Myrick
Leroy Scudder
Dan Tillman
Ralph Wetherbee
Don Williams

5 or Over
Jan Arroyo
Priscilla Behrens
Keith Binkley
Penny Bredemeier
Rosalie Bromann
Holly Combs
Becky Dodson
Gary Domzalski
Jan French
Rick French
Paula Gulbrandsen
Donna Hatfield
Roger Heasley
Betty Holcomb
Levia Holcombe
Gladys Holland
Roy Irving
Tish Jepsen
Esther Kammerling
Barbara Keeney
Mike Kiss
James Kovalik
Eleanor Kraus
Pat Kutilek
Don Lomasney
Jim Markle
Gloria Martin
Rita Matthews
Doyle McDaniel
Robert Messner
Thelma Neuen
Ida Newton
Larry Novak
Tom Ollendorf
Richard Olson
Pam Rhoads
Fran Romack
Margaret Roshko
Harriet Salios
Mavis Sanders
Pat Slater
B.J. Slinger
Robin Slinger
Gundel Sprouse
Carole Streeter
Lee Suderman
Guinevere Svoboda
Lillian Tanner
Marguerite Thompson
David Tilson
Lois Tuck
Mary Tucker
Joanne Willanger
Barb Williams
Wes Willis

5 Years or Less
Faith Aeilts
William Anderson
Cynthia Atoji
Mardelle Ayres
Bill Bauske
Cheryl Beeman
Kerry Binkley
Arthur Blakely
Patricia Bryda
Pam Campbell
Stanton Campbell
Doris Chase
Carol Ciezadlo
Greg Clouse
Douglas Crawford
Barbara Dowell
John Duckworth
Gary Duff
Victor Erickson
Jane Farnham
Timothy Fix
Mark Folkerts
Beth Funk
Christopher Grant
Priscilla Greene
Margaret Grow
Dorcas Hamilton
Lori Hart
Elizabeth Hartley
Kenneth Hawley
Joni Henderson
Paul Higdon
Dorothy Hoffer
Christine Hoffman
Bruce Holstrom
Marilyn Hoyt
Dorothy Hraback
Ricky Hudgens
Candace Johnson
Eileen Johnson
Elmer Johnson
Stephen Johnson
Steven Johnson
Dora Karwoski
Susan Larson
Ronnie Lee
Laura Le Gear
Laurie Loftin
Randy Maid
Donna Manning
Frances Martin
Kathy Martin
Brian McRae
Deloris Niedfeldt
Keith Ovitt
Susan Payne
Robert Perrone
Joel Peterson
Kathryn Powell
Sharon Quiggle
Dorit Radandt
Mary Radcliff
Patricia Rader
Jean Ramsey
Ronald Ramsey
Brenda Reiskytl
James Rew
Janet Ryker
David Salzmann
Jacqueline Schmidt
Kenneth Schroeder
Heidi Seabloom
Ronald Semran
Sandra Sepanski
Thomas Shaw
Eleanor Shell
Elizabeth Sheveland
Thomas Shumaker
Judith Simcox
Celette Skinner
Pat Skorburg
Richard Smith
Julia Snowdon
Lawrence Snyder
Joan Sohn
Sally Sorrill
David Souders
Noel Southard
Farrel Stauffer
Gordon Stevens
Sherryl Street
Mark Sweeney
Karen Talbot
Carolyn Thayer
Jeffrey Wahrman
Karen Walker
Douglas Walton
Louise Webster
Beth Wells
Juli Wesolek
Tom Wesolek
Rachel Wetzler
Shirley Wiley
Maude Williams
Halbert Wilson
Gerald Wit
Virginia Zick

1985

In February, SPPL sold its EP Film Service Division for $27,750 (Canadian) effective January 31, 1985; there were no acceptable offers at that point for the EP stores. Also Olive Blackman retired after 30 plus years, the last 19 of which she served in Payroll and Employee Benefits.

June found Lorraine Ackley being honored for the second time for outstanding service. In 1980 she had been honored as Employee of the Month, and five years later given the Outstanding Service Award. She began in January 1958 as a senior administrative secretary and in 1985 was marketing services manager. As one fellow employee said of Lorraine, "Her efficiency in handling details is something to behold! Her love for the Lord and dedication to SP over these many years is worthy of the award."

In July, Jim Adair was honored as the first SP employee to reach the 40-year milestone. President Hall spoke of his vision for the take-home papers line and for the establishment of Victor Books and presented him with a cash award of $750. Family members and friends gathered at Stouffers in Oak Brook to pay special tribute.

In August, Helen Gorges was honored as she joined the Quarter Century Club.

On September 26, Lloyd Cory celebrated the day he had been waiting for, according to *Spotlight*—his retirement. In a chapel program, it was recalled that he began working as a youngster for SP without pay, then at 12 cents an hour, but officially began as editorial production manager in 1948. For many years he served as a vice president, managing the Editorial Division. To start the celebration, Mark Sweeney and Jim Adair spoke of their appreciation for Lloyd, both as a worker and friend. President Hall presented him with a Sears gift certificate to buy a gasoline chain saw, to be used for firewood in Hot Springs Village, Arkansas, where he and his wife, Lois, would live.

To be in keeping with the times, the Personnel Department got a new name in October: Human Resources Department.

Margaret Armstrong Berg, administrative secretary, Victor Books, joined the Quarter Century Club in December, having come to SP from Ohio in 1960 after responding to an ad in a

Power take-home paper. She began in the Order Clerical Department, served as secretary to Bill Hall, then in 1971 moved to Sunday School Papers and later to Victor Books.

1986

Ruth Blair marked 30 years on the job in February 1986. She first worked as an order reader and more recently had taken on the responsibilities of purchasing secretary.

In March, Julie Walker returned as receptionist. She came to SP in 1956, then later served for 13 years as a missionary with the C&MA in Japan and Irian Jaya.

In May, *FreeWay* won the EPA Award of Excellence in the Sunday School Take Home category and was also cited as "Most Improved" at the EPA convention in Seattle. Mavis Sanders was "day chair" on Tuesday of the convention and was again named to the EPA board.

In June, Phil DiCicco, who came as a part-time Elliott machine operator in 1956 and continued in a variety of positions until 1961 when he became a full-timer as area supervisor of Mailing List, became a member of the Quarter Century Club.

At the CBA convention in July in Washington, D.C., SP won two first-place plaques for advertising promotional aids: Best Self-Mailer and Best Statement Enclosure. Ron Ramsey received the plaques. Ramsey was promoted to national sales director in September.

Also in September, Data Processing said good-bye to Martha Lincoln after 23 years at SP, and in October Marketing bade farewell to two high-profile employees, Art Blakely and Bob Messner (in January 1998, Bob, a pastor in Akron, Ohio, died following a massive heart attack).

Also in October, Curt Henrickson celebrated 25 continuous years with SP. He began working at the Lighthouse Christian Bookstore in California in 1960, became Long Beach shipping supervisor in 1961, and later returned to Wheaton as Order Processing manager. He became a senior vice president, as noted earlier, in 1980.

On Saturday night, December 6, SPPL (Canada) held its annual Christmas banquet. Earl Swanson was honored for 25 years of faithful service.

Teaching Materials for Urban America

ON FEBRUARY 17, 1964 SP welcomed Melvin Banks as a field representative in the Retail Distribution Department to specialize in service and sales contacts with African-American churches and denominations across the U.S. A graduate of Moody Bible Institute, Mel had gone on to Wheaton College, where he received both his undergraduate and graduate degrees. In the early '90s he was given an honorary doctorate by Wheaton College.

UMI CEO Melvin E. Banks, whose inner city literature ministry began at SP.

As the years passed, Mel and SP management talked about the need for teaching materials especially written and designed for urban blacks. SP leaders concurred with Mel that a new company should be established for publishing this material. In 1970 a board of directors was selected and Urban Ministries, Inc. was born. The new board consisted of Tom Skinner, a black evangelist who had been a gang leader in New York's Harlem district; Dr. Harold Garnes, chief surgeon at Harlem Hospital; Dr. Wilbur N. Daniel, pastor of Antioch Baptist Church, Chicago; Richard Linyard, vice president of Seaway National Bank, Chicago; Ozzie Edwards, Stanley Long, Charles Butler, Carl J. Wright, and SP's Wilfred Frykman, Jim Lemon, and David Hall. Bill Hall helped with the details of organizing and the production of new products.

It was all a boyhood dream of Mel's. As a boy of 12, he had received Christ as his Savior. Soon afterward he gave his testimony in a church on one of the back roads of Birmingham, Alabama. An elderly, white-haired black man heard Mel's testimony and quoted this Scripture to him: "My people are destroyed for lack of knowledge" (Hosea 4:6). The verse made a great impression on Mel, and he determined to yield himself to God so that he could be used to help bring the knowledge of His word to blacks.

With SP backing the new ministry, Mel began searching for an editor. At the suggestion of a mutual friend, he contacted Henry Soles, an African-American and a newspaper reporter from Scotch Plains, New Jersey. Henry had recently been offered a job as public relations director for the New Jersey Symphony Orchestra; it paid more than SP could offer but involved Sunday work, which was not to Henry's liking. With a heart for the work Mel had described to him, Henry accepted the Wheaton job, came as editor, and worked for about seven years, eventually becoming director of publications. Today Soles has a ministry of his own, including serving as chaplain for the Chicago Bulls.

First publications appeared in January 1971

The first publications, *Inteen* magazine and *Inteen Teacher,* were introduced in January 1971. Inteen received recognition as the magazine of the year in its category at the 1971 Evangelical Press Association convention.

Early UMI materials for African-Americans.

In 1971, Urban Ministries introduced *Direction,* followed by *Juniorway* in 1973, *Primary Street* in 1975, *Preschool Playhouse* and Vacation Bible School materials in 1980 and *Young Adult Today* in 1986.

Initially, all work was done at SP in Wheaton at SP's expense, but eventually UMI moved its operations to the Banks home and assumed responsibility for operating costs. In 1982 the publishing firm leased space on the second floor of 1439 W. 103rd Street, Chicago. In 1985 UMI expanded its operation to include the first floor of the 1439 building. In 1990 UMI moved to 1350 W. 103rd Street. In 1996 the firm moved into a brand new home at 1551 W. Regency Court in Calumet City.

Ever-increasing sales have been characteristic of UMI since its inception, CEO Banks reports. By 1998 the firm was serving well over 50,000 Sunday School teachers in the U.S., Haiti, Bahamas, and Nigeria. UMI, "The African American Christian Publishing & Communications Co.," has studied its market carefully to insure that the products and services offered to urban America churches are those desired by its audience. The firm now distributes through denominational publishing houses, scores of bookstores across the U.S. and through its sales forces consisting of telemarketing and field sales personnel.

In 1988, UMI developed a video/film division. Also UMI has Bible Application manuals, a series of leadership training books for use by lay persons within the church.

UMI employs 72 workers

In 1997, UMI employed 72 full-time and part-time employees. "UMI's management philosophy prompts us to develop our employees for increased responsibilities and to enlist their participation in most areas of the company's operation," according to Mel Banks. "In such a participative management style, building trust, loyalty and confidence is essential for both management and employees.

"The vision of a company where committed Christians can devote themselves to preparation of Christ-centered resources continues to grow as we minister to African-Americans. We are challenged to reach every black Christian church with Christian education products and services," he continues. "In accomplishing this mission, we recognize our responsibility to our Lord, employees, customers, community, and society at large."

Mel's son Reginald serves as manager for VBS products. His son Mel, Jr. left UMI in the mid-'90s and began a firm in Atlanta that publishes Bibles and other material for much the same market UMI reaches.

Ventures into Book Publishing

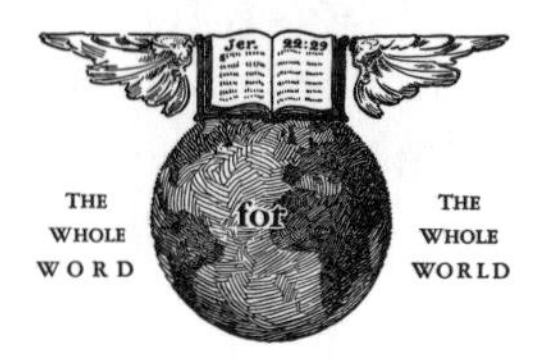

With his burning desire to get out "the whole Word to the whole world," Vic Cory, while at 800 North Clark Street, began a separate business to publish books by Bible teacher Dr. William R. Newell, as mentioned earlier. Under the label "Grace Publications," with a 100 West Chicago Avenue address, he published several books, including *Romans Verse by Verse* and *Revelation Verse by Verse*. This venture probably lasted till the mid-'40s, for Moody Press published Newell's *Hebrews Verse by Verse* in 1947, after taking over publication of the previously mentioned books. Cory's venture, not intended to be profitable, made the rich teaching of Newell available to believers thirsting for a greater grasp of God's Word. VEC took great delight in this.

The 1950s venture

In 1954 Scripture Press ventured into book publishing, hiring Henry Stair in April as editor, under Laurin Zorn, head of the Wholesale-Book Department. Zorn had directed Van Kampen Press before returning to Scripture Press in his marketing capacity. Stair came with 14 years' experience in Christian publishing, and spent the previous eight years as an editor at Van Kampen Press. SP published the first books in this venture in November 1954: *Man-eaters Don't Knock* and *Man-eaters and Masai Spears,* both $1 books by Charles Ludwig.

When Van Kampen Press went out of business in 1955, "Scripture Press took a big step toward becoming a major factor in the book publishing field," according to *Spotlight* for April 1, 1955, taking over 59 titles from the Van Kampen Press line. They included 19 titles authored by Paul Hutchens, 11 of them the latest "Sugar Creek Gang" books. Also there were six titles by Dr. V. Raymond Edman, president of Wheaton College, among them *Disciplines of Life* and *Delights of Life;* two titles by Dr. Merrill F. Unger, *Biblical Demonology* and *The Baptizing Work of the Holy Spirit;* Dr. Joseph Free's *Archaeology and Bible History;* Jim Adair's first book, *Saints Alive;* titles by such authors as Bernard Palmer, E. Myers Harrison, Dorthy Grunbock Johnston, and Craig Massey; and 26 titles by Dr. William R. Orr (32-page "Christian Guidance Books" on various impulse topics such as *The Key to Success* in the *Christian Life, How to Pray and Get the Answer,* and *How to Know the Will of God for Your Life).*

Lucille Nelson, who served in various key spots, tried several times to encourage management to add more adult books to its book program, but sensed a reluctance at higher levels for the company to become involved with authors who might be out of step with the "SP Flavor." Later, SP did several adult titles, including Roy Zuck's *The Holy Spirit in Your Teaching* and *Creative Counseling for Christian Camps* by Joy Mackay. Jim Adair recalls conversations with VEC probably in the mid-'60s who seemed warm to the idea of publishing a book by Edith Schaeffer when the name Francis Schaeffer was becoming widely known, but no move was made. It was the story of L'Abri, the ministry of Dr. Schaeffer in Switzerland, and how it got started. Until Victor Books began, SP, under the guidance of Bernice Cory, focused on children's books and resource books for teachers, including Children's Educational Books (per catalog) by such authors as Dr. Mary LeBar and Ruth McNaughton Hinds (in the 1950s & '60s, "Pattibooks," "Tiny Thoughts Books," "Learning Books," "Tiny Doings Books," and "Tiny Question Books"). SP did publish at least two adult books in the early '60s: *The Bible and Tomorrow's News* by Charles Ryrie and *Build a Happy Home with Discipline* by Henry Brandt and Homer Dowdy.

Adult electives trigger start of Victor Books

By the mid-'60s Stair had departed, and SP had disposed of most of the Van Kampen books. The company was virtually out of book publishing. Then management took notice of the fact Sunday Schools across the country were using books as adult electives. Gospel Light, under the Regal label, was publishing elective paperbacks and doing well. Scripture Press saw an opportunity and published several paperbacks in the late '60s and early '70s especially for use as Adult Vacation Bible School electives, including Paul Little's *Know What You Believe* and *Know Why You Believe* (both more than half a million in sales). Henry Jacobsen, SP adult curriculum editor, was responsible for these books. He himself wrote a book titled *The Good Life,* on the Epistle of James.

As early as March 1967, interest was building toward accelerating SP's book program. In an Executive Committee meeting, Jim Lemon, SP's marketing vp, gave some highlights of a conversation that he, Adair, and Lloyd Cory had had with Bob DeVries, editor of Moody Press.

SP Board minutes in April 1968[1] included reference to VEC's interest in developing a book publishing program in the paperback field. "Preliminary planning is underway with implementation contingent on staff and finances," the minutes stated.

Early Victor electives.

Executive Committee minutes for November 11, 1968 stated: "Question was raised if budget should take into consideration our launching into books. David Hall said we need to look at the total picture—books, new products, all of it—and then determine where the money available for R&D should be spent for the best return. . . . It was suggested that Lloyd Cory's editorial budget include books. A question was raised if we could afford to produce six titles during 1969. William Hall said to figure production costs at 10¢ a copy. Some consideration has been given to the categories of books we should produce, such as popular and electives, programs, and CE books, children's books. We should start with the highest potential volume titles. Release date should be CBA in 1969 as this is the best time to make quick sales."

The November 18, 1968 Executive Committee minutes stated: "The six titles a year mentioned in last week's notes refers to paperbacks similar to the Regal series. These would be over and above the present number and type of books being published."

Minutes well into 1971 continued to include mention of an accelerated book program, finding funds, and hiring a full-time editor. There was talk in Executive Committee meetings about trying to "hire a high-caliber person . . . as book editor" to be an area director reporting to Lloyd Cory, or as a division director reporting to the president. The minutes went on: "It was the consensus it would be better to hire a high-caliber person who knows the book field than to take a man who would require training."

On the side, there was talk of trying to hire Bob DeVries, but the Executive Committee finally settled on Adair and Stan Baldwin, according to Lloyd Cory's board report for July-September 1971. Adair and Baldwin, "SS people, are slotting portions of their time for [books]," the report stated. Adair, who had written several books, became editorial director of the new department. The report indicated that the department would produce as many as 20 32-page paperbacks, 4 adult elective paperbacks, plus leader's guides, 1 adult VBS paperback, plus a leader's guide, and 2 "special" popular paperbacks.

Lloyd Cory's board report for October 1971-January 1972 stated that "Victor Books is shifting into second gear. For CBA this summer we'll also have 9 32-pagers and a 64-pager."

The name *Victor Books,* honoring SP's respected founder, Victor Cory, was suggested by then Sunday School papers editor Bill Krutza.

The first books under the Victor label began appearing in 1972. The plan called for developing electives and popular titles in the 32-page series in the genre of William Orr paperbacks. Victor continued to publish such new Orr titles as How to *Keep Your Wife Happy, Are Demons for Real?*, and *How to Get Along with Your Teens.* Leader's guides were developed for such existing books as Paul Little's *Know What You Believe* and *Know Why You Believe.*

The Victor Books program did not start with much fanfare. SP's catalogs for 1972 and 1973 included only low-key mention of the electives.

Some highlights of the early Victor years

Warren Wiersbe wrote *Be Real* (1972) at the invitation of Henry Jacobsen, for use primarily as a VBS elective study. He had preached a series on 1 John and agreed to write the book because it wouldn't be a difficult task. "If Henry had asked me to do Ezekiel or a book I had not preached on, we would have had a problem," Wiersbe recalls. The original title of the completed manuscript was "On Being a Real Christian," but Jacobsen or someone else hit on the title *Be Real* (350,000). Harry Emerson Fosdick and another author, it was discovered, had books with Wiersbe's original title or something similar. Adair encouraged Wiersbe to continue with another "Be" book, resulting in the second, *Be Joyful* (500,000), in 1974. Little did anyone then guess that the series would continue, until today the "Be" books cover all of the New Testament and more than a dozen books of the Old Testament.

Evelyn Christenson got her start with Victor Books when Jim Lemon dropped some audio cassette tapes on Adair's desk and asked him to listen to them, to determine if their subject matter would make a book. Adair liked the idea and talked with Mrs. Christenson about writing a book that she wanted to title *What Happens When People Pray.* Adair persuaded her to change the title to *What Happens When Women Pray,* reminding her that women buy most books. Published in 1975, her first book became Victor's all-time bestseller (more than 2 million, plus many thousands in foreign languages). Viola Blake assisted her in writing the book and still receives royalty.

Evelyn Christenson, author of Victor Books' top-selling *What Happens When Women Pray,* greets a bookstore representative at a Christian Booksellers convention in the early 1980s. The book has topped two million copies. At right, VB editorial director Jim Adair.

Darien Cooper was referred to Victor by a bookstore clerk. Zondervan had turned down her manuscript that Victor titled *You Can Be the Wife of a Happy Husband* (1974), and it became one of Victor's top sellers (930,000).

Barbara Davoll kept knocking at SP's door, but curriculum editors who were developing children's books couldn't warm up to her material, until Adair made further contact with her at Word of Life in New York. From that contact developed the "Christopher Churchmouse" series that became highly successful.

LeRoy Eims, with The Navigators, had never thought of writing a book until Victor persuaded him to write a book on leadership. *Be the Leader You Were Meant to Be* (1975; 285,000) became his first book. At the same time Victor contacted **Walt Henrichsen,** also then with The Navigators, and he wrote the popular *Disciples Are Made—Not Born* (1972; 500,000).

Howard Hendricks broke into print with his first book, *Say It With Love* (1972; 314,600), developed from some of his taped messages, edited by Ted Miller on assignment. *Heaven Help the Home* followed in 1973 (418,000).

Joyce Landorf had published initially with Zondervan, but Victor's best-selling *Fragrance of Beauty* (sales figure unavailable) published in 1973 helped launch her. After her much publicized divorce and remarriage, Victor ceased distributing and publishing her books.

Bill Hybels had a series of sermons that were made into a book for SP's youth section titled *Caution: Christians Under Construction.* He wrote several adult books, including *Christians in the Marketplace* (1982; sales figure unavailable).

John MacArthur may have written initially for another publisher, but likely his first book was Victor's *Found: God's Will* (1977; 229,000).

Erwin Lutzer may or may not have first published with Victor, but at least Victor popularized him. His first VB book was *You're Richer than You Think* (1972; sales figure unavailable). Other VB books by Lutzer include *How to Say No to a Stubborn Habit* and *Satan's "Evangelistic" Strategy for this New Age.* All of his books have sold well.

John Pollock had published *The Apostle* with Doubleday, and Victor obtained rights to do a paperback version elective that was titled *The Man Who Shook the World* (1972) and republished under the title *The Apostle* (1985); he wrote *The Master* (1985) at Victor's request. Both books have done well in several formats.

Charles Stanley may have published elsewhere, but his two books—*A Man's Touch* (1981; sales figure unavailable) and *Handle With Prayer* (1982; 300,000)—were early books that he wrote.

Roy Zuck's first Victor title was *Barb, Please Wake Up,* about the tragic auto accident that left his daughter in a prolonged coma. When it occurred to Adair about 1980 that a Bible commentary by members of the Dallas Theological Seminary faculty would be a good addition to the Victor line, he conferred with Zuck and President John Walvoord, and they became editors of Victor's two-volume *The Bible Knowledge Commentary* (New Testament, 352,000; Old Testament, 303,000).

V. Gilbert Beers approached Victor Books about 1979, resulting in the publication in 1981 of his *Victor Handbook of Bible Knowledge.* It was considered a special addition to Victor's resource line of products. It was republished in a new handsome format in 1996 under the title *The Victor Journey through the Bible.*

A steady seller.

A change of command

With Adair slowed down by a severe case of asthma and the book program not progressing to the satisfaction of management, President Hall brought in Mark Sweeney, formerly manager of the Publishing Division of Moody Bible Institute. Hall designated Adair as "No. 2 man" to continue on as a senior editor, editing books and helping with book acquisitions. He retired in April 1988 but continued to work part time till 1996, ending his association with the company after 51 years.

Sweeney joined the Executive Workteam on May 4, 1981 as a division director, was elevated to vice president in 1983, and in 1994 became corporate vice-president/publisher.

After his arrival, SP began to work more vigorously with foreign publishers. Hall and Sweeney made annual trips to the Frankfurt Book Fair to talk with publishers about purchasing rights to books. Prior to this, German agent Winfred Bluth had handled all European contracts for Victor. In the early '90s, Sweeney gave Margaret Berg the job of working with foreign publishers, and he and Margaret made annual trips to Frankfurt. She made her final trip in 1996.

By the mid-'90s, the Book Division had annual gross sales in the vicinity of $11 million. When Sweeney resigned in 1995, James Elwell took over his post and held it till Victor

Books became part of Cook Communications Ministries in 1996 under the label ChariotVictor Publishing.

---

[1] See Appendix for excerpts from board minutes relating to launching of Victor Books.

[2] This sales figure and most other figures are estimates of sales as of 1997. SP reports in some instances do not include sales of early editions, and Cook reports in some cases do not include sales prior to 1996.

CHAPTER 19

Southern Baptists and Other Denominations

IN THE EARLY '60s, Willis Grimm, Laurin Zorn, and Harold Eavey laid the groundwork for imprints of lesson materials for denominations. Eavey worked out an arrangement with Christian Publications, the publishing arm of the Christian & Missionary Alliance, and Zorn brought Advocate Press, a Pentecostal Holiness publisher, into SP's imprint program.

In early 1966 Jim Lemon came to SP as Marketing vice president, and soon stepped up the imprint program. He put Grimm in charge of special markets, and eventually 32 denominations were under contract for SP to supply imprinted materials for at least one SS department and in many cases for most or all departments.

The imprint plan permitted black plate changes so that each account could delete certain material and add its denomination's desired theological emphases. The Salvation Army and Christian and Missionary Alliance were major accounts, along with the Church of God, Cleveland, Tennessee, the Baptist General Conference, and the Evangelical Free Church.

Lemon and Grimm saw a need among Southern Baptists and sought ways to make inroads into the churches of the denomination, largest of all Protestant groups. Battles were being waged by the moderates and the fundamentalists, particularly in relation to inerrancy and getting conservative professors into Southern Baptist seminaries.

SP tried getting to Southern Baptists through FreeWill Baptists in Nashville, Lemon recalls, but that failed. SP's financial people, as he saw it, took a dim view of the imprint venture, but VEC encouraged it. Eventually, Lemon and Grimm made contact with Dr. William A. (Bill) Powell, a Southern Baptist pastor who championed the cause of Bible inerrancy. He was executive director of the Baptist Faith and Message Fellowship which published the *Southern Baptist Journal,* of which he was editor. Powell and his team were sounding an alarm that liberal trends were being observed in the denomination. Dr. M.O. Owens, Jr., pastor of Parkwood Baptist Church, Gastonia, North Carolina, was chairman of the board of directors of the Fellowship.

As Dr. Powell traveled, he found many pastors and lay people disturbed by and dissatisfied with some of the curriculum published by the Southern Baptist Sunday School Board in Nashville.[1] In some instances these pastors and their churches had already begun to use Sunday School curriculum published by independent pastors. But many of them were unhappy with what they were using, and Dr. Powell often heard the question, "Why can't we have materials that are doctrinally sound and written from a Southern Baptist viewpoint?"

Undoubtedly some of those asking the question were aware that in 1891 the Southern Baptist Convention in establishing the Sunday School Board had made the following recommendation: "It is therefore recommended that the fullest freedom of choice be accorded everyone as to what literature he will use or support, and that no brother be disparaged in the slightest degree on account of what he may do in the exercise of his rights as Christ's freeman."

Powell suggests working with SP

In the summer of 1975, Dr. Powell recommended that leaders of the Baptist Faith and Message Fellowship consider working with Scripture Press. They met in the living room of Dr. Owens' home in Gastonia. In addition to Owens and Powell, present that day were the Rev. Robert Estes, the Rev. Aubert Rose, the Rev. Gerald Primm, and Harry A. Steele. The group agreed that the matter of providing literature based on the verbal inspiration and inerrancy of the Bible was indeed worth pursuing. They agreed that it would not be feasible to start a publishing house and write, edit, and publish suitable materials for all ages..

In subsequent meetings, the matter was further discussed, and Lemon told how Scripture Press lessons could serve Southern Baptist churches. SP would provide the basic manuscripts, which would then be edited by Southern Baptists chosen for the task of making the material fully agreeable to the conservative Southern Baptist mind. The edited material would be printed by Scripture Press in an attractive format and bear their chosen imprint. The materials would be shipped to customers from a distribution point in Georgia.

The group agreed to seek symbiosis with Scripture Press. They proceeded to secure a charter and form a corporation. The name of the new organization was The Baptist Literature Board, Inc. Owens was asked to serve as editor in chief; Powell was named executive director; and Harry Steele was named controller. The business address was 2439 Dodson Avenue, Atlanta, GA 30344.

An agreement was worked out with Scripture Press, and publicity about the project was sent to many churches. The *Southern Baptist Journal* carried a full page ad giving information about the new materials and offering evaluation kits. The response was favorable. Shipping of the imprinted lesson manuals began on November 1, 1976 from the Buchanan, Georgia warehouse. Then came a full-page news story from the Southern Baptist Convention accusing the Baptist Literature Board of being deceitful in claiming that the board was producing curriculum for Southern Baptists. Many of the state Baptist papers took up the cudgel against the Baptist Literature Board.

SP takes over

For about three years the working arrangement with Scripture Press continued. However, the overhead expenses were greater than the small, though growing, BLB business could handle. Sales continued to increase but so did expenses. BLB asked Lemon and other SP leaders to meet with the board to assess the situation.

The result was that SP in August 1980 assumed ownership of BLB, including indebtedness, and formed a for-profit

Delaware subsidiary with the same corporate name. The agreement was that the Southern Baptist directors would continue to exercise a major influence as to the content of the printed materials, while SP would handle the operational side. Formal agreement was approved on August 18,1980.

Lee Suderman became general manager in October 1983, and after he resigned in 1988, Doyle McDaniel, an SPPI field rep, replaced him. Finances and operational matters were coordinated and supervised from Wheaton by Curt Henrickson.

The ministry continues under the umbrella of Cook Communications Ministries. Those who were on the BLB Board now serve as advisors to the Curriculum Division of Cook. Sales for the year ending June 1997 were $529,193, and BLB was serving 743 churches. The Biblical Heritage curriculum, based on the *King James Version,* begun in 1995, was discontinued after one quarter at Cook, and users were given the option of switching to BLB, Scripture Press, or Cook's Accent curriculum.

---

[1] "Early History of the Baptist Literature Board," by Doyle McDaniel in *Baptist Focus* (1996)

CHAPTER 20

The Final Decade in the Wheaton

1987–1996

On the national scene, the year 1987 saw President Reagan accepting "full responsibility" on March 4 for the Iran-Contra affair, but later he denied knowing that profits from Iranian arms sales went to the Contras. On March 19, PTL evangelist Jim Bakker resigned after his affair with Jessica Hahn was made public and it was made known that he stole funds from his ministry. Oral Roberts began a campaign to raise $4.5 million to save his medical center. If it didn't happen, he claimed "God could call Oral Roberts home."

President Ronald Reagan

On January 23, 1987 at Scripture Press, Sam Postlewaite retired after nearly 25 years directing art design and production. He had taken the job of manager of the Art Department on August 13, 1962, and kept a watchful eye not only over SP products but those of Urban Ministries. More than 100 gathered to honor him at a dinner at the Back Door restaurant. Wayne Eklund presented a plaque of appreciation to Sam for his 17 years of service with UMI materials. On January 26, Bill Anderson, executive editor of the Editorial Division, became division director. Previously, he had served as west coast field rep for three years.

In February, the SPPI board approved a curriculum revision (packaging changes, not content) beginning in September 1988 and an associated funding proposal (a $900,000 line of credit) as presented in the written report, "Bible for Today Curriculum."

Later, the treasurer was authorized to sell 50,802 shares of common stock to the Employees Stock Ownership Trust (ESOT) at $18.80 a share and ESOT became leverage for securing a loan of $950,000 for the curriculum revision (student guides and teaching resources). These cosmetic changes that cost nearly $2 million did not improve sales, as had been hoped.

Also in February, the Advertising Department became an in-house agency called Pressworks Advertising, under the management of Brian Wills.

In March, records showed *The Bible Knowledge Commentary* was printed in three foreign languages—French, Hindi, and Russian. Also that month Doyle McDaniel became BLB's full-time general manager.

In April, Elsiebeth McDaniel, who had worked part-time at SP in the '40s and returned for full-time work in 1960, was honored at a retirement dinner at St. Andrews Country Club. Wes Willis presented her with a camera and congratulated her for her creativity and energy in producing products for children.

In May, the Board of Directors asked Gil Beers to visit Gospel Light concerning interest in a merger. GL's Bill Greig had expressed interest in the possibility of pooling resources toward a completely new Sunday School curriculum for publication in the year 2000. Nothing, however, came of the idea.

SP's campus in Wheaton was always admired for its flowers, especially petunias. In June, Faith Aeilts guessed closest to B & G's Steve Johnson's count, 4,610 pink and white petunias.

In August, employees staged the first of a Craft Harvest and Bake Sale. In September, Harold P. Halleen, 84, a former chairman of the SPPI board, died.

1988

On January 6, 1988, Marketing pinned a corsage on Lorraine Ackley in honor of her 30 years with SP. On February 17, Louise Rodman died following a heart attack. She joined SP in 1938 and worked for 37 years, the last 25 as Employment manager.

In early 1988, high-profile employees Floyd and Thelma Neuen retired and returned to Canada from where they had come. Retirement came for Thelma after 14 years, the last 8 being a member of the Cradle Roll/Nursery staff. Both the Neuens had joined the Canadian SP staff in 1966, and in 1973 Floyd came to Wheaton as dealer services manager. During the early 1960s, they had become increasingly involved in CE activities and were instrumental in forming the Toronto District Sunday School Association.

On April 28, Jim Adair, who came to work on *Power* in 1945, retired from full-time employment after 42 years, 9 months, and 4 days. On May 1, he started anew on a part-time basis as a Victor Books senior editor involved in acquisitions. He was honored at a dinner at Sharko's restaurant, with Dr. Warren Wiersbe humorously emceeing the event. Adair continued part-time work until SP closed its operation in Wheaton in September 1996.

On Friday, June 10, President David Hall marked 25 years with SP. Rod Toews, former minister of education at Peninsula Covenant Church, Redwood City, California, joined Marketing as educational ministries director in July.

In September, Joann Keith guessed in a contest that SP's electric bill from July 18 to August 16 was $8,938. She got a gift certificate for being closest to the actual—$9,223. On September 2, Olga Kononowa became the 11th employee to reach the 35th milestone and the current full-time employee with the longest service record. She had started work on September 8, 1953 as an accounting machine operator. At her retirement, she let it be known she had officially changed her name to Anne Conway.

1989

Ron Ramsey became executive director of SPM on January 30, 1989. Helen Gorges, it was announced, would continue to serve as administrative director, coordinating current programs, until she retired in May. She began her SP career in 1960 as Training Hour secretary. Helen later moved to Arizona with her housemate Edythe Draper and after a bout with pancreatic cancer died in January 1993.

In October, directors authorized the corporation to establish a subsidiary corporation under Delaware law, to be named

Vista Media Corporation, to acquire 80 percent of common stock for $105,600 and to lend $450,000 to Vista, later renamed Video Dynamics, Inc. This was later deemed a bad move, for about a year later the board authorized liquidating VDI "as soon as possible." It was estimated that SPPI would lose at least $1.3 million.

1990

In February, President Hall announced that SP had a newly designed logo. The new one and previous logos were displayed in the February 23, 1990 issue of *Spotlight*.

In March, Text Editing began setting final type for SP's products inside, whereas before, the Editorial Department purchased final type outside.

On April 27, retiree Henry Jacobsen, longtime editor of adult materials, died in Glendale, Arizona.

On May 21, SPPI directors approved Will Frykman's recommendation that Harris Hanson be named chairman of the board for the remainder of the current term, citing health reasons for stepping down. He would, however, continue as an officer, taking the post of vice chairman. The board accepted the resignation of David Hall from the presidency. (See end of this chapter for David Hall's summary of highlights of his term of office.)

Beers elected president

The board named V. Gilbert Beers interim president of SPPI, effective May 23, 1990. He was elected president on August 20, 1990. A former editor of *Christianity Today,* he had at that time authored five titles for Victor Books and numerous titles for other publishers. In other action by the board, the positions of senior vice president were dissolved and reappointments made for Curt Henrickson as vice president of Operations and Wes Willis as vice president of Strategic Planning. Lorraine Ackley was named administrative assistant to the president.

On August 20, the SPPI board approved President Beers' reorganization plan, "SP at the Crosssroads." Three divisions were set up: Victor Books; Scripture Press, producer of educational products; and Operations, provider of necessary operational and financial services for the other two divisions. Mark Sweeney was retained as vice president and publisher of Victor Books, and Curt Henrickson retained as vice president of Operations. The board ordered a search for a vice president and publisher of Scripture Press (the search was abandoned later, and the president assumed those responsibilities).

November brought the celebration of Margaret Berg's 30th year with SP. In early December, Lou Von Busch, head of B & G for many years, died at age 85 in Spartanburg, SC. His wife, Ruth, was an employee of SP from 1956 to 1971.

1991

In early January 1991, Bill Anderson, formerly of Marketing and Editorial, began new responsibilities as pastoral administrator at Christ Community Church, St. Charles. Jerry Wit departed after nine years as Marketing head. He had purchased a segment of Video Dynamics and began directing the operation of the video clubs under the name Family Video Plus. On Sunday, January 20, a memorial service was held at Moody Bible Institute for Harry Saulnier, the brother-in-law of Bernice Cory. He had been involved as a board member of SP from the beginning. Superintendent of Pacific Garden Mission for 46 years, he died on December 22, 1990 at age 88. And also in January, Marilyn Schaer, Human Resources director, marked 30 years at SP. She began a new job in April on the leadership team of the Sharon Glen Retirement Village, Wheaton.

February saw Rod Toews move up to become assistant to the president. Ruth Blair, for many years a secretary and later a proofreader, was honored for 35 years on the job. (She retired in October 1992.) Drew Clouse, son of Greg Clouse of Victor Books, was diagnosed as having childhood leukemia.

In May, Phil CiCicco, Office Management director, marked 30 years with the company. In June, Ray Bradshaw of Finance marked 25 years at SP.

At CBA in July, Victor Books won two Gold Medallions for *King Leonard's Celebration,* a children's book, and *Developing the Teacher in You,* by Wes Willis.

The SP family was deeply saddened upon learning of the death of Wayne Eklund on Wednesday evening, October 2. He had undergone surgery on March 8 for a malignant brain tumor. Wayne had served as vice president of the Purchasing Division and his leadership helped establish SP's relationship with a host of printers, designers, and suppliers. A Wayne Eklund Memorial Fund was later set up to provide scholarships for students at the Emmanuel Bible Institute in Romania.

Three employees passed impressive milestones: Curt Henrickson, vice president, Operations, 30 years, in October; Darrell Johnson, of Data Processing, 25 years, in November; and Marilyn Dunn, administrative secretary, Production, 25 years, in December.

1992

Wednesday, January 22, 1992 marked the first of annual pancake breakfasts for employees. President Beers, Mark Sweeney, and Curt Henrickson dished out the flapjacks, and employees wore their favorite sweatshirts.

Starting March 6, the first Friday of each month would be Casual Day, it was announced, and the day would begin with free coffee and donuts. (In January 1993, every Friday became Casual Day.) Also in March, Jan Burton, of Editorial, was undergoing tests to relieve severe pain. (She went through a long bout, recovered, and was one of the Editorial employees who later moved to Colorado Springs.) And Beers returned from England, where he attended the Christian Booksellers Convention. He brought back the news that SPUK was named runner-up publisher of the year.

On April 17, retiree Vic Anderson, who worked for the company for 37 years, died after bypass surgery. In May, *FreeWay* took honors as the top take-home paper in EPA competition, and *Teen Power* won an Award of Merit. Kyle Olund was editor of *FreeWay* and Amy Cox, editor of *Teen Power*. Also in May, retiree Lois Gustafson Buelow died. Sharon Noble, of the Credit Department, became a member of the Quarter Century Club.

With sales of curriculum continuing to slump, management began another effort in July to stem the tide. President Beers appointed veteran editor Joyce Gibson editorial director and worked with her to begin a new program to produce fresh lesson materials in keeping with the times, yet with the "SP flavor." Decision was to start from "scratch," resulting in the painful termination of the staff with the exception of several whose qualifications fitted the restructuring plan and the hiring of three specialists. In effect, the entire Scripture Press Curriculum Division was reorganized, including Production and Marketing.

After beginning the restructuring effort, the company began a desktop publishing program, intended to increase efficiency. However, the move to produce new curriculum came to a halt in 1996 because of increasing financial difficulties and when management realized SP would soon be under a new umbrella.

In August 1992, the SPPI board authorized purchase of the 1825 building and property from Washington National Insurance Company for $600,000. The terms: WNIC would lend SPPI 100 percent of the purchase price at 9 percent for 25 years. The board authorized a contribution of $600,000 to the Employee Stock Ownership Trust to pay off the leveraged loan for the curriculum revision. Also in August, announcement was made that the Marketing Departments of Scripture Press and Victor Books would assume responsibility for their own advertising services.

In a November board meeting, President Beers proposed a self-study of the two boards (SPM and SPPI.) By this time, the SPM Members were meeting in joint sessions with the SPPI and SPM boards. The study was later carried out.

1993

Lorraine Ackley marked 35 years at SP in January. The Operations Division was renamed the Corporate Services Division, Curt Henrickson announced in early February.

On February 8, retiree Lloyd Siegfried, who had worked at SP from 1937 to 1973, died.

In June, announcement was made that a 401(k) plan would replace SP's old retirement benefit plan, effective January 1, 1994. The new plan provided a base benefit as well as a matching contribution to encourage employees to plan and save for retirement. The old plan would be frozen as of September.

July saw the arrival of Barry Gardner as part-time financial consultant in Corporate Services. He had worked for Wheaton College, Congoleum, and Pepsico/FritoLay but had more recently been an independent financial consultant.

In August, the Sunday School Board (SSB) notified SP that SP had infringed on their trademark, LifeWay. Both SSB and SP had sought registration for LifeWay, using 1977 as the date of first use. In 1982 SP had declined opposition to the LW service mark registration but continued to use the name. In 1993 an agreement was reached that SP would discontinue the name LifeWay for its Christian school curriculum, and use Bible for Today. Gil Beers explored the possibility of an alliance between SSB and SP concerning LifeWay, but nothing happened. SP changed the name to Bible for Today.

Also in August, Ron Ramsey resigned as executive director of SPM to become senior pastor of a church in the Toledo area. Curt Henrickson was honored in chapel for his 35 years with SP. And in September, five employees with a combined 98 years of service retired: Dick Olson, from Production (17 years); Gloria Martin, Marketing (19); Jackie Schmidt, Proofreading (12); Ralph Wetherbee, field rep (23); and Ray Bradshaw, Finance (27).

In October, Dave Hurst, of Finance, joined the Quarter Century Club.

1994

President Beers announced organizational changes in January 1994. Mark Sweeney became corporate vice president and publisher and was given responsibility for the editorial, production, design, and marketing aspects of both the Scripture Press Curriculum and Victor Books Divisions, as well as for new areas of creative product development. He had served as vice president and publisher of Victor Books. Jim Elwell became corporate director of Marketing and Development. Bill Anderson had returned and was named director of trade sales; Brian Wills became director of Consumer Marketing; and Blake Ebel became creative director and manager of all advertising in the Pressworks Advertising. Directors authorized Beers to pursue the feasibility of developing a new 2s and 3s curriculum for release in September 1995; and if deemed wise to proceed, to spend approximately half of his time as president and half leading the development of the curriculum. Board action scuttled this plan in February 1995, when management revealed the company could not afford the change.

In February, at the recommendation of Doris Chase, Dan Wegehaupt joined SP as the new bookstore manager. Mrs.

Chase stepped down to became assistant manager. Also in February, a decision was made to begin the process of closing down SP's operation of Screen Printers in Warsaw, Indiana.

SP said good-bye in July to Alan Addy, especially known for his bass solos in chapel sessions, when he retired after 24 years in Merchandise Handling.

Joyce Gibson marked 35 years at SP in August.

On August 16, some 200 employees, board members, and retirees celebrated SP's 60th birthday at a luncheon at Radisson Hotel in Lisle. Lloyd, Dan, and Phil—three of the four Cory sons—attended. Lloyd provided personal anecdotes and Liz Duckworth, of Victor Books, gave a short narrative of the company history. Mark Sweeney reviewed more recent growth and development. Dr. George Brushaber, president of Bethel College and Seminary, was introduced as SPM's new board chairman. Dr. John Walvoord, longtime board member, challenged listeners to remember the SP corporate mission and to focus on cultivating a vision for the future of the ministry.

Don Bovey, director of Materials Handling, joined the Quarter Century Club in October.

1995

In April 1995, Arnie Bernsten, with Cook Communications Ministries for 25 years, became director of retail sales. Most recently, he had served as president of Christian Purchasing Network. Also in April, Mark Sweeney resigned his post as corporate vice president and publisher, and announcement was made that *Zelos*, a journal, three-month devotional guide, and magazine, would replace *FreeWay* and *Youth Illustrated* in September 1995.

In May, Arnie Bernsten was named vice president and publisher of SP, and Jim Elwell, vice president and publisher of Victor Books. Also in May, Liz and John Duckworth's twin son Christopher began chemotherapy for a rare form of bone cancer. He was the second child in the Victor Books family to undergo chemo; previously, Drew Clouse had been diagnosed with leukemia. Both boys were successfully treated.

At an all-company coffee break on August 21, SP honored Jim Adair and Bob Walker who had each been associated with SP for half a century. Also, President Beers announced that Curt Henrickson had decided to resign his executive staff position, effective October 1, and that he would continue in a part-time resource and supportive role to the president.

September found Victor Books curtailing the development of the Adult Education and SonPower youth resource product lines, eliminating jobs held by Pam Campbell and Carolyn Nystrom. Also, Lee Kloese, of Merchandise Handling, joined the Quarter Century Club, and Margaret Berg marked 35 years in November.

Spotlight for Friday, December 8 announced that on the previous Monday employees were informed that Scripture Press Publications and Victor Books would join Cook Communications Ministries in Colorado Springs. A Scripture verse accompanied the announcement: "My grace is sufficient for you; for My power is made perfect in weakness" (2 Cor. 12:9).

1996

On Tuesday, January 9, 1996, Bruce Adair and Dan Brokke, senior vice presidents of Cook Communications Ministries, conducted an informational session for SP employees. This was the first of several meetings related to the merger with Cook. The Scripture Press Employees Credit Union merged with the DuPage Schools Credit Union (now DuPage Credit Union), effective in April.

Myrna Hasse, of Victor Books Production, joined the Quarter Century Club in May and resigned in June to accept a position with a textbook publisher. Announcement was made that as of July 31, the Fullerton distribution center would no longer be in operation; shipping would be out of Elgin.

Issues of *Spotlight* until September 13, 1996 reported the exodus of employees, some to Colorado Springs and others to other jobs. That final issue of *Spotlight* before the official closing of the Wheaton building announced that Darrell and Anne Johnson had moved to Colorado, and that Ken Schroeder, Arnie Bernsten, and Jan Burton would soon transfer to CCM. In 1998, SPM continued to publish *Spotlight* from time to time, mainly for retirees and Quarter Century Club members. A 1997 issue listed former employees and the jobs they had found.

David Hall recalls highlights of his presidency

To broaden the scope of this history of Scripture Press, the author asked David Hall to summarize the highlights of his term as president. He graciously obliged with the following:

> Some of the activities during my leadership included the items which I will list. While I am sure that there were others, I, after a number of years, cannot recall definitively all of them.
>
> An overall observation is that during sales growth, the number of people employed by SP remained constant or declined through attrition. Also the sales shifted from retail to bookstores, distributors, and denominations. This was consistent with the industry at large.
>
> During this period there was a significant increase in Victor Books sales. This enabled the separation of the field sales force into book sales and curriculum sales. Also during that time, the kinds of books produced by Victor Books increased in number, adding to the initial adult elective line.
>
> The reorganization of SP Canada took place in the early 1980s, with SP Canada becoming a taxable organization. During subsequent years, the Canadian operation became a distributor for a number of other U.S. publishers, including Multnomah Press and Nav Press. This enabled an increase in the field sales staff to both churches and bookstores throughout Canada. Also during that period, SP Canada acquired Evangelical Publishers, a firm that worked primarily in publishing and in retail with several bookstores in the Toronto area. At the peak of the 1980s, there were more than 90 people employed in all the areas of SP Canada.
>
> Scripture Press U.K. was the SP curriculum distributor in the British Isles. Its representation in that area was primarily through weekend training conferences in churches. Moody Press came to SPPI, asking whether their books could be distributed in the British Isles through SPUK. This resulted in the establishment of distribution for a number of U.S. publishers. The additional sales enabled SPUK to add a field staff to represent the firm throughout the British Isles.
>
> The growth of Victor Books was enhanced because of the increased representation, and this led to the publishing of British editions of some of the more popular VB books, along with some of the titles of the other publishers the firm represented.
>
> Representatives of management of SP Canada and SP United Kingdom came to the Wheaton office on a regular

basis to be involved in the planning activities for future growth of all Scripture Press.

The Baptist Literature Board was formulated to meet the requested need of conservative churches in the Southern Baptist Convention. The imprinted curriculum distribution started in east Georgia and later moved to Atlanta under the ownership of Scripture Press. Doyle McDaniel was brought in to oversee the growth of that organization.

Scripture Press' entry into the Christian school market came as a result of a relationship with Association for Bible Curriculum Development (ABCD) of Pasadena, California. With their leadership retired, ABCD became a part of SP, with direction given by Joyce Gibson.

Scripture Press was involved with a number of international groups who, by permission, translated SP curriculum into their languages. Also SP's English material was distributed in many countries. I had the privilege of visiting translators in Belgium, France, Holland, Korea, Japan, and Hong Kong, as well as visiting distributors in Australia and Singapore.

Because of the international ministry of SP, we were invited to be one of three Christian publishers to display at the Moscow Book Fair in 1988, resulting in the translating and publishing of one of the first Christian books in the USSR, *How to Really Love Your Child* by Dr. Ross Campbell. This book was published and printed by the government during a time before the demise of Communism. We were also invited, along with a select number of other publishers, to the ceremonies of the official recognition of a Christian publishing company and the opening of the first Christian bookstore in Yugoslavia. This publisher also translated some of our books.

Christian Booksellers Association, in their growth, recognized the importance of the vendors in their area of retail store work. In 1980, CBA reorganized its board, allowing for the first time vendor board membership. SP was recognized as a strong supporter of CBA, and CBA invited me to be the first board member representing the publishers in the industry. After I served on the CBA board, the CBA Service Corporation was formed, and I was on the board for ten years, serving for three years as chairman. I continue to serve on the CBA Foundation board of directors.

Scripture Press has been heavily involved in the Evangelical Christian Publishers Association (ECPA) from its beginning. Will Frykman was one of the founders of ECPA, and Mark Sweeney and I each served on the board and as president during a term.

The primary comment coming from users, both retail and bookstore, was the dependability of the material based on the Word of God. SP stood strong during a time when many publishers were producing products that were thin in content, questionable in biblical soundness, and produced primarily for sales dollars. SP's strong ministry orientation was recognized by many throughout the world, and this resulted because of the strong staff who loved the Lord and viewed their work as ministry and not just as a job.

An Overview of Scripture Press Sunday School Curriculum

by Joyce Gibson

(Former editorial director of the SP Curriculum Division)

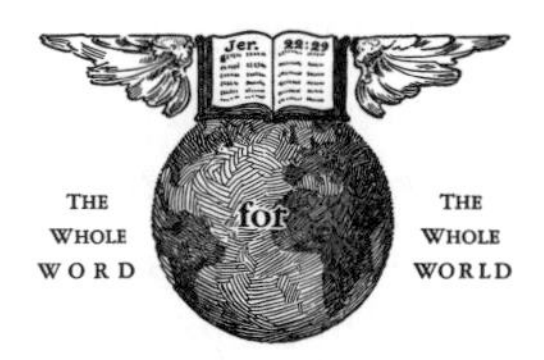

As detailed in the Prologue, in the early 1930s most of the Sunday Schools of America were following what was known as the uniform lessons. It was a curriculum dating back to 1872 that provided about 30% coverage of the Bible, with the same passages being studied in all age levels. Concerned Christians noted that people who had attended Sunday School most of their lives still did not know the essentials of the Bible nor understand how it applied to their lives. The lessons simply were not meeting the mental and spiritual needs of students. Liberal theology dominated the field of Christian Education. Spiritual famine was at hand.

To meet the spiritual hunger in America's Sunday Schools, Scripture Press All-Bible Graded Lessons were prayerfully developed to provide 12 years of systematic, life-changing Bible study. Dr. Clarence Benson's students at Moody Bible Institute worked over a period of 8 years to prepare a "model course, which would give consecutive, comprehensive, and complete instruction in the Bible." Each of the 624 lessons in the All-Bible Graded series was "chosen with the greatest care to conform to the psychological and pedagogical laws that govern the development of the child and adolescent."

The beginning

In a great step of faith, the Scripture Press curriculum was launched in 1934. "Teaching the whole Bible—with Scripture content of the lessons geared to the needs and abilities of learners" became the motivating vision. Scripture Press writers eagerly prepared lessons that would get God's Word into the hearts and lives of students. The goal was to provide Bible instruction that would be true to the Scriptures and would relate the Bible to the life of each student, motivating a personal response to the Lord. The philosophy behind all SP materials was briefly epitomized by three salient claims: All Scripture Press lessons are *Bible based, Christ-centered, and pupil-related.*

The Corys: "The Lord has done great things for us, and we are filled with joy" (Ps. 126:3, NIV). Pins on the map represent Sunday Schools using ABGS lessons, probably in early '40s.

The curriculum not only taught the facts of Scripture but also helped prepare students to live for Christ. Scripture Press believed that "no other church agency is as effective as Sunday School to help prepare people—young and old—to meet Jesus." The goal of the lessons was to teach for transformed lives that would grow out of a personal relationship with Jesus Christ. Each lesson had two purposes:

(1) to provide Bible instruction that related the Word to the life of each student, and

(2) to motivate a personal response to the Lord so that both teacher and student would live the Word because they loved Christ. Mrs. Cory often referred to this essential element in the lessons as "arousing the want-to."

Teachers rejoiced to have their eyes opened to God's Word. Many received Christ as Savior as they prepared and taught the lessons, and hundreds of their students also became true Christians. Churches wrote for more products—tools for evangelism, for building up new converts, and for equipping believers to serve.

One of the unique features of the All-Bible Graded Series

was its departmental grading system, in which the curriculum was divided by departments (rather than single years) based on normal ability groupings. A brochure distributed in 1961 highlighted the advantages of departmental grading:

1941 lesson manuals.

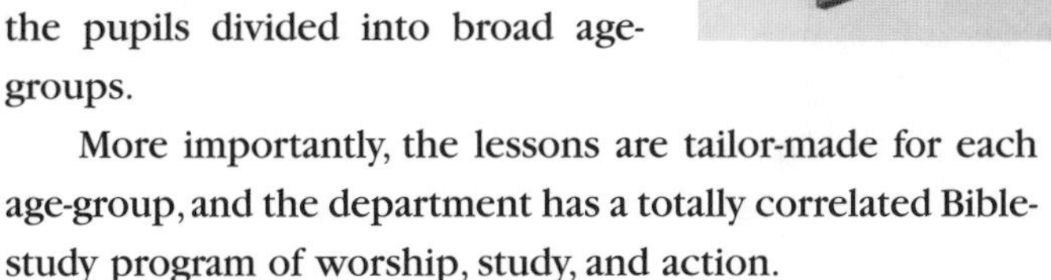

> Under the All-Bible plan, not only are the pupils divided into broad age-groups.
>
> More importantly, the lessons are tailor-made for each age-group, and the department has a totally correlated Bible-study program of worship, study, and action.
>
> See how this plan works out for you in a very practical way.
>
> 1. Departmental grading is adaptable to any size school.
>
> 2. Is flexible for age, class, and ability groupings . . . helps pupils learn better.
>
> 3. Provides theme-related worship services that set the spiritual pace for each Bible lesson and add impact to one truth.
>
> 4. Gives teachers and departmental superintendent a common aim throughout the Sunday School hour.
>
> 5. Makes possible practical teacher training in regular departmental workers' meetings. Teachers pull together as a team when they have one common teaching aim.
>
> 6. Allows for one correlated film or other visual aid to be used throughout a department (not possible in a department having different lessons).
>
> 7. Provides a unified memorization program for all ages in each department.

As God blessed SP with sales, money was available for Marketing to provide training in local churches and at conventions. Under the leadership of Dr. Bob Cook in the 1950s on into the '60s, the CREDEX (Christian Education Extension) Department regularly sent out staff and consultants to inspire people to serve Christ through Christian Education and to train them in the use of Scripture Press curriculum. Dr. Bob would counsel workshop leaders, "Ask God to use you to bless the people. He will take care of the sales."

The impact of these staff members and consultants has been remembered for years. Among them were Sherman Williams, Marjorie Ford, Jack Bradford, Norman Townsend, Ed and Frances Simpson, Roy Zuck, Peter DeGraff, Willis Grimm, Ray Syrstad, and later, Winona Walworth, Joanne Colson, and Larry Richards. In Canada, Earl Swanson, Gloria Akin, and David Bell spread the Scripture Press story, while in Britain, God used Lillian Swanson and Martyn White to build Sunday Schools through personal contacts and training programs.

Curriculum's Distinctives

Other publishers also introduced curriculum that was an improvement over the old uniform lessons. Churches began to make evaluations and comparisons. Though Scripture Press continued to view its curriculum publishing as a real ministry, it could not avoid being caught up in the business climate of competition between publishers. The challenge of meeting competition demanded that SP's distinctives be highlighted with a clear explanation of SP's balanced theological position and a defense of its Christian Education philosophy.

As SP's curriculum grew to serve over 70 denominations and many undenominational groups—ranging in their doctrines from strict Arminianism to stalwart Calvinism—editors needed to avoid criticism for being too hard or too soft on theological issues. Much time in Editorial and Marketing involved discussions about these and educational issues, such as the merits of SP's departmental graded lessons versus the competition's closely graded curriculum, whether curriculum should deal with social issues, or if it should provide for student testing for Bible knowledge.

In the early days, many of these letters were referred to the Church Sales Department for reply. Clara Sander, a veteran customer relations professional with years of experience at Scott-Foresman and a heart of compassion for teachers in local churches, headed the department. Mrs. Cory responded to the more challenging letters with an earnest desire to help the customer understand SP's position. Always sensitive to the turn of a phrase that could avoid an unwarranted criticism, Mrs. Cory carefully combed the manuscripts, promotional pieces, and advertisements to forestall negative responses and reinforce SP's uncompromising commitment to the truth.

In the late 1950s the Editorial staff had grown to keep pace with the increasing volume of products: Sunday School, Vacation Bible School, Training Hour, Children's Church—with correlated resources, such as Gospel-graphs, Suede-graphs, Mission-graphs, and music. It was time for Mrs. Cory to take steps to ensure that "Scripture Press flavor" would permeate every page of the products and promotion. What constituted "Scripture Press flavor" was somewhat of a mystery to new editors, but was always clear to Mrs. Cory and Lloyd. Gradually the SP Style Manual was developed, urged by Dr. Bob Cook in 1957. He saw a need for it not only for writers and editors in Editorial but for advertsing people.

New products.

It began with qualifications of an SP writer and/or editor, which included spiritual and theological qualifications as well as educational. Other pages included preferred ways to state concepts, carefully hammered out to be acceptable to the wide range of churches using the curriculum while conveying SP's uncompromising commitment to God's Word and making the claims of Christ clear and compelling. (As the Style Manual was expanded through the years, it tended to deal more with editing style than with the nuances of stating the truth plainly but without offense.) Mrs. Cory often stressed by personal example and admonition that the lessons must be "bathed with prayer." She longed for editors who would be writers after her own heart. She joked about the four Ms that took promising editors from Editorial: mothers, marriage, moving, and maternity.

Lifestyle issues, such as appropriate attire for girls and women and length of hair for males, Sunday sports, and mention of movies, became so significant that churches, and sometimes whole segments of denominations, dropped the curriculum when they were offended. Other issues, such as position on Communism, war, ecology, ordination of women, and race became such hot buttons that churches occasionally imagined weakness or outright error in lessons when teaching on these subjects wasn't there.

A committee was appointed to compile what became

known as "The Red Flag Notebook." This useful policy manual gave SP editors subjects to be avoided, subjects to be constructively opposed, subjects to be treated cautiously, and other subjects to be instructed on positively.

Product Revisions

Curriculum is unlike most other publications, which are printed and sent out to customers as completed works, and may be reprinted many times without revision. True, curriculum needs to be complete in the sense that it has a scope and sequence of content that can be understood by the customer. However, in our ever-changing society, if curriculum is to be related to the student, it must be updated as student interests and needs change, as trends in education impact ways students learn, and as programming in churches change.

In the late 1960s the pressure to make product changes was increasing. No longer was it enough to craft carefully-worded lessons, distribute dynamic sales promotion pieces, and provide inspiring workshops and sales presentations designed to build confidence in SP. The company had to answer with actual product changes.

For example, SP's response to the pressure to move to closely graded curriculum in the elementary levels was to produce tri-level graded student manuals while continuing to offer the curriculum on a departmental basis. This met the need for many churches. A different student manual was provided for each of the three grades in the Primary and Junior Departments. But all three student manuals in a department centered around one Bible lesson each Sunday. In this way, students in all three grades studied the same lesson on a given Sunday, but each learned on his or her own level of abilities and learning skills. This innovation enabled SP to retain its prized distinctives of presession activities, departmental worship, and a take-home paper, all correlated with the lesson theme.

At the Junior level, SPs highly acclaimed Gospel-graphs had been written into a number of Sunday School and all VBS lessons. Increasingly, users objected to the complicated figures and dated artwork. With reluctance these flannel-backed visuals were dropped in favor of other teaching aids. The Gospel-graph, an innovative visual approach created by Mrs. Cory, had provided solid doctrinal backbone to the Junior lessons. Though over the years some customers have begged to have these visuals made available again, it was never possible.

At the youth level, SP's response to the pressure to move to more life-related topical studies was to completely revamp the youth philosophy and develop new products. Ardith Hooten Bradford, working under Roy Irving and with Larry Richards, developed a solid youth curriculum, which was immediately accepted in churches. *Youth Illustrated* won the approval of teens around the country.

Aids for reaching young hearts.

SP decided that it was time to look at other departments for possible revision. From High School down to the Nursery Department, all lessons were evaluated. A new scope and sequence was designed at each level to meet the needs of the learners of the 1970s.

A committee was formed to develop a prospectus that would form an umbrella presentation for the entire line of Scripture Press curriculum and related products, highlighting SP distinctives, SP commitments, and SP identity. The committee was made up of Bernice Cory, Lloyd Cory, Wilfred Frykman, Roy Irving, Larry Richards, Roy Zuck, and Jim Lemon. When completed, the prospectus highlighted six outstanding features of the All-Bible Curriculum:

Scripture
Evangelism
Departmental grading
Guided discovery learning
Leadership development
Correlation

Approximately half the prospectus dealt with general principles and the other half on ways these principles were worked out in specific curriculum areas. More than 25 years after it was produced, it continued to provide the most reliable explanation of Scripture Press curriculum distinctives.

Years of hard work by a dedicated staff in Editorial and Marketing had produced a completely revised curriculum line that could potentially fulfill the desires of almost every Sunday School. Management thought it was time to stop the costly revisions and pick up cycles of the lesson without changes. However, almost immediately new requests came from Sunday Schools, and once more SP had to respond with costly product revisions.

In the late 1970s the issues changed. Sunday Schools wanted either KJV or NIV-based lessons. They wanted the elementary lessons to accommodate Primary, Middler, and Junior Departments (known as the 2-2-2 plan). Some were insisting on gender-neutral language. Others were asking for photos and art illustrations that reflected our ethnically diverse society. Many wanted the Sunday School experience for children and youth to be activity-oriented rather than structured like a school classoom of a previous decade. Teachers demanded less complex and time-consuming lesson preparation. Extensive editorial changes and adaptations were tried, but often failed to silence the voices of discontent.

An All-Bible Curriculum Task Force was appointed with Roy Irving as chair, with Don Crawford, Phil DiCicco, Norma Felske, Elsiebeth McDaniel, and Robert Messner as hard-working members. In May 1983, it presented a report, calling for extensive research into the needs of teachers, ways to lower production costs without reducing product marketability, and increased consumer awareness of All-Bible Curriculum products and services in order to gain a larger share of the Sunday School curriculum market.

Lessons for all ages.

A concentrated effort was made to simplify the teacher manuals and to unify the lesson structures. At the same time Editorial moved from the typewriter to the computer. Then SP turned to the student guides, investing in costly redesign of all manuals, most with four-color illustrations. The investment of time and effort did not pay off in the increased sales, as had been anticipated.

Some in the field of Christian Education were announcing that the day of dated Sunday School curriculum would soon be over. The steadily declining unit sales for more than a decade seemed to confirm this sobering prediction. SP held to its conviction that there was still a ministry through Sunday School, and that curriculum resources could still meet a real need in the churches. However, the problem was how to update the products when the product investment dollars were shrinking.

A New Challenge

In 1990 President Gil Beers challenged Scripture Press with a two-pronged program for curriculum: (1) to "harvest" in every possible way—sending products through with absolutely the minimum revision cost, and (2) to execute an exciting revitalization of the curriculum, especially through an all-new design of the Teaching Guide. Trends in society and in the church needed to be recognized if the lessons would be effective in reaching the needs of both teachers and students.

A review of customer comments gives a perspective of benefits desired in a revision:

1. Teaches the Bible at the students' learning level
2. Is quick and easy for teacher to prepare
3. Is easy to organize and manage the class session
4. Offers enough options to choose from, to customize material for the class
5. Has low cost
6. Offers strong life application
7. Holds students' interest
8. Provides activities at the students' ability levels

A full-day session was scheduled for each age level, with the curriculum editor and a field representative presenting to the Curriculum Managers Team a historical perspective of that age level's curriculum, including principles on which the curriculum was originally based and product changes that had brought the department to where it was, a report from the field representative, feedback from Marketing, Finance, Production, and Research Departments—all to prepare the team to make specific recommendations for product revitalization.

The insights gleaned from these sessions formed the basis of an Editorial Position Paper that was presented to management. The paper called for minimum revisions in all products except the teaching guides, which would be completely redesigned and rewritten.

The goal was to create a new teaching program that

would guide teachers through a logical and understandable lesson development. It would lead students to make meaningful, personal decisions to respond to the life-changing truths that had been presented in the lesson.The challenge would be to accomplish this while accommodating the expressed desires of teachers to have easy-to-prepare lessons with teaching methods that involved students in physical activities.

The expectation was that new teaching guides would both retain existing customers and draw new customers. With increased sales, monies would become available for much more extensive revisions—hopefully, an all-new curriculum with all-new products designed to meet the needs of the next century.

Once the Editorial position paper was approved, plans were made to move quickly into the first stage of the revitalization program.

Age-level specialists replaced most of the editors as product developers. Larry Richards served the elementary levels, Dewey Bertolini the youth levels, and Gil Beers gave his efforts and many years' experience to the early childhood levels.

Editorial moves into desktop publishing

The newly designed teaching guide was introduced. It had the appearance more of a magazine than a textbook. Photographs of the appropriate age levels leaped off the pages. The first page of each lesson introduced the lesson to the teacher—not from an educational point of view but from the heart of the lesson-writer, showing how the Bible content of the lesson had impacted the life of the writer. A positive element of enjoyment in God's Word ran through the pages, motivating teachers to infuse the Sunday School hour with delight for the students.The center column on each page alerted the teacher to methods and needed resources, and allowed space for the teacher to add notes. Many teachers praised the innovations.

SP responded to Marketing requests to move to the 2-2-2 plan for elementary, providing Primary curriculum for Grades 1-2, Middler for grades 3-4, and Junior for grades 5-6.

Zelos, a combination of student guide and take-home paper, was introduced for the High School.

Primary Days received a dramatic new look and was slanted editorially to the reading and ability levels of first and second-graders.

An Editorial product review and five-year plan showed the existing status of all products and made proposals for changes and additions at every age level over the five-year-period—and beyond. High on the priority list was an all-new Junior curriculum with a new take-home paper for grades 5-6 and an all-new curriculum for 2s & 3s.

Vision glowed for ministry through the proposed revitalization program. Enthusiasm for product growth and market expansion flourished, but the dollars simply were not available to implement the plan. On one hand, in light of serious slippage of sales, it would seem that the vision of the Corys was not being fulfilled. But on the other hand, teachers continued to be fed and motivated, and students were being blessed as the Holy Spirit used the Word of God to transform their lives.

For example, in November 1997 a teacher wrote anonymously from lengthy experience teaching the lessons:

> "I have really enjoyed the Scripture Press curriculum for years. The basic reason is the Bible content. It is there! Thank you for the years of staying true to God's Word. I enjoy the Bible Truth and Life Response in the lesson overview—they're great. I pray about my class that these truths will come across. They help keep me focused. I also like the various activities suggested. There are many to choose from, and I need that. I pray about which activities would be best for my class.
>
> "The material has made it easy to present Christ and bring students to a decision point. We are getting more and more unsaved children in. Today this is vital! Sunday School is not what it once was. We are getting a real mix of the culture. The life-shaping Focus (lesson approach) is super. It usually applies to my life even before my students!
>
> "Thank you for being so faithful."

"SP Flavor"—who can define it?

"SP Flavor" was often mentioned in relation to Scripture Press teaching materials but it was difficult to define. Following is a list of ingredients constituting what likely added up to "SP Flavor." The list came from a brainstorming session involving SP editors and marketing personnel, led by Bernice Cory.

We want lessons that . . .

- present a living, loving Savior and the Bible as a Book to live by
- reach head, heart, hands
- follow a child on all levels
- stir and stimulate
- create an at-homeness in God's Word
- promote empathy
- make discoverers out of pupils
- take into account the unevenness of growth
- involve pupils
- result in a changed being, constructive thinking, diligent doing
- combine lesson-learning with personal growth
- encourage problem-solving
- lead pupils to God's Word to solve their problems and find their answers
- train pupils in every essential of Christian growth
- meet major needs of each age
- touch on all areas of Christian living
- weave in Bible memorization with events in today's world
- create active listeners
- result in long-term decisions
- involve the home
- enlist cooperation of parents
- have a built-in goal
- are evangelical, educational, effective
- incorporate new methods, interest-arousing variety, no all-of-a-pattern programs
- present individualized ideas to reach varying temperaments
- are trend-setting
- pioneer in new teaching ventures
- put over truths through planned correlation
- are tested, timed, and timely for today
- dated, to keep up with history in these hurried days
- readily adjust to different sized churches
- make for aggressive discipleship
- create intelligent church leaders
- produce poised, articulate pupils, not ashamed to witness for Christ
- provide readiness for meeting life's tests
- instill a built-in will to win
- reinforce and strengthen Christian resolves
- develop Christian loyalty
- unify Christians
- lead Christians to participate and cooperate
- induce pupils to give with understanding
- bring out local talents
- arouse desire to serve the Lord
- indoctrinate pupils with virile portions of God's Word
- enable pupils to know how to lead friends to Christ
- encourage pupils to search the Scriptures
- bolster ability to take reproof and correction from God's Word
- train in righteous living
- help conform pupils to God's will in thought, purpose, action
- equip pupils "for every good work"
- stimulate pupils to be spiritually creative
- incite pupils to keep coming to Sunday School
- fix attention on what God says is important
- encourage communication with God through simple, natural prayer

What Ever Happened to Scripture Press?

The author of Ecclesiastes put it simply: "There is a time for everything, and a season for every activity under heaven: a time to be born and a time to die" (3:1-2, NIV). Scripture Press was born in 1932 and made a dramatic change at the age of 65 years in September 1996. To many employees, it seemed like a death. But the good news is that when the doors closed at the 40-year-old Wheaton building, Scripture Press curriculum and Victor Books continued on under the umbrella of Cook Communications Ministries, Colorado Springs. And, happily, the building that some regarded as almost hallowed was not bought from Cook by a builder, who would have demolished the building and erected houses or condominiums, but by Wheaton College, meaning, it appeared, the property would be used "For Christ and His Kingdom."

SP had seen its best year in 1974, when the profit margin peaked at about 6 percent; in those days employees rejoiced at generous bonuses at Christmastime. Later, in 1994, gross sales peaked at about $20,000,000, but the profit margin was an unsatisfactory 4 percent. Compared with the most profitable publishers in the religious field, SP lagged far behind.

The merger of the grand old company had roots in a 20-year decline in curriculum sales and accumulated debts. Till the early '90s, accounting records, unfortunately, gave an unclear picture of the gravity of the situation. This was soon remedied.

An Editorial plan to attempt to reverse the decline was considered in 1979. The key thought then was to simplify materials for both pupils and teachers. Reading levels were down in public schools, and teachers wanted simpler manuals to lessen the time of preparation for teaching. Materials would contain more pictures, larger print, wider margins, and shorter words, sentences, and paragraphs. Bill McVey, a textbook designer whose basic skills were in the editorial realm, was recommended to work with editors, first in simplifying, unifying, and improving the appearance of teacher manuals plus a few other products for pupils. This plan was rejected by management as being too costly.

About ten years later, as mentioned earlier, curriculum was given a cosmetic change that cost in the vicinity of $2 million, all borrowed, but this move did little to change the downward spiral of curriculum sales.

In regard to other losses, President Beers put it in these terms in a board report in 1991:

> Historically, no subsidiary has brought substantial amounts of money to our parent corporation, and several have brought substantial losses. At the moment, these represent enormous holes in our treasury bucket. Video Dynamics, for example, has drained off more than $1,200,000 during the last year! For many years, our Canadian operation has lost substantial sums of money. . . . Scripture Press United Kingdom is not a subsidiary, and as such cannot return a profit to us corporately except through the modest profit we get by selling products to them. . . [For years, SP made financial contributions to SPUK.] Scripture Press Ministries owns SPPI stock and thus is not a subsidiary, but there are cash flow requirements from SPPI to SPM and in that sense allocates corporate funds to something other than future corporate development. The combination of these has for many years kept SPPI cash poor and thus unable to develop products for the future.

Management saw that SPPI was not in a position to borrow a large sum of money to make major revisions in curriculum or to create a brand new line of lesson materials. To aggravate the problem, the other part of the company, Victor Books, was long thought to be subsidizing curriculum, but when management took a more careful look through an "overhead allocation study," it showed that the book division was losing large amounts of money, and curriculum, though in decline, was still highly profitable. So SP had the unique situation of having a stable division losing money, and a declining division making money. Long range, neither could truly help the other succeed without major financial help.

In troubled waters

In a summary for the boards in February 1995, President Beers made it clear that in 1990 he had taken over captaining a ship in very troubled waters. As a result, he stated, "the SP administration changed as a response to a concern for more concerted and more open planning for the future." It began a new chapter in positioning SP. He continued:

> Our challenges have been many . . . and painful. . . . I think we have most of those conquered. But we are not "out of the woods" yet. In some ways, as we think of growing the company toward a new future, we may indeed face our greatest challenges. Impossible? No.
>
> Tough? Yes, really tough.
>
> In addition to internal challenges, we have faced a growing collection of external challenges, not the least of which is an enormous competitive challenge from companies that are industry leaders. During the past 4 1/2 years, I have personally felt we could revitalize dated curriculum. I still believe we could, but we have reached a crossroads—where the lack of resources and the continuing decline intersect. We must deal with that issue now, not next year.
>
> A number of factors have converged in the last two years or so to bring us to a point of urgency. Is it a crisis? It's premature and even unwise to use the word *crisis* now. But if we do not take rapid and decisive action, it will become a crisis. Today, I would ask that we use the term *urgency.*

17 steps taken in positioning SP

Beers went on to list 17 steps that had been taken since June 1990 in positioning the company. The steps included:

a. Reducing the number of executives from seven vice presidents to two corporate vps reporting to the president

b. Reducing the full-time staff from 180 in 1990 to 159 in 1994

c. Disposing of entities that were draining resources and equity (Video Dynamics, Beacon Distributing and Mainroads [Canada], Screen Printers, and the Canadian building—all at a $4+ million loss)

d. Providing major revitalization in curriculum (improved teaching guides; new adult curriculum; completing the Bible Heritage, all-KJV line for Baptist Literature Board; *LifeWalk* devotional curriculum; new youth publication, *Zelos*; 2-2-2 grading Primary through Junior; many smaller improvements in product and production of products, including going to desk-top publishing)

Beers' 1995 report stated that, despite a good cash flow in 1994, the company had an operational loss of about $100,000 and a loss, after audit adjustments, of $1.4 million. (For complete details of this report, see "Summary of Where We Are," February 29, 1995, Appendix.)

By late 1995, the company was in a definite crisis. Plans that were to have helped begin reversing the decline of curriculum sales—a new 2s and 3s course that the president himself was to engineer—had been dropped, because $550,000 of SPM funds were to have been used and going ahead with the plan was considered too risky. President Beers recommended to the board "that our best option [is] to team up with a partner who [can] provide capital, a more stable product picture, and which would be compatible with us." The board concurred.

Mergers had already occurred in the Christian publishing field, involving larger publishers. Thomas Nelson generated one of the buyouts, purchasing Word for $72 million in cash, according to *Business Wire,* making Nelson/Word the largest player in the Christian publishing field. Though the two companies retained their separate names and catalogs, many of their operations were combined. In 1997 Word moved its corporate headquarters from Dallas to Nashville.

Zondervan was bought out in 1988 by Harper-Collins, a publishing segment of Australian billionaire Rupert Murdoch's empire. Employees later tried to buy the company, but the effort failed and Harper-Collins solidified its control.

In relation to the desire of Beers and some members of the board to merge SP with another publisher, over the months several firms came into the picture. Some wanted to buy the entire company. Others preferred to buy only one division. Management believed it essential to merge or sell the company in its entirety.

An attractive offer from Cook

Then along came Cook Communications Ministries with an attractive offer. Much discussion and prayer followed. Suggestions were made that the company could start over on its own with a sharp cutback in the number of employees. Beers, however, felt this would be more painful than a merger, and not feasible because of a lack of financial resources to revitalize curriculum. Also suggestion was made to keep Victor Books operating as a separate entity or sell the division and keep the rest of the company intact.

Some board members cringed at the idea of merging with Cook. After all, in years past Cook was regarded as being on the outskirts of Evangelicalism and not at all well regarded by SP leadership and editorial employees. But Beers offered evidence that there had been a change at Cook, that the leaders, headed by President David Mehlis, were evangelicals and that Cook had swung back to a conservative theological position. Finally, feeling comfortable with a merger with Cook, the board approved the sale. According to the official record, the sale was to David C. Cook Publishing Company, which operates as Cook Communications Ministries, Inc.

Prior to the decision, there was great unrest among employees. Some employees began to look for other employment. One employee in mid-management had just a year earlier moved his family into a new home. He was extremely anxious. Fortunately for him, he had had a long-standing offer from a firm in another state and because of the uncertainty of the future at SP, he took the job.

SP to merge with Cook, morale low

When the announcement finally came that SP was being merged with Cook in Colorado Springs, morale at the company hit rock bottom. Many felt they had been betrayed. Some wondered why management hadn't called for days of prayer, as had happened in the early days of the company when the company faced serious problems. Beers points out that signed confidentiality agreements and the need to keep negotiations private prevented public disclosures. More than one person believed that God began removing His hand of blessing when the company discontinued publishing VBS lessons and even more when management decided to hold chapel services less frequently than on a daily basis, as had been the custom from the 1930s.

David Mehlis, president of Cook Communications Ministries, and Gil Beers, the last president of SP and now president of SP Ministries, sign letter of intent for acquision of SPPI by CCM, Nov. 30, 1995.

Addressing employees, Beers stated that he believed God had provided a way to save the SP curriculum and Victor Books through the merger. He explained why the merger was necessary, but it was difficult for most employees to grasp why such a drastic step had to be taken. Representatives of Cook came to help boost morale. As many as possible who wanted to move to Colorado would be hired, they promised, suggesting that as many as 40 jobs were open, in addition to jobs that would be created by the merger.

The agreement was finally signed on February 29, 1996. Cook purchased 223,048 shares of common stock of SPPI (63.7 percent of all issued and outstanding shares of common stock) owned by SPM. The remaining shares, 127,293 (36.3 percent of the total shares), were purchased from ESOP, and employees were extremely pleased when they received their checks some months later.

Cook made a strong effort to make the merger as painless as possible. Several Cook executives, including President David Mehlis, came to Wheaton to address employees and introduce them to the Colorado firm. They talked of many job openings, focused on housing in Colorado Springs, and spelled out procedures for moving employees who would join the Cook organization. They offered generous severance packages to those choosing not to make the move. For example, senior management employees were assured of their salaries for two years even if they chose not to move to Colorado Springs. Long-service employees below the senior management level were assured of paychecks for a year.

Thirty-three employees eventually took positions with Cook, 27 going to Colorado or "on the road." Those who moved their families did so at Cook's expense. Most of the SP sales staff were hired to sell SP curriculum, though in 1998 two salesmen, had taken other employment.

Cook Communications Ministries, Colorado Springs.

Six SPers remained in the Wheaton-Elgin area, working either in Cook's Elgin office or in the SP building warehouse, which Cook leased from Wheaton College after the college purchased the Wheaton property. Two of those who were working at Elgin later took jobs at Wheaton's Tyndale House, Doug Walton and Dave Horton, joining Mavis Sanders, who had been hired as a publicist.

As this is written in mid-1998, Cook continues to market SP curriculum under the Scripture Press name, along with six other lines of curriculum. A new, attractive SP catalog has been distributed. Upgrading of the curriculum was under discussion in early 1998. Jan Burton (curriculum) and Don Alban *(Power for Living)* are the only editors from the Scripture Press Editorial Division who went to Cook. Joyce Gibson continues some curriculum work in Wheaton.

Cook now publishes books under the ChariotVictor label. VB editors who went to Colorado Springs are Greg Clouse, Liz Duckworth and Barb Williams but only Clouse remains. Gil Beers joined Cook part-time as vice president of ministry development and also serves in Wheaton as president of SPM.

---

[1] "Report of the President to the Board of Trustees of SP Ministries," May 20, 1996.

SP Ministries Today

Ministering as a private operating foundation after the settlement of the tax case in 1962 and as a public charity since 1982, Scripture Press Ministries (corporate name changed to SP Ministries in 1994) today takes the Gospel into prisons, strengthens the ministries of pastors in third-world countries, and reaches out in other ways to the uttermost parts of the world, helping fulfill the Great Commission. As recounted earlier, in former days as Scripture Press Foundation, the ministry focused almost exclusively on the Sunday School, though the foundation did supply copies of *Power* for prisons and veterans hospitals through Power for Others, begun in 1948 as Tomorrow's America Fund.

SP Ministries

SPM President V. Gilbert Beers, in the Foundation's February 1998 board meeting, put the SPM purpose/mission in these words: "Our ministry exists to provide biblical resources which help people receive Jesus Christ as Savior (evangelism); understand and apply His Word (Bible learning); grow in belief, character, and conduct (life-building); walk with Him as obedient followers (discipleship); and enable and empower for life and leadership (training). This is not meant to be an official statement of mission, but to articulate what I think our purpose encompasses."

Since the sale of SP to Cook Communications Ministries in

1996, SP Ministries has been blessed with a strong endowment, resulting in the outreach programs that it carries out today. This endowment pays all overhead and fund-raising costs for SPM, permitting 100 percent of donor income to be applied to programs.

Within the confines of prisons across the U.S. live men and women desperately needing the healing message of the Gospel. Their world is characterized by hatred, bitterness, and death. It is indeed a dark world where the only hope is the light of Christ. SPM is there, working hand in hand with chaplains and others by providing them materials for teaching, training, and sharing the message of God's love. For example, SPM provides *New Life Study Testaments* (35,000 in 1997), an easy-to-understand, 850-word controlled vocabulary New Testament; *Free for Sure* Bible Studies (32,000 in 1997), a 4-book series of studies in John's Gospel written especially for prisoners; and *Power for Living* (approximately 650,000 individual copies in 1997), a paper carrying the Good News through real-life stories. In addition, SPM's mini-library program helps chaplains build reference libraries they can rely on for their work. In early 1998 SPM supplied chaplains with 2,600 mini-libraries consisting of six books each, even more than the 1,600 libraries shipped in 1997.

The George Del Vecchio story

George Del Vecchio received a death sentence for a crime he was accused of and came to Christ in prison in 1978. *Power for Living* papers supplied by SPM were instrumental in his opening his heart to the Savior. George grew by leaps and bounds as a believer, his cell became lined with Christian books and commentaries. He often would go to sleep at night listening to Scripture cassettes to drown out the constant yelling and clanging of keys. A chaplain once wrote that George's cell was an "altar of intercessory prayer and his typewriter a pulpit of evangelism and encouragement." Though strong efforts were made to have his death sentence commuted, Illinois Governor Edgar denied the request and George was executed in late November 1995. While on Death Row, George told SPM visitors Gil Beers and Janet Peluso:

"I know the terrible pain within the heart of a man who has

killed. But I'm fortunate that by the grace of God, I was led to the Cross. That's why I hope you'll keep on sending Christian literature to those of us behind bars. It helped make the difference in my life. It was one of God's tools to change me."

Mission statement

In November 1996, the Board of Trustees adopted the following statements:

- The mission of SP Ministries is to provide communications products and services based on the Scripture and designed to build lives for Jesus Christ.
- Our mission is global and transcultural, primarily to people who cannot afford our products and services. We minister to all ages, especially to children. Where possible, we seek to multiply our ministry's effectiveness through strategic partnering.

SPM trains and equips nationals

SPM finds that one of the most efficient and effective ways to spread the Gospel is through the training and equipping of nationals. Who can better understand how to minister to a group of people than someone already part of the culture? SPM's job then is to educate these people as well as provide them with the right tools to do the work. SPM is involved in training and equipping pastors and others in Africa and Asia. Together with educators, SPM is building up men and women to take the Gospel to their own people. And through its mini-library program, SPM is equipping them with some of the most reliable, practical resources available.

Norman W. Dixon, principal of Moffat College of the Bible, Kijabe, Kenya wrote:

"There are no adequate words to express the impact that this [reference books] ministry has had for our graduates as they go out into ministry. Most of our graduates will begin with salaries of $30 per month, and when they reach the top of the pay scale they will earn less than $50 a month. You buy few books at that rate. The books they take with them will serve as their library for the next 30 years of ministry."

In 1997, in partnership with SIM, SPM and its team of supporters helped supply 16,000 pastors of the Evangelical Church of West Africa each with a mini-library of 39 reference books, SPM supplying two of the books, *Twelve Prophetic Voices* and *Pastors at Risk,* for each set. The books were on a "most wanted" list drawn up by African church leaders. SPM partners opened their hearts wide, giving over $27,000 to pay for the books.

In another project in 1997, SPM supplied some 450 African Bible school graduates with 450 sets of Bible reference books. Each of these sets would cost the graduate a year's salary to buy. Donors supplied money for SPM to buy these books at cost and to ship them.

An outreach to children

Since the merger of SPPI with Cook that triggered more funding, SPM has begun an extensive outreach to children. There's a strong focus to help send Good News to street children of Latin America, as agencies strive to help them materially, resulting in sending 30,000 *Picture New Testaments* in Portuguese and Spanish and 100,000 *Life of Jesus* booklets to be used to tell them of the Savior. Also through a TV series called "Fabulicious Day," reaching an estimated 20 million homes in Russia, SPM and its partners in early 1998 were helping provide follow-up literature to reach children. Plans were afoot to televise the series next in Ukraine. In May 1998 SPM was discussing plans to supply *Picture New Testaments* for workers to give to children in Cuba, a country believed to be more open to the Gospel since the visit of Pope John Paul II there in early 1998.

SP Foundation organized and approved

In 1997 the trustees of SPM approved the organization of a separate nonprofit corporation under the sole control of SPM to be operated exclusively for the benefit of, to perform the functions of, and to carry out the purposes of SPM. Named SP Foundation, it is governed by a board with experts in money management, investments, fund-raising, and development, while at the same time the SPM Board focuses on ministry. The new foundation makes grants to cover SPM's overhead and other operational expenses. This allows SPM to use one hundred percent of donor income for its literature outreach programs.

SPM leases space

After the sale of the SP property by Cook to Wheaton College, SPM leased office space in the east wing of the 1825 building and space in the warehouse. Rest rooms and an archives area (where copies of this book will be kept) were added in space formerly part of the SP bookstore. Currently the office is maintained by a small staff headed on a daily basis by Janet Peluso, administrative director. President Gil Beers spends half of his time overseeing SPM and the other half of his time working for Cook as a vice president in charge of ministry development.

In addition to President Beers, the SPM Board of Trustees in 1998 was comprised of the following: Dr. George K. Brushaber, chairman; Harris H. Hanson, vice chairman; Lorraine J. Ackley, James R. Adair, Lloyd O. Cory, Wilfred C. Frykman, David L. Mehlis, R. Dean Stone, and Robert A. Walker. Janet Peluso serves as secretary to the board and Curt Henrickson as treasurer. David A. Bell and Dr. John F. Walvoord are Advisory Life Trustees.

The SP Foundation Board of Directors is comprised of Beers, president, Brushaber, Hanson, and Barry L. Swenson.

A  B  C  D  E

F  G  H  I  J

K  L  M  N

SP MINISTRIES BOARD MEMBERS

A
Lorraine Ackley
Former Administrative Assistant, Scripture Press Publications
Former Corporate Secretary, SPPI & SPM (Joliet, Illinois)

B
James R. Adair
Former editor, POWER/line Papers
Founding director, Victor Books (Wheaton, Illinois)

C
V. Gilbert Beers, Th.D., Ph.D.
President, SP Ministries
Former president, Scripture Press Publications (Elgin, Illinois)

D
George K. Brushaber, Ph.D.
Board chairman, SPM
President, Bethel College & Seminary (St. Paul, Minnesota)

E
Lloyd O. Cory
Former Editorial vice president, Scripture Press Publications (Hot Springs Village, Arkansas)

F
Wilfred C. Frykman
Former president, Scripture Press Publications & SP Ministries (Carol Stream, Illinois)

G
Harris H. Hanson
Board vice chairman, SPM
President, Cathedral Press (Long Prairie, Minnesota)

H
David L. Mehlis
President, Cook Communications Ministries (Colorado Springs, CO)

I
R. Dean Stone
Executive Director, International Network of Children's Ministry (Englewood, Colorado)

J
Robert A. Walker
Former publisher, *Christian Life* Magazine (Boca Raton, Florida)

SP FOUNDATION BOARD

K
Barry L. Swenson
Vice President, Mill Bank Corporation (Chicago, Illinois)

(Other SP Foundation Board members, all pictured: Beers, Brushaber, and Hanson.)

ADVISORY LIFE TRUSTEES

L
Rev. David A. Bell
Retired senior pastor, Metropolitan Bible Church (Ottawa, Ontario)

M
John F. Walvoord, D.D.
Chancellor and former president, Dallas Theological Seminary (Dallas, Texas)

SPM ADMINISTRATIVE DIRECTOR

N
Janet L. Peluso
Also corporate secretary, SPM & SPF (Wheaton, Illinois)

SPM continues to keep in touch with retirees

Since the closing of Scripture Press in Wheaton, SPM has kept in touch with retirees. From time to time retirees receive issues of *Spotlight* with the latest news of interest to them. An annual feature is a reunion. The second reunion of retirees since the sale of SP was scheduled for September 11, 1998, and these special people were to be the first to receive copies of this book.

SP Retirees at annual gathering September 12, 1997 at Hilton Hotel, Lisle. Front row: Pauline Siegfried, Pat Skorburg, Marilyn Dunn, Ruth Blair, Flora Anderson, June Cronk, Bernice Bosmann, Lorraine Ackley, Corinne Strating, Stella Miles, Olive Blackman, Eleanor Krause, Mavis Sanders. Second row: Willis Grimm, Phil DiCicco, Norma Felske, Grace Anderson, Ginny Zick, Joyce Gibson, Ruth Von Busch, Pat Kutilek, Joanne Willanger, Elaine Grimm, Beth McCulla, Martha Lincoln, Lynn Hoyt, Ruth Shrigley, Ernie Arroyo. Third row: Lloyd Cory, Jim Adair, Bruce Bucklew, Rodney McClelland, Will Frykman, Al Cronk, Dave Hurst, Don Crawford, Joan Sohn, Myrna Hasse, Margaret Berg, Dick Olson. Back row: Lee Kloese and Sam Postlewaite.

Down Memory Lane with Former Employees of SP

MANY FORMER SP EMPLOYEES, especially retirees, responded to an invitation to share memories for this book. Here is what they wrote:

Eunice Fischer, Rich Hill, Missouri

As I think back over my years with Scripture Press, I see a strong family tie. I think the daily chapel service was a means of bringing us together. I remember chapel services on Wabash Avenue and on College Avenue, Wheaton. These are my fondest memories.

Eunice Fischer, 1995.

I also remember the move from Clark Street to Wabash Avenue. The Convention Department had a little glassed-in area on Wabash Avenue, far removed from any window. Air didn't seem to circulate much, we thought. But when we went to a distant window and opened it, workers on the far end of the building complained of a draft. I remember discussing it with Lois Gustafson (later Buelow). She said it was "drafty"; I said it was "stuffy." Play with the windows was finally settled. Only Lowell Lewis, purchasing agent, was to touch a window. That was changed when the company moved to Wheaton to the comfort of air conditioning.

I never revealed this to anyone before, but when I felt actually starved for a breath of fresh air when we were on Wabash Avenue, I would walk down the stairway to the street, open the outside door, crane my neck as if looking for someone coming from the north (while breathing in deeply). And then I'd turn and crane my neck looking for someone coming from the south (and take another deep breath). Revived, I went up the stairs to my small office.

I like to remember the petunias outside the Wheaton building. I remember a surprise party we had for Clara Sander. I remember so many happy times at gatherings in the Cory home.

I remember Dr. Bob Cook's loving ways. He would walk down the way, stop at someone's desk and say, "I'm on your side."

I remember kindnesses shown to me when I was sick in the Wheaton College infirmary for a week or so. My former supervisor, Mr. Bob Walker, and his wife, Jean, came to see me. I felt the prayer support of the SP family.

Yes, I'd say a strong family tie, that brought SPers together, is the thing I remember most. I came to SP in September 1945 and left after eight years in the Convention Department when I felt led to get more schooling. In 1957, I returned again to work with Lloyd and Bernice T. Cory in Editorial. This gave me what I needed in editorial experience when I felt the Lord in 1959 led me to Cook, as they were revising their curriculum. Now ONE family!

Nora Newman, Atlantic, Iowa

Note: Nora died in October 1997, 12 days before her 94th birthday. In March 1997 she wrote:

As a student at Moody Bible Institute in the early '30s, I attended classes taught by Clarence Benson on Christian Education. I learned that he and Victor Cory would be publishing the All-Bible Graded Series. They had opened an office close to MBI. This was one room. The filing system was a shoe box, and supplies occupied the center space at night. When the Corys came to work in the morning, the office supplies were moved to the hallway to make room for the personnel. When I inquired about working there, no, they were not hiring anyone at that time.

I graduated from MBI in 1935. The time following, I spent a year with the Southern Highland Evangel Mission presenting the Gospel in the mountain area of Kentucky. A coworker and I walked miles up the hollow to a primitive one-room school to bring Bible stories to the children. Sunday School was held in our house, which was provided by a mining company for the use of the "Sunday School women."

I then taught in the rural schools in Iowa for a few years. In 1941 I enrolled in summer school at Wheaton College. I returned to Chicago in the fall and in October applied for the second time at Scripture Press. Gladys Siegfried interviewed me, and I was hired as a file clerk in the Order Clerical Department.

After 19 interesting and meaningful years, I retired as Order Clerical department head. They were updating and making changes in management. I felt the Lord was leading me to take a responsibility I had been considering. Mother lived alone in her home in Iowa and was losing her vision. In 1961 I retired from Scripture Press to be with her in her time of need.

Something amusing:

A group of women department heads and key people shared a table in the lunch room at noon. On birthdays we did something different. Once Jeanette Carlson Grove brought a large watermelon all decorated with lighted candles. The melon was delicious, the fellowship uplifting.

Something very special:

Morning chapel services each weekday. A time for a short devotional and prayer. Just what we needed to begin our work in the Lord's service.

Gladys Siegfried Halleen, Horseshoe Bend, Arkansas
"Some Enduring Personal Memories of Scripture Press" (her title)
SP at 800 N. Clark St., Chicago:

I didn't really apply for a job at Scripture Press. I believe my sister-in-law Marian, then office manager, must have mentioned to VEC my experience working in our Elmhurst school superintendent's office, plus my SS teaching, and work as program chairman of the Fundamental Young People's Fellowship citywide youth meetings, and VEC was impressed. Little did I know about what I was getting into for so many years! I started work April 1, 1939 with mixed emotions—the excitement of starting a new job with a Christian company, plus shock and sadness of hearing that same weekend that the popular speaker I had booked as our speaker for the Fundamental Young People's Fellowship (FYPF) annual conference at Cedar Lake, Indiana (the Rev. P.B. Chenault, pastor in Iowa and president of the MBI Alumni Association) had been killed in an accident with a drunken driver. Later, young Robert Cook (yes, RAC) agreed to fill that speaker need.

Early impressions of the SP office:

• The small SP staff and family feeling . . . about a dozen full-timers, but additional temporary workers during the quarterly shipping seasons and to help with mailings promoting SP publications.

• Daily devotions and prayer time started each morning, led by the Corys and employees (you didn't say No when it was your turn!). We prayed for God's guidance, for Him to send in the right applicants for certain jobs, and for needed funds and materials, such as . . .

. . . the time we had bags of quarterly mailings to customers and prospects, and no money for postage . . . and God sent the needed money.

. . . the times we needed bolts of colored flannel for flannelgraph Bible scenes and suppliers had no stock—but God "had contacts" and met the needs through unexpected sources.

. . . the time paper was in short supply, and we needed enough to print one of the publications. We prayed! The very same day a crate of paper fell off a truck and had to be trimmed in size. Someone phoned SP to ask if we could use it. Turned out it was exactly the right size, weight, and quantity needed for our job. Again, God had answered!

• Outstanding Christian leaders often visited SP and spoke during our devotional times (VEC had a rare talent of meeting and talking with a wide variety of people at conventions, etc.). Occasionally, some of these outstanding Christian leaders visited and were invited to join the staff in a fun time. Vance Havner visited one time and came to our SP picnic in a park. Percy Crawford and the Pinebrook Radio quartet were our guests at a special employees luncheon (preceding their being featured at the FYPF rally in Moody Church).

Postwar years included many "firsts" (still at 800 N. Clark):

These were the years of very rapid expansion in the

Sunday School and Vacation Bible School lesson series for all ages, SS take-home papers, visual teaching aids. We were constantly introducing publications for different age groups. Just a few "firsts" in those years:

• First SP catalog of SS supplies and teaching helps

• First SP bookstore (sixth floor)

• First of many new teaching aids: Gospel-graphs and Suede-graphs

• First flannelgraph demonstration/workshop at SP (for MBI Founder's Week visitors)

• First SS magazine started

SP helped start the Christian Booksellers Association. I still recall attending a luncheon meeting of representatives from other Christian publishing companies, held at a Loop hotel. The meeting went well until the hosts discovered that the delicious dessert had an interesting flavoring not usually found at church dinners. They called the waiter and registered a complaint. But the waiter reappeared soon with a tall bottle as proof that the dessert was OK. The label clearly showed the vineyard name, "Christian Brothers."

SP's move to Wabash Avenue, 1947:

This move led into a BIG expansion period for SP (1947-56). At first our bookstore was on the second floor of our new location at 434 South Wabash. Several years later we took the big step of opening a street-level store at 135 South Wabash, across the street from the Palmer House. Billy Graham made a special appearance there on our opening day! Our film producer captured this historic event on film.

We got into film productions featuring SP lesson materials, and several films emphasizing the important ministry of Sunday Schools: "Stars in Your Crown," "Acres of Diamonds," and "Doorways to Decision." These films were loaned out for showings in church across the country.

Until this period of SP's history, we still had no field representatives to contact the rapidly growing Christian bookstores and denominational headquarters around the USA or in Canada and England. I was drafted by Bob Walker to make what he called "hand-holding trips" to dealers out west and later another trip to the east to visit our accounts there. Later we did a trip through the South, conducting VBS workshops for dealers.

When SP finally added our first field representatives to the staff (Bob Bear and a bit later, Willis Grimm), I was very relieved and happy to get back to my regular job and office.

SP's move to Wheaton, 1956:

Wheatonites objected fiercely to a printing company moving in and wrecking the streets with big, heavy trucks (that's how they interpreted "publishing").

We continued to produce more SP promotional films after the move into our new building in Wheaton. That was my "most fun" assignment . . . until one very memorable but sad day when our camera and sound expert, John Meredith, died suddenly as he prepared cables and equipment to start our next promotional film!

I felt that the two decades after SP moved to Wheaton were interesting and full of challenges . . . but, at times, unsettled and confusing . . . probably due to the frequent changes in personnel at management level. But I think we "long-timers" always knew that no one could ever fill the Corys' shoes!

Lucille Nelson, Tahlequah, Oklahoma:
I joined the SP staff as Victor Cory's secretary at the end of September 1947, so worked only a few months at 800 N. Clark Street. One of my first goofs occurred when I opened the mail, and from one letter fell pieces of a check. When I read the salutation of the letter, I realized that it wasn't addressed to VEC. Instead, on checking the address, it stated, "Mrs. Victor E. Cory." I immediately took the letter to BTC's secretary and explained what had happened. A short time later, BTC rushed past me into VEC's office, and I could her complaining about anyone but her own secretary opening her mail! The next day I apologized to BTC. She was very nice, and said she was sorry she reacted so badly, but she was upset more by the return of a check she had sent to a relative, and took it out on me.

A few days later, I took some dictation from VEC. Among the letters was one to Dorothy Braun. I started typing the salutation, and then wondered if he addressed her as "Dear Dorothy," or "Dear Dr. Braun." I simply typed "Dear" and decided to complete the salutation when VEC returned to the office. However, when he returned, he took all the letters, signed them, and told me to get them into the mail right away, which I did. It wasn't until I was filing the carbons that I saw my unfinished salutation. I told VEC what had happened. He smiled and said, "I know Dorothy Braun quite well but not well enough to simply call her Dear." I told him I'd write a letter and explain what happened, which I did. Dorothy replied with a very gracious letter, and we became quite good friends after that. However, after that booboo, I wondered if I'd keep my job. But I did.

When we moved to 434 South Wabash, the offices were not finished. They lacked carpeting, some offices hadn't been finished, etc. I can remember VEC going around from office to office, with long carpet samples getting folks' opinions as to color, grade, etc. of carpeting. I don't know whose opinion he followed.

When the small dining room was finished, VEC saw to it that there were free sweet rolls and coffee for several weeks. Guess that was to woo all of us who went out of the building for breaks.

I greatly enjoyed the annual banquets which were held to commemorate the growth of the ministry. At first these were held in the 434 S. Wabash offices, but as the business expanded, they were moved to hotel banquet rooms. These were always festive affairs with committees appointed to handle decorations, the program, guest lists, etc. VEC always had a part in these, at which time he displayed his charts showing the growth of various products through the years. These were most impressive. The programs always had skits, as well as an inspirational message from some key speaker.

Before the Wheaton building was erected, the architect presented colored drawings of the outside of the building, including the flowers along the sidewalk leading to the front door, the prayer tower, etc. Those of us who admired them were skeptical that they were just an artist's drawing and that the building would never look as beautiful. But it did.

Remember the prayer tower, which the architect, who was Jewish, thought would be a symbol of the organization, and could be used for daily prayer? However, it never was as far as I know. The steps going to the top were finally closed off so that children coming into the building could not climb up them. We prayed in our chapel services and elsewhere.

Some of the folk I especially admired:

VEC, who said he didn't need to know much as long as he

had men on the staff who were knowledgeable in their fields. However, VEC was no dummy. He had two engineering degrees, and believed in continuing education. He encouraged me to take many courses to improve my skills and knowledge, which I greatly appreciated.

R.A. Ginter, who was our controller at 434 S. Wabash. He held a tight rein on expenses, and initiated the first real budgets. We were all saddened by his sudden death.

B.T. Cory, who headed Editorial and insisted that all publications have the "SP flavor."

R.A. Walker, our sales manager at 434 S. Wabash. While I was awed by his bruskness, I was impressed by his understanding of the market and how to reach it.

E. Clara Sander, Gladys Siegried, Ruth Mead, and many of the other women at 434 impressed me. They were all women of dedication and tremendous ability for the jobs assigned to them.

James Adair, who VEC thought highly of, and often said, "He will go a long way."

I could name many, many more "special" people, but I'll let others do that.

William J. (Bill) Petersen, Grand Rapids, Michigan:
I will never forget those summers of 1945 and '46. Those were the summers of my first job, as a shipping clerk at Scripture Press, 800 N. Clark St., Chicago. As a 15-going-on-16-year-old, I was wide-eyed with awe and excitement. For me it was a great adventure from the start of my commute on the Chicago, Aurora and Elgin electrified train in Elmhurst, to my transfer in Chicago's Loop to the el, then to the Chicago Avenue station, the walk to the Clark Street building, and then the elevator ride to the SP offices.

If I remember correctly, Scripture Press rented the fifth and sixth floors. Executive, editorial, and clerical offices were on the top floor; order-picking, shipping, and mailing were on the lower floor, where I worked.

I joined several full-time employees like Vic Anderson, a few Moody students who worked summers, most of whom were relatives of executives or editors, part-timers like Dan and Paul Cory, Harry Dahlberg, and Warren Zorn. I got my job because my folks went to the same store-front church as Lloyd

Siegfried, who headed the shipping and receiving departments, as I recall.

My immediate boss was Emil, who blended Ben Franklin-like aphorisms with Scripture in such a skillful way that sometimes you didn't know which was which. I don't remember Emil's last name [Hudacek], but I remember one of the first things he said to me as we looked down five floors of a gaping elevator shaft: "You are not replaceable. It's possible that some Sunday School quarterlies might topple over and fall down that shaft. That would be too bad, but that might happen. Sunday School quarterlies can be replaced, Bill, but you are not replaceable."

We took a lot of quarterlies up and down that elevator, unloaded from trucks on the first floor, up to the fifth floor to the bins, then packed and posted and put in mailing sacks and taken down again to the post office. I learned a lot about packing merchandise and about mailing machines that summer. I learned a bit about geography too. I still remember that there was a Baptist church in Grand Rapids called Wealthy Street that could afford hundreds of quarterlies, and an active church in Kissimee, Florida. I always accented the first syllable of the town's name.

Perhaps the most memorable aspect of the fifth floor was the magic stairway at the back. It led to the sixth floor where the important people worked. It wasn't really magic, of course, but yet, whenever we heard anyone descending it, all the heads in the shipping line turned in unison to see who it might be.

As a teenager, I was specially interested in some of the female summer workers who worked on the sixth floor. They would bring down orders to be filled each morning and afternoon, but maybe they came down more often than that, just to be admired. Occasionally, if Lloyd Siegfried wasn't on the premises, the girls would be greeted with admiring whistles. One time—which happened to be the last time we whistled—the teenaged girl was followed a few steps later by Bernice Cory.

We also behaved ourselves when Louise Rodman, the personnel director, whom we called "Louie the Rod," came down the stairs. She had a distinct authoritative step to her descent down the stairs. We learned to recognize it because she brought our paychecks.

But I was in awe as some others descended those magic stairs. I remember one elderly gentleman who came down quite slowly. He was William R. Newell, author of a couple commentaries we mailed out and known even more for his gospel song "At Calvary."

I was also in awe when Bob Walker or Alvera Johnson (later Mickelson), who edited *Sunday* magazine, came down those stairs. (I think it was still *Sunday School Promoter* the first summer, and then the title was abbreviated later.) Occasionally, Jim Adair came down. He was the young newspaper reporter who had just been hired to work on SP's new Sunday School papers called *Power* and *My Counsellor.* When Victor Cory came down, he always seemed in a hurry. He usually had a jaunty bounce to his step except when he was accompanied by a missionary or a teacher from Moody Bible Institute.

No, I will never forget those summers, particularly 1945. Two momentous things happened in '45. In August, World War II ended, and I remember how everyone gathered around the radio on Lloyd Siegfried's desk, to hear the news of the announcement of Japan's unconditional surrender. In September the Cubs won the pennant and everyone in the shipping room, except for Vic Anderson, who was a Cardinals fan, rejoiced. But they were sad when the Cubs lost the World Series to Detroit in seven games.

Ruth J. Blair, Glen Ellyn, Illinois:
I am enclosing copies of a poem I wrote titled "I Prayed for You." It was inspired by a chapel message at SP. I don't recall who the speaker was: it might have been Roy Zuck, Bob Cook, or one of the Corys. But the person challenged us with the thought that if someone should come to our mind during the day for no apparent reason, or a missionary should come to our mind repeatedly, it might just be the Lord telling us that this person needs prayer. I don't know how many times I have thought of this when I have thought of someone for no reason.

I prayed for you today, my friend.
I knew not what the need may be;
but since your name came to my mind,

I knew that God was prompting me.

It may be that you do not know
the life that He alone can give;
And that by taking it by faith,
You look to Him and you can live.

It may be in some foreign land
that you are laboring for Him there.
God may have laid you on my mind
so I would turn to Him in prayer.

It may have been an illness then
that gripped your body with its pain.
So if your name comes to my mind
I'll take you to the Lord again.

Darwin Dunham, missionary to Tanzania:
In the late 1960s and into the early '70s, I did the layout design and art for *Teen Power.* Budgetary constraints dictated using hand-separated color art to reduce production costs back in the old "pre-computer graphics" days! This intricate, involved process calls for using a series of overlays and flaps placed over an under drawing to produce both two- and four-color printed illustrations and drawings.

I found this work both challenging and informative. I learned much about the multicolor reproduction process that I did not learn in art school or in doing conventional art (separated by the four-color photographic process of that time).

I went to Tanzania as a missionary artist with AIM in 1972 to help in literature production for East Africa. My experience with *Teen Power* enabled us at Inland Press to print our first full-color illustrated calendar. The press staff was very excited to see that calendar entirely produced by our own personnel and equipment.

I am thankful to the Lord for allowing us life experiences that will bear fruit not only in the present but also in other times and places.

Phil DiCicco, now employed by Christianity Today
(Item requested.)

On Tuesday, April 24, 1973, the day before Mrs. Cory's funeral, Dave Hall, Ed Liden, and I decided to fly to Ottawa, Ill. for lunch. This is something Dave did routinely. It was the second time I was up in the air with him. He belonged to a flying club and had regular use of a plane. I remember before we took off at DuPage Airport that the door on the pilot's side did not close properly. So we secured it on the outside with a piece of rope. We took off successfully and landed on a grass strip at the Prairie Lake Hunt and Golf Club, where we had a nice lunch and good conversation.

On our take-off toward home, the plane was not lifting for some reason (we did not eat that much!). I remember it well: the plane bumped along the strip but did not lift. Dave said a few words as he saw his problem. Up ahead were power lines. If the plane did finally lift at this point, he would likely smash into them, he concluded. So all he could do was land or stop the plane. The problem was that at the end of the runway was a small lake, called Prairie Lake. He hit the brakes, and the plane skidded into the water, ending up about 50 or 60 feet from shore.

Whatever we said at that moment I do not recall. I do recall that Dave, because of the door problem, could not get out of his side. I was in front next to Dave and panicked trying to loosen my safety belt and open the door on my side. Either Dave or Ed leaned over and opened the door before water filled the cabin. We all jumped out and began to swim toward shore. I had on a full suit of clothes and heavy dress shoes. I started out rather well but soon became exhausted trying to swim (and I am no great swimmer!). I saw Dave, and then Ed [wearing a brace on at least one leg], get to shore and collapse. I shouted, "I'm not going to make it!" For at that point I was starting to go down. I struggled up to the surface, and remember yelling several times, "Help! Help!" and seeing Dave still collapsed on shore and Ed running toward a boat with a young man.

I kept going down, flailing my arms trying to stay afloat. I saw Ed and the young man putting a boat in the waster, and then saw them coming, but the boat capsized! I kept struggling and reaching, and saw Ed and the lad again, paddling the overturned boat toward me. Suddenly, reaching, I felt someone, Ed, grab my hand and pull me up onto the overturned boat.

They paddled to shore and dropped me on the ground. Still conscious, I felt glued to the ground and was aware of people around me. I remember hearing Dave saying, "I thought we lost Phil."

I was taken to the clubhouse, given oxygen, and wrapped in warm blankets. We were then all taken in an ambulance to a hospital in Ottawa.

Later I wrote in my journal:

> I owe my life to Ed and the lad who brought the boat to pull me out of the water. I could not have made it by myself. I know that if no one had come to my rescue that I would have drowned. I relived the trauma of that event over and over. At the hospital as I lay waiting for dry clothes and the car to take us home, it was like a video playback over and over.
>
> I guess my mind did what most people's minds do. I began to think about my family and my children. The reality of death was so near and close. It was frightening and I kept wiping tears from my eyes.
>
> That night when I got home I was tired and could not eat. I was restless and took a tranquilizer. While I lay trying to sleep, I sang songs of praise to God. (I must have been a bit delirious.) My son, Mark, came in later and said, 'Dad, did you know that you sang every song in the hymn book?'
>
> I had a great joy of life. God had spared me. The next day my thoughts turned not so much to the events of the day before, but their meaning for me. I knew that I might not have been alive had not the Lord guided. I knew that God was merciful to me. I had to ask why.

Thankfully, all of us were able to attend Mrs. Cory's funeral on Wednesday afternoon, despite our bruises. Dave served as a pallbearer.

Jim Adair, Wheaton, Illinois

"There's an ad in Carl McIntire's *Christian Beacon* that may interest you," a friend told me in a phone call 'way back in 1944. She knew that my mother had been praying that I would get into "Christian journalism." At the time I was a news reporter working for the *Asheville* (N.C.) *Times.* Though I never saw the ad, the phone call prompted me to apply for the job that Scripture Press had open.

In November of that year I came to Chicago to be interviewed by Laurin Zorn, who had created two Sunday School take-home papers, *My Counsellor* for junior-age boys and girls and Power for teenagers. Our interview was cut short when Zorn got a phone call that his mother had died. Meantime, I wrote an article for *Power* on Peter Cartwright, the colorful Methodist circuit rider preacher of the 1800s.

After a long wait, I received a letter from Zorn, offering me the job as associate editor of *Power,* and I accepted. About that time I was invited to play golf with Billy Graham, and learning that I was a newspaper reporter, he suggested that I get in touch with Youth for Christ and apply for a job to work on its new magazine. I told him I was already committed to SP.

The night before I left by train for Chicago in mid-July 1945, I attended a Bible class taught by guest teacher Dr. William R. Newell, and he prayed that God would bless me on my new job. My C&MA pastor, Julian Bandy, predicted I would soon return to Asheville. But God had other plans, giving me 51 years with Scripture Press, including 9 years working part time after my retirement dinner in April 1988 emceed by Warren Wiersbe.

World War II was ending, and the train I took from Asheville was crowded with GIs, many with their wives. I traveled with the assistant pastor of my church, John Dunlap, who later established a flourishing C&MA church in Norfolk, Virginia. We both had Pullman berths but gave up one for a GI and his wife, and John and I crowded into one berth.

My starting salary was $35 a week and soon was raised to $40. Some years later—perhaps in the late '50s—my salary was $165 a week, my weight 165, and my bowling average 165!

In Chicago in 1945, as a Southerner from a small city, I needed friends. At 800 North Clark Street, Clara Sander made special efforts to make me feel welcome, and, as mentioned in an early chapter, SP's innovative advertising manager, Andy Jessen, befriended me and introduced me to Wisconsin's Door County, which eventually became a favorite vacationland for me and my family. Zorn, a feisty, mustached man, introduced me to handball at the Lawson YMCA, where I lived for the first three months. (Several SP men worked out at the Y on a regular basis.)

If memory serves me correctly, it was at the Lawson Y that the Evangelical Press Association got its start. Though not officially organized until 1948, the organization grew out of earlier meetings held at the Y that included Dr. James DeForrest Murch, editor of NAE's *United Evangelical Action,* who became EPA's first president; Bob Walker; and Russ Hitt, who worked at Moody Bible Institute.

Russ came to work at SP some years later. Once I rubbed him the wrong way. It was my practice to bounce a list of titles for *Power* stories off various people, and I dropped into Russ' office. We discussed titles, and suddenly Russ burst out, "Get out of my office!" I never knew just what I had said that offended him; I simply continued to sit there till he cooled off. Russ and I later became good friends. On trips to Philadelphia over the years, I had lunch with him and Bill Petersen, his assistant, when Russ was editor of *Eternity* magazine. He and his wife, Lillian, came to open house at my wife's home in Philly to see our twins, Mary Sue and Martha Lou, a few months after they were born, and Russ presented them with silver dollars.

I greatly enjoyed my lengthy term as editor of take-home papers. When Zorn left SP two years after I arrived, Bernice Cory became my boss, but she gave me free rein, much as Lloyd Cory did when I reported to him. Several times a year I was on the road interviewing people for *Power* stories. My most memorable trip was in the '60s, on assignment by VEC, to visit the Janz Brothers evangelistic team in Germany, a story-gathering jaunt that also took me to Switzerland, France, and England.

An SP trip took me to California for my first visit there. I especially remember flying on a Douglas DC-3 prop plane for many hours with Ken Anderson, who wrote for *Power* and later established Gospel Films. A friendship that developed with writer Bernie Palmer took me to the far reaches of Saskatchewan for stories, to a camp where he and his wife spent summers; there I interviewed a Christian mountie and an Indian trapper, both for *Counselor*.

SP played a part in my meeting my wife, Ginnie. SP artist Ed Pike became one of my best friends. We did things together, including producing the *PGM News* for Pacific Garden Mission Superintendent Harry Saulnier, brother-in-law of the Corys. After almost 50 years, I continue to do this work. In the summer of 1954, I invited Ed to go fishing with me; however, he planned to go to Moody Church Week at Canadian Keswick, near Toronto. We compromised and did both. It was at Keswick that Ginnie caught my eye when she sang in a trio with two of her sisters at a meeting. A date for a snack at a restaurant triggered our corresponding, and my arranging story trips that took me to Philadelphia, to interview such people as Dr. C. Everett Koop, then chief surgeon at Children's Hospital, and Dr. John Brobeck, a respected professor at Penn.

For a year or so we did not correspond. When Billy Graham held his 1957 Crusade in Madison Square Garden in New York City, Ginnie and I got together again. Conveniently, she was visiting her brother Ed, a Bronx pastor, and Ted Miller and I were in New York to get story interviews at the Crusade. Ginnie and I attended the Crusade one night, but the next night I took an airline stewardess whom I had met at a CWI conference at SP at 434 South Wabash. Afterward, I asked Ted who was the best pick in his estimation. Ted wrinkled his brow as he thought for a moment, then said he favored the stewardess, adding, "Ginnie's too silly." (Forgive me, Ted, for recalling this!) Ted is known for his discernment but long ago realized, after getting to know Ginnie, that he had not given the best advice. He graciously served in our wedding as one of my groomsmen, along with SPers Harold Eavey and Lloyd Cory.

When I began to think of proposing to Ginnie, I wrote to BTC in 1958 when she was on a trip to England and asked her to pray. I valued her as a special friend who would pray that God would show me if I should propose to Ginnie. Her prayers obviously paid off, for we were married in Philadelphia on July 4, 1959.

When I was selected to head up the new Victor Books program, I began the task, looking to the Lord to lead me. I had written and compiled several books, and that probably was one reason I got the assignment. I had come to SP in much the same way. Apparently all others who answered the *Beacon* ad had little or no qualifications. I had no book experience, except as mentioned, but God saw me through. I enjoyed the work, though perhaps not as much as I enjoyed editing, traveling, and writing for the papers. I phased out of papers entirely in 1975 and devoted my full time to books. There was indeed more pressure. Marketing wanted so much to have good books to sell that Jim Lemon took a strong interest in helping recruit authors, and we took many trips together.

When SP brought in Mark Sweeney to head Victor Books, it came as a blessing in disguise. God had used me and had enabled Victor Books to become an integral part of the SP picture. I had been battling a prolonged bout with asthma, and it was good to be relieved of the pressure. I enjoyed those last years in my acquisitions role, along with some editing.

I am glad that many of the books that we published years ago continue to be published under the ChariotVictor label, books such as *What Happens When Women Pray, You Can Be the Wife of a Happy Husband,* and *The Bible Knowledge Commentary.* To God be the glory!

Anne Harrington DeWolf, Dunnville, Ontario

God taught me a great deal during my 12 years at Scripture Press, which found me over that period editing three different Power/line papers.

One afternoon I interviewed a 13-year-old boy in his Wheaton home for a story in *Young Teen Power.* He sang with his parents and sisters, the Musical Murks. A few years ago I had the privilege of meeting this former story subject, and heard him sing with his own family. What a thrill, some 30 years later, to realize that the Lord is using Bill Murk in a music ministry of his own!

Shortly after taking over as editor of *FreeWay* (December 1973), I attended the Urbana Missionary Conference. I felt very insecure at the idea of taking over a paper edited previously by Jerry Jenkins. (*How does one fill his shoes?* I wondered.) But the Lord knew I lacked confidence and arranged for me to interview Don Curry, a medical student from western Canada. Don had accepted an invitation to speak to the students at the Inter-Varsity conference. (The interview took place on the floor in the crowded Inter-Varsity office, and the FreeWay article that resulted was titled "Take the Risk."

Don told me that he was a quiet, studious, and withdrawn

person, but he had learned that God can stretch a person's resources beyond his or her natural abilities. One of his stretching experiences was speaking to the 15,000 students at the Urbana Conference. He based his presentation on the parable of the talents.

"Christ was speaking to me in the parable," he said. "I was one of the servants. . . . I had been given talents to invest. I can't use the excuse that in Christ's Great Commission I have nothing to offer. I have been given a talent to invest for His glory." Through the parable, God revealed that faithful investment, not ability, was rewarded. He challenged the students to prove God's trustworthiness and ask Him for stretching experiences. "Ask Him to place you in positions where you must rely on Him," he said. "Dare to risk—and discover yourself and your Lord."

Don's message hit home to me and gave me confidence that God would enable me to fulfill my duties as editor of *FreeWay*. (I later heard that Don Curry, M.D. went on to serve the Lord in India.)

In 1976 I met John, and we were married the following year. I have many fond remembrances of a company-wide shower given for me by my coworkers and friends.The unique program included a skit introduced by "Dragnet" music, and a personalized edition of a *Power* paper prepared by the creative editorial staff. One of the editors, Rick Gilmore, served as photographer and took many photos to commemorate the special day. After the shower he admitted he'd just discovered there was no film in the camera!

Not long afterward, I was asked to take over *Power for Living,* becoming the paper's first woman publication editor. One memorable story was called "Little Margaret Is Looking Up" (3/24/80), which was a joint effort of myself and Jim Adair, who conducted the interview in Philadelphia with the subject, Margaret Woodruff. She was born with a genetic disturbance of the endocrine gland. She stood only 4' 6" tall, and worked for the U.S. Defense Department for 25 years. She often thought of her mother's advice to her as a child: "Margaret, the Lord made you. . . . No matter what happens, always look up, never down."

Though Little Margaret's life was not easy, she was well-liked, had a great sense of humor, and enjoyed helping others.

When people asked her if her furniture was scaled down, Margaret replied, "No! Rather than scale my furniture down, I scale myself up."

Now whenever I face hard situations, I think of Margaret's words, and also try to "scale myself up!"

Al and June Cronk, Barneveld, Wisconsin

We became employees of Scripture Press in 1957, arriving from northern Minnesota, where we had done home-mission work for ten years. At the time we began work, we had experienced some difficulties and problems in Minnesota that were stressful and discouraging. Mr. Frykman and Miss Rodman, along with all the dear folks we worked with, welcomed us with hearts full of Christ's love. The encouragement and blessings of each of those individuals meant more to us than we could ever explain!

Throughout the 24 years we were part of the SP working family, we always praised God for His people there, working side by side to get His Word out. The Lord used SP to build us up and give us strength and ability to serve Him!

When our children decided to give us a 50th wedding anniversary celebration in 1987, they felt the logical place to get together was at Scripture Press, 1825 College Avenue in Wheaton. However, just before the event was to take place, the "Great Flood" occurred, and it seemed impossible to believe that we could carry out plans for the occasion. But, like the postal service, "neither high water, mud and dirt, nor any other impediment" stops the SP people from their appointed commitments! We were warmly welcomed to a beautifully cleaned and shined up chapel and lunchroom area. The event was a wonderful one, and we shall remember SP's part in it with much appreciation!

Lee Temples, New Tribes missionary in Venezuela

I thank the Lord for Scripture Press, as the work that I did there helped prepare me for the work I am now doing here in Venezuela. Emil Hudacek in the Scripture Press print shop was a real help and explained things there to me. All the work that I was involved in at Scripture Press has been a great help to me now.

Leaving the jungle, we moved to Puerto Ayacucho in 1975

to take over the print shop. The work here consists mainly of printing primers in the tribal languages, lesson materials, portions of Scripture, hymnals, and some office forms that are needed here in the offices.

We first started out using a mimeograph for all the work. Irene did the typing of the stencils, I would proofread them and put them together, and begin copying them on the mimeograph. (For printing of the book of Matthew in the Piaroa language—1,000 books—I turned the handle over 330,000 times!) We are now using a Risograph and a Xerox copier for the work.

We have been here for 31 years and have seen the Lord do great things. We can only say, "Thanks, Lord, for the way You led while at Moody, Scripture Press, Bryan, in Chicago, and here in Venezuela."

I thank the Lord.

Ted Miller, Wheaton

Back in 1953 when I joined the editorial staff of Scripture Press' Sunday School Papers Department, a new vocation of Christian journalism was pressing into religious publishing. Its writers, of which I was one, were trained in newspaper and magazine fields, and its audience was anyone who might read about spiritual truth that worked in everyday situations for ordinary people. It was the right time for SP's people-oriented, action-filled periodical *Power* to flourish in the booming Sunday School movement of the '50s.

Featuring personal stories of individuals' conversions to Christ and adventurous narratives in serving God, *Power* rocketed to the top in readership among Sunday papers, as more than 400,000 copies were being read every Sunday for many years. With current dates and real places and events, it demonstrated God's intervention and power in people's daily lives.

For me as an editor and writer, *Power* meant the steady opportunity to learn about and meet little-known and famous people who discovered and described the wonderful changes God had made in their lives.

The spouse of a murderer, a crippled seller of shoelaces and pencils on Chicago streets, a Greyhound bus driver, Senator Mark Hatfield, singer Beverly Shea, speaker-writer Francis Schaeffer, among countless others, told me how Christ became the center of their lives and God used them to reach out to others. Their true stories thrilled me and proved God's reality and goodness.

So ten years of service—I never thought of it as work—strengthened my faith and launched my Christian journalism career. I moved to Tyndale House to edit its new magazine, *The Christian Reader* [actually, Ted's idea and creation], for 23 more years of publishing the living truths of Christian faith. And in retirement today, I'm still grateful for the very accurately named *Power*, which became *Power for Adults,* then *Power for Living* that continues to introduce readers to the amazing power of Christ for making new people.

B.J. Slinger, Wheaton, now with Christian Service Brigade

I especially remember the many worldwide friends who visited in chapel, presenting their vision for Sunday School ministry. The employees of SP recognized the need for prayer, and for most of its history, held *daily* chapel services, dedicating each new day to God's work. A frequent highlight through the years was to host Sunday School curriculum translators from around the world. SP Ministries was responsible to coordinate the translation and development of the All-Bible Curriculum into scores of languages. Often these educators would meet with the in-house curriculum editors to discuss ministry needs in their respective countries.

The staff was encouraged to meet dedicated Christian workers using the lessons to reach children and adults for Christ. For example, I remember inspirational testimonies in chapel from the following missionaries: Irene Pao, Hong Kong; Jeannie Lockerbie, Bangladesh; Yvonne Gibson, South Africa; Leon and Inke Willems, Holland; Meta Knecht, Holland; Clement Kroeker, Belgium; and Marj Ford, Germany.

Marj Ford, Yucaipa, California

First, I recall some quotes and comments by some of my favorite, famous SPers. I remember Lloyd Cory's comment, "Marj could write if she'd stop talking long enough." And when he was introducing me in an SP chapel service: "Marj Ford, who talks 100 words a minute, with gusts up to 180."

Early on, at my first SP banquet, held in the Congress Hotel, after the waiter removed my unfinished salad course while I wasn't looking, Mary LeBar's advice was:"You've got to hover."

I remember Dr. Bob Cook's telling of driving his old car sans brakes on Michigan Avenue (during his student days), ending with: "God takes care of fools and little children, and I was no child." Or again, as he walked with me from the hotel to a bus station in Canada, when my suitcase of visual aids and workshop notes was in a car across town and might not make it on the bus with me, he teased, "Now you'll have to trust the Lord."

Perhaps it all began when I was 15 years old, totally frustrated and bewildered, trying to get a Sunday School class of 20 or so squirming, often crying preschoolers to "sit still and listen" in the basement of the little church I grew up in. I sent for a book I read about in a magazine called *Patty Goes to the Nursery* Class by Mary LeBar. When it came, I followed it to the letter, and "it worked!" I learned to become a better teacher, understanding preschoolers and how to make the Bible relevant to them at their level of interest and comprehension. The fulfillment through working with little children for the next six or seven years spurred me on to be a teacher beyond Sunday School, first in public elementary school, then "teaching teachers how to teach" and finally students at the German Bible Institute in Seeheim, Germany.

I came to Scripture Press "through the back door." My professor and mentor at Wheaton College, Dr. Lois LeBar, told me that SP was considering hiring someone in the Convention Department to represent the company and do teacher training in local churches. She and Mary LeBar took me to meet Dr. and Mrs. Cory at their Wheaton home one Sunday night after church. Robert Walker, head of Distribution, was also there. Later that summer before my graduation from Grad school, I took the old "Roarin' Elgin" from Wheaton into Chicago to 434 South Wabash for an interview with Miss Louise Rodman, director of Personnel. She informed me that my having been interviewed by the president, editor-in-chief, and head of Distribution *before* going through channels in her department was most unusual!

After August graduation from Wheaton, I returned home to California, where I talked with a number of people about a position as a Christian school teacher or Christian Education director, but no offers came. Finally, I prayed, "God, for me to know Your will, let someone else make the decision for me." Shortly thereafter, a letter came from SP, offering me the position in the Convention Department.

Taking that as the Lord's answer for me, I traveled back to Wheaton and reported for work at 434 South Wabash on November 1, 1953. It was stimulating for this small-town girl, working in the Chicago Loop, in the big-city hustle and bustle, albeit in the sheltered Christian environment of Scripture Press... shopping on lunch hour or after work, eating chicken paprikash, sweet-sour red cabbage and apple strudel at the little hole-in-the-wall Romanian (or was it Hungarian???) restaurant up Wabash, riding the Chicago, Aurora and Elgin and the "L" to work.

My job was to plan, set up, and conduct Sunday School training workshops, later called "Leadership Training Institutes," as a service to churches of many denominations, in order to teach their teachers how to teach better and to introduce them to good teaching aids. I traveled three weeks out of four, beginning in a local church on Sunday and conducting sessions for workers in various age groups through Friday evening. Then it was on to the next church. My first assignment was to Paducah, Kentucky, which I had only heard of in a country song, "The Duke of Paducah."

As the years passed and our service expanded, I led workshops with as few as one or two Nursery teachers or as many as 10,000 (once) at a state convention. I traveled at peak time as much as 35,000 miles in one year.

At the age of ten, as a Sunday School pupil myself, I had made up my mind to be a missionary, a childish resolve that influenced my educational choices through high school, college, and graduate school. When I accepted the opportunity to work with Scripture Press—"in the U.S. for pay"—friends questioned, "Whatever happened to your call to the mission field?" After the first three weeks, helping Sunday School teachers learn how to teach the Bible and lead pupils to Christ, I knew that I had found my mission field. That conviction motivated my work for the next ten years I remained at Scripture Press.

The freedom of serving the Lord and churches through the Christian Education Extension Department (CREDEX as it was later dubbed by Dr. Bob Cook) defined our ministry.

Supported by the "missionary margin," as Dr. Victor Cory liked to call the profit margin of the company, we felt free to provide pastors and workers help and encouragement with no pressure to "sell books" or the materials. We just made available to them the teaching aids to do the best job of teaching the Bible and soul-winning—the choices were theirs. I was and am convinced that the All-Bible Graded Series of Sunday School materials and the ABVS for Vacation Bible School provided the best courses and helps available.

During my 25 years as teacher at the German Bible Institute from 1965-1991, I continued to use the ABGS teacher and pupil manuals in Christian service work done by GBI students, whom I taught and supervised. The materials had been translated into German by fellow missionary John Peters. I worked and became friends with the German editor, who adapted ABGS children's materials for the Church of the Nazarene in Germany. When I occasionally conducted local church or area training institutes in Germany and Switzerland, I conducted demonstration teaching sessions, using the ABGS lessons in German.

Looking back, for me one of the "perks" was knowing many "great" people—some on a first-name basis, like Dr. Bob Cook, Dr. Howard Hendricks, Dr. Roy Zuck, Drs. Ed and Frances Simpson, Drs. Lois and Mary LeBar, Dr. Lois McKinney, Dr. Clate Risley [executive director of the National Sunday School Association, murdered in a parking lot in Chicago] and, of course, the Corys (not by first names but as VEC and BTC). I was privileged to be on a convention program with Gospel Light founder Dr. Henrietta Mears, many church leaders, college presidents, professors, and pastors, both "great and small." I even joked occasionally about someday having a mink stole and outlandish hats like Dr. Henrietta wore.

My first boss was the Rev. Al Sedgwick, a quiet, caring man, who greatly encouraged me on the new job. His successor, the Rev. Sherman Williams, inspired and motivated all of us. Under his capable leadership, we improved our service, our outreach, and at the same time developed a deep loyalty to SP and a sense of family. Old friendships have lasted over 40 years, in many cases. Sherm Williams, Dr. Robert Walker, and Dr. Bob Cook, as well as SP's founders, Drs. Victor and Bernice Cory, were great people, both in the work and spiritually, who helped me succeed and who shaped my life. How true the Corys' theme song for themselves and SP, "God Leads His Dear Children Along."

My last tour of Scripture Press was with the Corys, Lillian Swanson, Stan Mooneyham in England and Scotland, in September 1963, on my way to Germany, where I served with Greater Europe Mission for 27 years.

Scripture Press and its people, who were my mentors and coworkers, were and still are "family" for me.

Martha Lincoln, Olney, Illinois

(Written on request to provide information about the introduction and use of computers in the Data Processing area.)

My work experience before SP was all in data processing. I started with the U.S. Treasury Department, and later worked for Caterpillar Tractor Company and Domestic Engineering, a publishing house. I was hired by SP in September 1963 to fill a vacancy in the Data Processing Department. Harold Eavey sent me an application form, and I was interviewed by Mr. Bratkovich. At the time of my employment, there were two keypunch operators, Marie Friesen and Ruth Erickson Bos. The equipment from IBM included a card sorter and a 402 tabulating machine, plus the keypunch units.

As I remember it now, the quantities and catalog numbers of items sold to various dealers and churches were keyed in with a state and area code and were also coded whether retail or cash. Dealer orders were coded as to regular, denominational, and foreign. After the orders were keyed in for each day, they were sorted by machine and then read into the 402, which gave totals by the various coded channels and listed the information in an easy-to-read format. Sales analysis by channel, state, area, etc. were then sent to Dave Hall in Accounting. During my first weeks on the job, I worked with IBM consultants and Dave Hall very closely.

When I first started, our group of employees were in a small section along the northwest corner of Order Clerical. As new reports were added and requests for additional applications were coming in, new equipment was added and eventually more employees. We added verifying equipment, a reproducer, collator, and interpreter. Each of these units required input by the use of 80 column cards with holes punched in them by the keypunch operators. Each of these pieces of equipment had what were called boards which I wired to pick up data. This was "programming" at the very earliest levels. Eventually, all of this equipment would become obsolete as new technology was available. Of course, when we expanded equipment and personnel, space became a problem.

Our first move was to the east wing, where years later Victor Books was located. We used a large room in that area. My memory bank does not include the specific dates we were moved from one area to another but will hopefully supply the steps we took in the correct order.

Mr. Herb Sterling was hired as a programmer/director, I believe. We leased a main frame computer from IBM with tape drives and disc. An air-conditioned large room was enclosed along the west side of the building wall, with an aisle between Order Clerical and our department. We expanded the keypunch operators to a second shift. We used mostly Wheaton College students for this part-time job. Others from SP were trained as programmers/operators. Dick Merrill and Bev Jaderston were two of them, along with Merrill Hoyt. I believe computer time was sold to others in the area to help pay the cost of the lease, and it also more fully utilized the equipment.

When Mr. Sterling left, I believe, about that time Curt Henrickson became involved in decision making for the future computer needs of SP. Executive Computer Systems (ECS) in Oak Brook was brought in as consultants with a long-range plan. ECS consultants worked mostly with Accounting, Credit, and Order Clerical. Several of their programmers designed systems, wrote new programs, and documented and flow-charted everything. Step by step, we turned the computer work over to ECS and thereby phased out the need for the equipment we had at SP. We still had several keypunch operators, and the card output from them was picked up by ECS at night and the reports were delivered to us the next morning. Our role was changed from operations to checks and balances and also distribution of reports received, plus being sure the jobs were all ready at pick-up time.

With the large computer removed from SP, our space needs changed also, so we moved again. We were now in approximately the same area where we started—the northwest corner along the wall beside Order Clerical. A partition was erected to give Order Clerical and us more privacy and it cut down on the noise factor.

We then changed to tape units, made by a company called Viatron. These would eventually replace the keypunch units. These units were faster, more accurate, and a better medium of storage than punched cards. Curt Henrickson was always on the "cutting edge" of new technology, and the Viatron was ahead of competitors in that field. Unfortunately, because of poor management in their company, their progress did not keep ahead of competition later on.

When ECS was phased out, a contract was reached with Bill Forsythe, who had formed his own company, to run our jobs and write new programs for SP exclusively. He had formerly worked for ECS and knew our system well.

SP had then leased Datapoint equipment and we were developing an in-house programming staff which would eventually allow SP to bring all jobs back to be run by our employees. After we finalized our contract with Bill Forsythe, Cathy Lyons Meissner, Priscilla Behrens, Mike Kiss, and others took over the work, and we had come full-circle, back home, doing our own processing.

At the beginning, Order Processing and Customer Service were the first areas to have their individual Datapoint terminals. Programs were developed where order blank forms were simulated on the screen, which facilitated order-taking over the phone. They were keyed in faster, easier, and more accurately, as employees were trained in new methods.

Approximately a year before my retirement, Ken Schroeder was hired. He increased the programming staff and expanded the use of terminals throughout the company to decentralize the Data Processing function. He worked with other departments to enable them to input and maintain their individualized systems. As Curt Henrickson's executive work load increased, he began separating himself from responsibilities in data processing.

It was a slow, deliberate, methodical progression from manual centralized input to high-speed technology and a totally distributed system.

It was very rewarding to see it all unfold, fall into place, and know that I was allowed to play a small part in it. My major role was getting the work done through people management. I was blessed with a great boss, a wonderful company, and the best employees entrusted to me. I retired in September 1986, 23 years out of the middle of my life. God is so good!

Willis Grimm, Tahlequah, Oklahoma

Most of the human interest incidents connected with SP in my experience were on the "field" rather than in the office.

One incident that I told on several occasions involved our bookstore dealer in Peoria, Noah Roeschley. He called Laurin Zorn on a Wednesday afternoon to tell him that his large order had arrived but that the Shipping Department had sent Primary manuals instead of Beginner manuals. This was for an important church, so if SP would send the replacement special delivery, he would pay the extra cost.

On Friday afternoon, Noah called to say the order arrived, but it was still Primary, not Beginner manuals. This church was so important that if SP would refill the order and leave it where he could pick it up on Saturday, he would drive to Wheaton to pick it up.

On Saturday, both LJZ and Bill Hall were there to greet Noah, and the three of them went to the warehouse and filled the order. Saturday LJZ got a third call from Noah, saying, "We still have Primary manuals."

It was a rare instance in which orders were not filled properly.

Elaine Grimm, Tahlequah, Oklahoma

It was a big step for me to come to the city of Chicago to work when I finished business school. Because the chief accountant, George Sharp, was from my home town, I was placed into the Accounting Department, which he headed. Back in late 1946, Scripture Press was having some financial difficulties. I remember that each week the controller and chief accountant would go over the financial situation to see how much we could pay on the big accounts, such as those who printed our materials. However, there never was a time during my years that the payroll was not met. At that time, the books showed that Mr. and Mrs. Cory held back their salaries so all others could be paid.

When the move was made from Clark Street to 434 South

Wabash, I was promoted to the position of secretary to the controller. R.A. Ginter (none of us knew him by a first name), a man who was all-business, was the controller at that time, and I learned much from him. I worked with him on the company budgets, and it was a thrill the time he said, "Do we dare to budget $1,000,000 in sales?" We saw that budget materialize, and for years after that sales figures went up each year.

In those early days, an annual banquet was held which was a highlight of the year. The usual theme of the banquet was the same as that year's Vacation Bible School theme. Different people were given opportunity to use their talents. One year the theme was "Greater Heights," so we made miniature mountains out of papiermache. Eleanor Wiers was in charge of decorations. At these banquets, Dr. Cory would show his annual charts displaying progress in sales.

Scripture Press was unique in that the employees were almost like a family. One group which had close fellowship was the women department heads and the executive secretaries. We tried to get together on birthdays and do different things. One time we celebrated a birthday with a luncheon in the park, using a watermelon with candles in place of a birthday cake.

At SP many close relations were formed with some ending in marriage, such as in the case of Willis and me. Now that we are retired and receive our monthly pension checks, we are reminded of how gracious God was in allowing us to work for Him at Scripture Press.

Marian A. Clark, Thornton, Colorado

I was a new bride moving to Chicago in June 1954. The big city, tall buildings, elevators, etc., were all quite fascinating. That elevator at 434 South Wabash was something else, and quite an experience! We enjoyed the CTA elevated from the North Side and later the South Shore railway from Hammond when we ministered at Bethel Bible Church.

Bob had worked at Scripture Press while attending Moody Bible Institute, and while I visited him in April, I had an interview with Miss Louise Rodman. (She was one of the first persons Bob met at SP, too!) Later, we both worked full time for the company.

Miss Rodman was a gracious personnel director and consented hiring me to work with Lois Gustafson (Buelow) in the Customer Service Department. Stella Miles (Smiles as she signed her name) was the efficient and friendly switchboard operator.

My employment with SP was replaced by motherhood in September 1955. However, I have many happy memories of my early days with a fine company. (Marian returned to SP in 1974 and retired in 1991.)

Ginny Zick, Elmhurst, Illinois

I really enjoyed working at SP and meeting so many people, even though it was a short time of about eight years. One of the men I always admired and respected was Wayne Eklund. He was such a friendly person and so easy to talk with. I was only at SP and the switchboard for a short time and I was told never to leave the board unattended. One morning during chapel, I received a call from the wife of one of our men. She told me she was very ill and wanted her husband to come home right away. I was new in the company and did not even know who this man was. I was frustrated but felt this lady needed help. I left the board and went to the rear of the chapel and Mr. Eklund was standing near the door. I told him the situation, and he went to get the husband and took him home. I was afraid, though, for I thought I would lose my job for leaving the board unattended. Mr. Eklund came to me later that day, and I was sure he was going to fire me, but instead, he said it was good that I left the board because this lady was very ill.

I have worked in many places, but I have so many fond memories of Scripture Press and its employees.

Lorraine Ackley, Joliet, Illinois

Memories gathered over 40 years at SP were revived as I sorted through archives. Louise Rodman was a superb reporter—she included lots of people and company history in *Spotlights*. We owe thanks to those who preserved *Press Proof* and *Spotlight* for 48 years.

I'm sure SP-life for employees who relocated to Wheaton was quite different from life at 800 North Clark and 434 South Wabash. I'm glad my SP career began so near the big move from Chicago. I heard lots of talk about SP's early years and people, so I almost felt as if I had been part of that period of the company's history.

I'm thankful to have known the Corys—great people in many ways. SP was their life, not just in the office, but all their waking hours. VEC and BTC were "one" in their total devotion to the Lord, to the Sunday School, and to the curriculum and products that would lead people to Christ and help them grow in Him. I hope you sensed this as you read the preceding chapters.

One totally embarrassing incident, though humorous in retrospect, was when I pushed Louise Alfors down the hall of "mahogany row" in a secretary chair after hours. Who should appear out of nowhere but VEC! Louise gulped and said, "B-b-but, but it's after 4:30."

VEC enjoyed teasing. He used to tell me I was just a toddler when SP started. (Well, I was a little beyond, but it sounded good!) One night when I picked up my purse to leave, it was SO heavy. He had put a stapler in it. Sometimes when I asked him for a piece of correspondence he had, he'd say, "I'll bring it to you." That meant, "You don't need to watch me go through the piles on my desk to find it." It was a learning experience to read copy (mostly advertising) after he, BTC, and LOC had edited it. Mrs. Cory's motto was "Improving on improvements." I think it was VEC's too.

Doris Chase, Denver, Colorado

Managing the bookstore required a lot of team effort around SP, and I want to thank the departments and individuals who helped me countless times.

I am reminded of the special events the bookstore undertook to draw interest and bring in customers. Each annual sale was a tremendous amount of work, and the bookstore staff gave so much of themselves for this event. Building and Grounds were there for our many needs, and the Warehouse worked all year long getting products ready. Accounting spent hours balancing money with register tapes, *Spotlight* kept employees informed, executives were there to back us, Marketing polished our advertising, Office Services photocopied and mailed thousands of pieces, the switchboard handled hundreds of calls, Ministries helped with clean up and boxing leftovers to use in their outreach. All departments and individuals became loyal customers. It was challenging to see sales grow each year and bring such excitement and ministry to the community. We could not have done it without each one at SP.

My years at SP were rewarding, challenging, and a great experience. I will always be grateful for the opportunity to serve the Lord at Scripture Press!